Errata for Back to the Basics of Teaching and Learning: Thinking the World Together

D. W. Jardine, P. Clifford, & S. Friesen (Eds.)

D0819315

Back to the Basics of Teaching and Learning

Thinking the World Together

Back to the Basics of Teaching and Learning

Thinking the World Together

David W. Jardine
Patricia Clifford
Sharon Friesen
University of Calgary

2003

LAWRENCE ERLBAUM ASSOCIATES, PUBLISHERS
Mahwah, New Jersey   London

Lawrence Erlbaum Associates, Inc., Publishers
10 Industrial Avenue
Mahwah, New Jersey 07430

Cover design by Kathryn Houghtaling Lacey

Library of Congress Cataloging-in-Publication Data

Jardine, David William, 1950-
    Back to the basics of teaching and learning : thinking the world together / David W.
Jardine, Patricia Clifford, Sharon Friesen.
        p. cm.
    Includes bibliographical references and index.
    ISBN 0-8058-3980-1 (pbk. : alk. paper)
    1.   Education—Philosophy. 2. Teaching. 3. Learning. I. Clifford, Patricia (Patricia
Anne) II. Friesen, Sharon. III. Title.

LB14.7 .J365 2002
371.1'001—dc21
                                                                                    2002029486

Books published by Lawrence Erlbaum Associates are printed on acid-free paper,
and their bindings are chosen for strength and durability.

Printed in the United States of America
10   9   8   7   6   5   4   3   2   1

Contents

Foreword

William E. Doll
Louisiana State University

This book is, by any standard, amazing. It plays, in a wonderfully hermeneutic manner, with common themes in an uncommon way. A question—what is basic?—and an instance—a young, second-grade girl doing a math problem—entwine and recurse themselves in double-helix fashion throughout the whole book. As the authors—David Jardine, Patricia Clifford, and Sharon Friesen—say, they wish to propose the audacious idea that "if you do rich, good, disciplined, living work with children" [notice these adjectives please] that bugaboo of bugaboos, tests, "are no problem" (p. 8). In fact, to the degree that we worry about and teach for tests, we deprive the learner of the very chance to learn. Learning comes from being immersed, fully, in a situation, not from counting the number of correct answers on a test.

In the simplicity of traditional, linear, reductive thought, basics are those building blocks via which all knowledge is built. When pressed to analyze these, reductionists break the big blocks into smaller and smaller units until arriving at what we all "see" as self-evident. Any second-grade child must know her math facts, those single digit quantities (1 through 9; zero really does not "count") that make up all addition, subtraction, multiplication, and division problems. Again, in this simple world of school mathematics, powers, roots, recursions, iterations, fractaled dimensions do not count. Only *we* count, in simple, linear terms.

A story: Jardine, Clifford, and Friesen begin their book with "A Classroom Tale." A young child in the second grade is pondering an addition or subtraction question (boths and middles are excluded in this world of second-grade arithmetic worksheets). The problem is:

Joan went to the post office. She mailed five letters and three packages. How many more letters than packages did she mail?

The *relevance* of this question, shall be passed over. Playing with the fingers of David Jardine, who, seeing a puzzled look on the child's face, came over to help her, and as an illustration for her problem held up five fingers on his one hand and three on his other hand. Looking at his fingers and bending down two fingers of the five extended, as well as extending two fingers on his other (three fingered) hand, the child easily and loudly said 'Two!" But she was still puzzled. "Did I add or subtract?" she queried. The directions, simple as they were, asked her to describe whether she added or subtracted. An answer of both was not acceptable. But it is both the child did—pulling down (subtracting) two fingers on one hand, while pushing up (adding) two fingers on the other hand. But alas, the worksheets (textbooks, curriculum guides), in their desire for simple basics, neglect to bring forward the complex and most interesting and truly mathematical relationship between addition and subtraction. What is more basic to mathematics than relationship? If mathematics is not about (logical) relationships, what is it about? Relationships, though, were an excluded option on this worksheet.

What other options are excluded in our reciting the mantra—"Back to Basics"? The authors do not wish to dismiss what is basic; rather they want to examine the concept from a hermeneutical perspective, to provide "a more generous, more rigorous, more difficult, and more pleasurable image of what 'the basics' might mean" (p. 3) [Note, again, please the interesting adjectives grouped together]. And indeed the authors have provided a journey that is generous, rigorous, difficult, and pleasurable. As one wanders through the book, with its provocative Preambles (this is a book to journey in) one questions not only the basics but many educational slogans and shibboleths. One does indeed re-imagine the whole concept of schooling and the potential power that exists in a classroom filled with the fullness and richness of creative experience. Children are creative, adults are creative, life is filled with creativity—life is itself creative. "Treat the work of the classroom as full of intellectual vigor and possibility" (p. 7), say the authors.

Classroom vigor and possibility come from seeing anew, from seeing hermeneutically. In seeing hermeneutically one looks to read any particular event in terms of its fullness, its wholeness, its richness in undeveloped, even unseen, potential. Relationships are, to borrow a phrase from Alfred North Whitehead, the *really real* of life. It is this reality, in all its marvelous complexity, Jardine, Clifford, and Friesen ask us to accept. And they show us, over and over again, in chapter after chapter how this reality exists in every classroom, in virtually every teaching situation.

However, lest one think this book is only about teaching situations, let me mention a deeper thread of thinking that runs through the chapters. The authors, especially Jardine, are well versed in Gadamerian hermeneutics, and his ideas on the fullness of life's experiences and the changing visions differing cultural traditions and generations have, permeates their thought. Thus to look at an issue like "the basics" differently, interpretatively affects not only the way we might teach addition-subtraction but will also affect "how we live out" life itself and especially our relationship with our children (p. 210). Such an effect brings with it a host of ethical issues about how we treat the planet with which we live, how we treat those who are other to us (ourselves the others, other), how we treat our children, and how we treat that which we call knowledge.

This is in many ways an inspiring book—a what-can-be book—but more than that, it is a book which asks the reader to deal with "hard questions," ones which probe the meaning of life. To read this book is to be transformed. I invite all readers to partake of that journey.

Preface

No learned or mastered technique can save us from the task of deliberation and decision.

—Gadamer (1983, p. 113)

Education is laboring under and image of "the basics" that is no longer viable. This image involves ideas of breaking things down, fragmentation, isolation, and the consequent dispensing, manipulation, and control of the smallest, simplest, most meaningless bits and pieces of the living inheritances that are entrusted to teachers and learners in schools. The exhausting and exhausted arguments that swirl around this image of the basics are always full of urgency but rarely bring much prospect of relief, pleasure, or hope to the life of the classroom. What is often ignored in such arguments in that the designation of such things as "basics" is a deeply ethical decision regarding what comes first, what is valued, and what will count in the lives of the students and teachers in the work of schooling. As the burgeoning information age swells all around us, this image of basics-as-breakdown can cope with this eventuality only by accelerating the already-manic pace that some schools set, even for the youngest of children.

What would happen to our understanding of teaching and learning if we stepped away from this image of basics-as-breakdown? What would happen if we took seriously the critiques of breakdown that come from contemporary hermeneutics and from ecology and took to heart from these critiques different possibilities for re-imagining the basics?

Imagine if we treated *these* things as the basics of teaching and learning: relation, ancestry, commitment, participation, interdependence, belonging, desire, conversation, memory, place, topography, tradition, inheritance, experience, identity, difference, renewal, generativity, intergenerationality, discipline, care, strengthening, attention, devotion, transformation, character. Imagine if we treated as *basic* to teaching and leaning listening openly and generously to each other, not just to a healthy and sane understanding of other, but also of oneself. If we treated *these* things as basic to teaching and learning, students and the living questions they bring from their lives to the life of the classroom become imaginable as basic to the living character of the disciplines entrusted to schools. Moreover, the work that is very often thinly and dully outlined in mandated, grade-level, subject-specific curriculum guides becomes understandable differently. Schools can be treated as dealing, not with the dispensation of finished, dead, and deadly dull information that students must simply consume, but rather with troublesome, questionable, unfinished, debatable, living inheritances and with the age-old difficulty of how to enthrall the young with the task of taking up the already ongoing conversations of which their lives are already a part—the "conversation that we ourselves *are*" (Gadamer, 1989, p. 378).

Under this ecological-interpretive image of the *basics,* both the young and the old are transformed: The young become essential to the sane and healthy "sett[ing] right anew" (Arendt, 1969, p. 192) of the world and the world becomes a living array of "tried and true" knowledge which is only true to the extent that it is open to being "tried" yet again, here, now, with this child's question, experience, or concern. We are convinced that our children want "in" to the real work of this living inheritance, and that the image of basics-as-breakdown belies this vital desire, ending, often, with boredom, cynicism, and violence.

This book is about an ecological-interpretive image of the basics. Between us, the three author-editors have 70 years of classroom teaching experience, from 2-year-old children to graduate students older than any of us. The reason for mentioning this is specific and difficult. It is not enough to simply propose a different theoretical-philosophical basis for thinking about the basics. It is necessary to interpretive work—*basic* one might say—to show how such a different treatment might work itself out in the lives of teachers and learners. But this doesn't mean simply running through a long list of examples of a theory that is already fully understood and meaningful *without* those examples. It means showing, again and again, how new examples enrich, transform, and correct what one thought was fully understood and meaningful. This means, simply put, that our research is *interpretive* in character. It also means that the classroom events that we are interested in are themselves *interpretive* in character.

This text will be valuable, we believe, to practicing teachers and student-teachers interested in re-imagining what is basic to their work and the work of their students. Through its many classroom examples, it provides a way to question and open up to conversation the often literal-minded tasks teachers and students face. It also provides examples of interpretive inquiry which would be helpful to graduate students and scholars in the areas of curriculum, teaching, and leaning who are interested in pursuing this form of research and writing.

This book is the product of 10 years work, work that has been generously supported by the Social Sciences and Humanities Research Council of Canada, as well as the Izaak Walton Killam Memorial Fellowship Fund. The former provides the three of us with valuable financial support and the latter provided me with an even rarer gift—the gift of time which, in these days of accelerating rush, was welcome indeed. We would also like to acknowledge the careful work of the reviewers of this text—Geoffrey Milburn, University of Western Ontario, William E. Doll, Jr., Louisiana State University, and David Flinders, Indiana University, who caught all those embarrassing things that are so hard to find by oneself.

Thanks also to the staff at Lawrence Erlbaum Associates, Inc., first for agreeing to publish this work and second for taking such good care of both it and us as we proceeded.

We would especially like to thank Dr. William E. Doll for graciously agreeing to write a foreword to our text. He has been a tireless supporter of our work over the years and a good friend.

> *Something awakens our interest*—this is really what comes first!
> —Gadamer (2001, p. 50)

This Preface was drafted in mid-February, 2002, a few days after Hans-Georg Gadamer's 102nd birthday; he died on March 13th. For several years, the same joke has come up in my yearly graduate course on his text *Truth and Method* (1989): Hermeneutics might not be true, but it seems to be good for you. The foregoing citation comes from an interview with Gadamer at age 93. It remains an inspiration for us to hear from this old man that *this* might be first: being compelled by the world and awakened to have living questions of one's own, full of deliberation and decision. We thank Gadamer for his example and his work.

The cover of this book is a painting by a first-grade student taught by Sharon and Pat during their tracking of Coyote (see chap. 2). It is called "Thinking the World Together." We found it an excellent image for the movement from breakdown to interpretation that we have been pursuing in our work: Thinking of the rich and generous ways that things belong together, how each seeming "part" needs to be experienced interpretively, *as* part of a whole. Each part—each child's work or voice, each thread of mathematical nuance, each grammatical oddity, *is* "the whole" from just here. Thinking the world together is therefore not an invitation to woozy, holistic generalities, but an invitation to take up particular things with care and love and generosity, with an eye to how things belong somewhere and have come from somewhere—shared and contested spaces and voices and ancestries that define who we are in often mixed and contradictory ways.

Finally, this book is dedicated to the teachers and children who are suffering in the confines of a form of schooling premised on breakdown, and to the teachers and children who have taught the three of us so much about what an enlivening and pleasurably difficult thing teaching and learning can be, once the basics are re-imagined.

All author royalties from the sale of this book will be donated to the Calgary, Alberta, Canada branch of the Kids Cancer Care Foundation.

—*David W. Jardine*

Introduction:
An Interpretive Reading
of "Back to the Basics"

David W. Jardine
Patricia Clifford
Sharon Friesen[1]

> *The issue isn't finding new terms to replace old terms. The old terms are fine. It's a matter of seeing the old terms differently, shifting away from both nominalism and realism to rhetoric and metaphor.*
> —Hillman (1991, p. 42)

> *Our curricula, textbooks, and teaching are all "a mile wide and an inch deep." This preoccupation with breadth rather than depth, with quantity rather than quality . . . [leads to a] splintered character and poor work. How can we develop a new vision of what is basic?*
> —Schmidt, McKnight, and Raizen (1997, pp. 3, 11)

TO BEGIN: A CLASSROOM TALE

During a recent round of practicum supervision, I (David Jardine) happened into a Grade 2 classroom. The children were filling in a photocopied worksheet, purportedly dealing with questions of addition and subtraction. Here is an example of the question layout:

---

[1]Many of the chapters in this book are co-authored. In each such chapter, the term "we" refers to "the authors" unless otherwise designated. When a single voice is used in such chapters, the authors are identified after the first use of the term "I."

There are four horses in the field. Two of them run away. How many horses are left in the field?

Beside each question was a little black-line cartoon (in this cases, of horses), a line upon which to put your answer, and, above this line, a plus and a minus sign, one of which you were instructed to circle, to demonstrate the operation you used in solving the question.

One student waved me over. She said, "I don't understand this one at all." The question she had trouble with was this:

Joan went to the post office. She mailed five letters and three packages. How many more letters than packages did she mail?

Eager to help out, I squatted down beside the student's desk and put up five fingers on one of my hands and three on the other.

"Ok," I said, moving the appropriate hand slightly forward in each case, "she's got five letters and three packages. She's got more letters . . ."

The student suddenly grabbed the thumb of my "letters" (five digits extended) hand and bent it down. She then bent down my little "pinky" finger as well, leaving three fingers extended. But then, with a puzzled look, she considered my other (three-fingers-extended) hand. Carefully, she pulled my thumb and little "pinky" finger up, now leaving five fingers extended where there were three, and three fingers extended where there were five.

"Two!" she said, a bit too loud for the enforced quiet that worksheets inevitably demand.

"Yep, two, you've got it."

The student looked back down at the worksheet's requirements. Suddenly, this: "But, you know, I'm not sure. Did I add or subtract?"

The two of us talked, hushed, about the work she had done with my fingers, moving them up and down, adding, subtracting, taking two away from five and then adding two back on to three. Back and forth. She and I finally agreed that *this question of hers was really good*: "Did I add or subtract?"

"You have to do both," she ventured.

She and I also agreed that the other questions on the worksheet are too easy. "You just have to *do* them" she whispered, as if this was some secret knowledge that perhaps we'd better not let out.

ANOTHER BEGINNING: "BACK TO BASICS"

There is a long-standing allure to the idea of "back to the basics" in educational theory and practice. It drives not only reactionary school reform movements (e.g., Berk, 1985; Holt, 1996) and critiques or defenses of "liberal" or "progressivist" education (e.g., Grumet, 1993; Lazere, 1992). The idea of "the basics" also subtly underwrites how curriculum guides are conceived and organized; it defines how disciplinary knowledge is envisaged and delivered; it determines what the work of the classroom is understood to be; it provides images of how children are thought of regarding their participation in and necessity to the work of the classroom; it lays out what teachers are expected to know and to do, and how teaching and the assessment of teachers' and children's work are organized and evaluated. Even more subtle, but far more pervasive, powerful, and diffuse is the use of "basics" as an often unexamined, incendiary clarion in public discourse and the public press (Freedman, 1993).

In this book, we don't want to give up on the notion of the basics, despite the fact that it is too easy in these postmodern times to condemn the very idea of "basics" as all too modernist, all too Eurocentric, all too pretentious and grating on the ear. We agree with James Hillman: The old terms are fine. What isn't fine is that educational theory and practice seems stuck when it comes to imagining that what this term *basics* might mean in the living work of teachers and learners, except in the taken-for-granted and exhausted ways that the profession has inherited. Many of those in educational theory and practice have lost the ability to hear in this old term the myriad of alternate voices that haunt and inhabit it.

Rather than turning our backs on this troubled inheritance, in this book, we want to understand its meanings, motives, and desires, and we want to learn how to spot its (often unintended) appearance in the hallways and classrooms of schools and in the languages used to talk of teaching, learning, curriculum, and education.

But we want to do more than this: We want to offer what we believe is a more generous, more rigorous, more difficult, and more pleasurable image of what *the basics* might mean. Following the work of contemporary hermeneutics, we are not going to offer this alternate image as somehow naïvely "really" the basics, and demean the inherited version as "not really the basics." All we want to show, as Lewis Hyde (1983) suggested, is that "the way we treat a thing [like 'the basics'] can sometimes change its nature" (p. xiii). We want to ask: What might seem most important to us? How might we talk differently? How might we act differently? What new or ancient roles might we envisage for ourselves and our children in the teaching and learning and understanding of the disciplines that have been entrusted to us in schools? What, in fact, might "understanding" mean, given this alternate image of "the basics"?

In the rest of this introduction, we sketch out some of the key ideas in the commonplace, traditional, taken-for-granted version of "the basics" and how the version we will be exploring, what might be called an interpretive or hermeneutic version of the basics, operates on different fundamental assumptions. As demonstrated in detail next, even though talk of such fundamental assumptions might sometimes seem abstract and too distant from the tough and troubled realities of the classroom, it is never simply a matter of differences in philosophy. This difference in fundamental assumptions leads, of necessity, *to very different concrete classroom practices in our schools.*

TRADITIONAL AND INTERPRETIVE IMAGES OF "THE BASICS"

Education is being driven by an analytic idea of "basicness" inherited from a limited, literal-minded, and outdated version of the empirical sciences. This idea can be simply stated even though its consequences are profound: That which is most real or most basic to any discipline we might teach are its smallest, most clearly and distinctly isolatable, testable, and assessable bits and pieces. In the tale cited earlier, the worksheet that the child was doing had clearly isolated and made testable the child's understanding of the different operations of addition and subtraction. And, even if we find troubles with that particular worksheet and its wording or its reliability as a measure, under the auspices of this analytic idea of "the basics," the aim is to improve it by more clearly, carefully, and meticulously marking off, isolating, and separating distinguishable knowledge, skills, and attitudes. With such improvements, a particular child's mastery of specific knowledge, skills, and attitudes can thus be equally clearly, carefully, and meticulously tracked, tested, and assessed. Children's abilities regarding such masteries (and, via provincial or state testing scores, the accountability of teachers, classrooms, and schools) can be then unambiguously rank-ordered, from first to last. Furthermore, as happens in the city of Calgary in Alberta, Canada, such rank-orderings are published in the local newspapers in the name of the public's "right to know" about the performance of their children's schools. And this, in consequence, sets off, every year, energetic, but always eventually exhausting and exhausted debates, often full of more heat than light.

In this book, we contend that such fragmented "basics" are, in fact, *abstractions* that are the *outcomes* of a highly complex, theoretical, analytic process. In an odd turn of events, what is in fact an abstract and arcane product of analysis is believed to be what must be taught chronologically first, to the youngest of children. Under this idea of the basics, therefore, educators not only deliver *to the youngest of children* the products of a highly specialized theorizing; at the same time, both common sense and the work of developmental theory show that (in particular) young children *are not especially party to this form of analytic thinking.* School children are therefore subjected to the outcomes of a form of abstraction that they themselves cannot especially understand.

An image that is often invoked here is one of "breakdown." In order for something *to be itself* and not be unwittingly mixed up with other things, it is necessary to *break it down* into its component parts. Therefore, *to understand something* means *to break it down* (Jardine & Field, 1992; Weinsheimer, 1987) and to learn how to "control, predict and manipulate" (Habermas, 1972) the now-subsequent relations between such components. Therefore, in order *to teach something* (to young children especially), it becomes necessary to *break it down.* Moreover, if students in a classroom encounter difficulties in understanding some phenomenon we have broken down, we must *break it down even further.* We must, for example, further subdivide the subskills, further simplify the reading material or the mathematics questions or the science tasks we give children. And, failing this, if it cannot be commandingly broken down, it must simply be erased altogether. As that second grader's teacher suggested when shown what the conversation was about regarding the mathematics worksheet, "Yes, that question is confusing. I'll take it off the sheet next time."

We need to be clear about this. Whether that Grade 2 girl "correctly" circled the "correct" operations on that mathematics worksheet is reasonably easy to unambiguously assess, once mutual agreement is reached regarding which answers will count as correct. Assessing the quality and worthwhileness of the brief conversation and the mathematical and pedagogical potentials it might have held is a different matter. That conversation is full of ambiguity, leading questions, interventions, exaggerations, possibilities that are not especially easy to control, predict, and manipulate. Counting up the number of correct circlings on that worksheet is easier, quicker, more efficient, and clearer than exploring ideas of how addition and subtraction are inverse operations and that, mathematically speaking, one is not even *comprehensible* without the other. Talking about the inverse character of operations opens up large, contested, ongoing, and interweaving conversations that have defined and troubled the history of mathematics. We can be much more decisive and assured about that worksheet's "mark" than we can about the more elusive question of whether this conversation (if properly followed up) might "mark" this child's memory and learning and confidence. Marking such worksheets is less troublesome than the pedagogical and mathematical quandary of whether this "belonging together"—"you have to do both"—should be raised with the whole class and if so, how a teacher might properly do so. And this is to say nothing of the terrifying question of whether this child intended or understood any of this *at all.*

Moreover, as many student–teachers have courageously admitted, the mathematics worksheet is easy for *teachers* to "correct" by counting the circlings. What isn't so easy is for an individual teacher to face the question of whether he or she actually *understands* this mathematical "belonging together" and whether how well each beginning or experienced teacher might be able to handle him- or herself in the face of this child's questions.

In our Grade 2 tale, the adult who engaged that girl treated her questions as *mathematically interesting*. It is not helpful, at this point, to ask, for example, "Were they actually mathematically intended, or just calls for attention?" What is of interest in an interpretive treatment of "the basics" is this: Once this girl began to take up the possibilities that the conversation offered—all the images, for example, of putting together and taking apart 2 and 3 and 5, which started to sketch out for her the beginnings of a rich topography of relations—it became clear that *treating* her questions in this way, with mathematical interest, was beginning to change their nature. The playful, however-much-attention-getting game of moving fingers back and forth, up and down, was beginning to show something of a living mathematical relatedness that could begin to be opened up if it was treated a certain way.

The motives or the results of treating the basics-as-breakdown should not therefore be simply rejected outright. It is undeniable that *sometimes* breaking things down is *precisely* what is pedagogically required in the day-to-day work of schooling, or in dealing with specific difficulties of particular children. However, we contend that under the inherited image of "the basics," breakdown has become no longer a *response* but a *premise*: "Breakdown" runs ahead of teachers and learners and turns the living field of mathematics, for example, into something broken down in such a way that, paradoxically, it is now *all* problems. We know, for example, of an eighth-grade student doing pages of problems in a mathematics textbook and looking up the answers in the back of the book, who asked a teacher who drifted by, "Is *this* what mathematicians do?" And we know of a former head of a university mathematics department who told us that he could not recognize his own discipline in the work most children do in schools under the name of "mathematics education."

Once things are broken down into isolated, seemingly unrelated fragments, the only work of the classroom seems to be monitoring and management. As one student–teacher frighteningly reported: "In my practicum placement, *every* lesson is a lesson in 'classroom management'." Once the richness, rigors, and relatedness (Doll, 1993) of the disciplines are broken down into fragments, there is nothing to hold students' or teachers' attention in place and, of course, attention wavers. That Grade 2 girl just may have been seeking attention, but one of the reasons for this is that that mathematics worksheet did not deserve or especially need much attention. If teachers continually place such worksheets in front of children (we've witnessed settings where *eight* such sheets were done before morning recess), *of course* there will be discipline problems, because any of the ways in which *the work that students and teachers are doing* might have some "discipline" to it that might sustain attention have been eradicated ahead of time, all, again, in the name of this abstract idea of "the basics-as-breakdown."

An interpretive reading of "the basics" inverts this situation: It is only by working *in the midst* of the living discipline, for example, of mathematics and in the face of this living child's beginning venture into that terrain that a sound *pedagogical* judgment can emerge as to whether "breaking things down" might be needed here, now, in the face of these mathematical questions she has posed to us. It is only if you "know your way around" the territory of the "belonging together" of addition and subtraction that you can "hear" that Grade 2 girl's query, not as a problem (with her, with the wording of the worksheet, with the instructions given, etc.) but as a mathematically interesting question. This is, in fact, how hermeneutics understands the idea of "becoming experienced" at something, having been "around" (*peri-*) and having become someone because of such experience, someone "experienced" in mathematics. Having learned to live with trying to treat children's questions as full of mathematical portend (this was, after all, a mathematics class), one gradually becomes "experienced" at hearing the nuance and difference that each new situation brings. As Gadamer (1989, pp. 353–358) suggested, becoming experienced, hermeneutically understood, means become more and more sensitive to the fullness and uniqueness of experience itself, ready to experience the difference that *that* Grade 2 girl's questions bring to this troublesome, living human inheritance.

But of course, there is a paradox here. This going movement of "becoming experienced" occurs only if you treat the work of the classroom as full of intellectual vigor and possibility, and not as full only of problems that need fixing. Treated interpretively, the question of the belonging together of addition and subtraction is not a *problem*. That Grade 2 girl did not have *a problem*.

Therefore, it is not simply that the way you treat a thing can sometimes change its nature. There are implications in this interpretive treatment of "the basics" for how teachers and student–teachers might become experienced in treating that child's query as mathematically interesting and not simply as a problem that needs repair. And, just to throw in another twist: That Grade 2 girl *herself* was, in some small way, being taught how she might treat *her own* questions, not as problems that need repair, but as mathematically opening and interesting.

In this book we expand this interpretive treatment of "the basics" with images from the philosophy of ecology (e.g., the work of Wendell Berry, 1983, 1986, 1987, 1989, 1990; Snyder, 1977, 1980, 1990, 1995). This discipline has provided the authors with a rich language of relations, ancestry, interdependence, ideas of place and living, sustainable communities and the "continuity of attention and devotion" (Berry, 1987, p. 33) these matters require and deserve. Ecological discourse has helped us fill things we have experienced as teachers: the idea of sticking with a subject, a topic, a place (like the belonging-together of addition and subtraction) and not fragmenting, trivializing, or cheapening it for the sake of our own efficiency; the task deepening our understanding of the topics we are teaching and not taking the easy way out; the long lesson of learning to live with what we've learned about this place and these relations, learning that others have lived here before, deciding, then, what we shall do with this odd inheritance by linking it up with all its relations and histories and hidden kin.

This book is full of tough questions: What does it mean to conduct oneself well in the living, difficult "territory" of mathematics or science or poetry or the depths of a novel? What does it mean to lead our children carefully and generously into such territories? How can teachers, with some grace and sense of proportion, help students understand that their work can be a real part of the life of these places, and can make a real difference? What does it mean to become "experienced" in such matters? What are the dangers here? What is the good news? What, too, does all of this have to say about the nature and place of "educational research" in such matters?

Between the three of us, we have 70 years of teaching experience, and we have seen such rich, pleasurable, difficult interpretive work occur in real, ordinary school classrooms, with real, ordinary children and teachers. We have also seen that *even state-mandated testing scores go up* when such rich, pleasurable, difficult interpretive work is done. So this alternate, interpretive version of "the basics" is not proposed as an alternative to such tests. We are proposing something a wee bit more audacious: If you do rich, good, disciplined, living work with children, the (basics-as-breakdown) tests are no problem. If you "teach to the tests," the very idea of "good work" might seem like a great idea but a waste of precious time (Jardine, 2000). Or, worse yet, we either become cowards and say simply "who is to say what good work is?" or we come to identify "good work" with the efficiencies of basics-as-breakdown test-passing.

Obviously, that Grade 2 girl's questions did not have tags on them that say "this one is good." Those involved in educational theory and practice have all had enough of *that* sort of moralizing pretense and all of weakening, argumentative "who is to say" exhaustion that ensues. However, as teachers, we *are* faced with a choice as to what we ought to do. We can say that that Grade 2 girl was just looking for attention, or that the worksheet has a wording problem. However, if we are prepared to take this risk ourselves, that second grader's questions *can* be treated generously, as really good mathematical questions that open up a pedagogical territory worth of teachers' and students' attention and devotion.

WHAT FOLLOWS

We began this introduction with a classroom tale because of a central interpretive tenet: In attempting to understand the life of the classroom, it is never enough to simply put forth general principles, frameworks, or ideas. Ideas, hopes, presumptions, and prejudices about teaching, learning, children, and curriculum must face what Gadamer (1989, p. 38; see also Jardine, 1992b) called "the fecundity of the individual case." The individual case of that Grade 2 girl's questions is not merely an instance or example of something fully understood beforehand. Rather, her questions, treated interpretively, have the potential to "co-determine, supplement, and correct" (p. 39) what we have heretofore understood, thus adding themselves to the ongoing experiences of mathematics we might then pursue. Individual cases are thus treated, not as individual and individualized narratives in interpretive work (this would simply further entrench a new locale of "breakdown"). Seemingly isolated and individual cases are treated as sites where the discipline of mathematics that schools have inherited is in the process of being "set right anew" (Arendt, 1969, p. 192).

We have been using the example of mathematics in this introduction for a specific purpose. Mathematics, as only one of the many disciplines with which schools have been entrusted seems most amenable to the image of basics-as-breakdown. Moreover, the inverse is true. Mathematics seems *least* amenable to ideas of ancestry, topography, place, relation, generativity, conversation, and so on. Mathematics is "the hardest nut to crack" and has therefore become, for the authors, one of the most interesting challenges to face in an interpretive treatment of the basics. In this book, we often deal again with mathematics (see chaps. 6 and 7), but by no means exclusively. We explore child development (chaps. 2, 4, 7, and 12), science curriculum (chaps. 4 and 5), teacher education (chap. 8), novel studies (chap. 11), new information technologies (chap. 5), writing practices in the classroom (chaps. 1 and 3), ideas of curriculum integration (chap. 9). We also deal with another phenomenon central to interpretive work: how both language and taken-for-granted understandings of children and adults and the work of schooling are filled with bloodlines and histories and images that often far outstrip any individual desires, hopes, or intentions (see chaps. 2, 4, 8, and 10). We also explore in some detail the nature of interpretive inquiry itself as a form of "educational research" (see chaps. 2, 4, 9, and 12).

Portions of this book were written over a 10-year period, under shifting and varied circumstances, and the ideas sketched out in this introduction are our version of what has been slowly emerging over that time. Because of this, we have decided not to deal in detail with each individual chapter in this introduction. Instead, we carry forward some of the emergent ideas sketched out in this introduction by providing a Preamble before each chapter—some thoughts that will knit together how we have come to treat our work as revolving around what we suggest is a more generous, more rigorous, more pleasurable idea of "the basics" in teaching and learning.

Preamble 1

In ancient Greek mythology, *Chronos,* the god of time, was known for eating his children. One of the most common laments about the sort of classroom work proposed under an interpretive treatment of "the basics" is this: It all sounds wonderful, but there isn't enough *time,* given the realities of today's schools. These realities are many: state-mandated testing, the wide diversity of students in school classrooms, the increasing demands placed on teachers over and above the demands of teaching, the sheer amounts of material that have to be "covered," the seemingly waning attention spans of "kids these days," and so on.

We believe that this feeling of not having enough time is real and these laments are quite genuine. However, we also believe that this feeling is, at least in part, *the product of "basics-as-breakdown."* The logic as we see it is this.

Under the logic of basics-as-breakdown, each task we face in classrooms involves a lesson (or, as suggested in chap. 1, a "lessen") organized around an apparently isolated curricular fragment. Because this is understood to be the case, there is no time to deepen our understanding of or dwell upon any one fragment. There is no urge to slow things down and open them up, because there is simply so much else to get done and so little time. Moreover, *as* an isolated fragment, no one fragment *requires* such slowing down. As Wendell Berry (1987) suggested, for this fragmentary way of being in the world of the classroom, "time is always running out" (p. 44). As such, many classrooms (and, in fact, in so much of contemporary life) is caught up in an ever-accelerating "onslaught" (Arendt, 1969) of ever-new activities and the odd equation of some sort of fulfilment with becoming caught up in such frenetic consumption. Many teachers and children are thereby condemned to constantly striving to "keep up" and to taking on the *failure* to keep up as nothing less than a personal or pathological problem involving lack of effort, lack of skills, improper attitudes, or not having read enough books or been taught enough "useful" things in teacher education programs. As the pieces become broken down more and more, the only hope of at least *attempting* to keep up is *acceleration.* Talk of slowing things down, dwelling over something and deepening our experience of it begins to sound vaguely quaint, antiquated, and simply unrealistic (Jardine, 2000).

Many teachers and student-teachers are living in settings that do not understand, let alone promote, the possibility of a continuity of attention and devotion either to children or to the disciplines with which they are entrusted. Time itself becomes broken up, fragmented under precisely the same logic of fragmentation that breaks down the disciplines into broken-basics and breaks down our children into "special needs" (see chap. 2) and "developmental levels" (see chaps. 2, 4, and 7; see also Jardine, Clifford, & Friesen, 1999).

Interpretively understood, however, things are quite different. Each task faced in the classroom is precisely *not* an isolated fragment which must be quickly covered and then dropped in order to get on to the next bit. Rather, classroom and curriculum topics, conversations, and events are treated as ways in to the whole of the living inheritances that have been handed to teachers and students in schools. One is never "doing" an isolated fragment, but is always "doing" the whole living field *from* a particular locale. That Grade 2 girl, in her questions about adding and subtracting, had found an opening into the whole discipline of mathematics *from* this particular vantage point. This is how "understanding" is understood in hermeneutic work: Particular events are "read" or "treated" *as* a part of some longstanding whole to which it belongs and from which it gains its sense and significance. So, for example, in chapter 1, when the curriculum topic of "time" arrives, it is not treated as one more thing that has to be "covered." Rather, it is treated as a cluster of shared and contested and age-old bloodlines in human life which deserve some continuity of attention and devotion. Moreover, when individual students' quandaries and questions about time arise, they are not treated pathologically, but are treated as addressing these bloodlines and each person's place within them. Thus, teachers and students alike are treated as if they are *already deeply part of these bloodlines,* such that dealing with "time" as a topic in school is at once exploring our own implications within it.

Once this image of classroom work takes hold, something strange happens: Time seems to slow down. More than this, as Friesen and Clifford, the authors of chapter 1, have often heard about the various classrooms where they have cotaught, not only are things not especially frenetic. In an odd way, on the face of it at least, very little seems to be happening.

This first chapter is, in part, a description of what the work of slowing down looks like and how, when it works, such slowing down involves opening up large bodies of relations and ancestries. Therefore, what seems at first like slowing down over one fragment or one child's experiences in fact turns out to be the opening up, from this one fecund (Gadamer, 1989, p. 38) locale, great areas of pleasurable and difficult classroom work, for students and teachers alike.

Chapter 1

A Curious Plan:
Managing on the Twelfth

Patricia Clifford
Sharon Friesen

> The Mock Turtle went on:
> "We had the best of educations in fact, we went to school every day."
> "And how many hours a day did you do lessons?" said Alice, in a hurry to change the subject.
> "Ten hours the first day," said the Mock Turtle, "nine the next, and so on."
> "What a curious plan!" exclaimed Alice.
> "That's the reason they're called lessons," the Gryphon remarked; "because they lessen from day to day."
> This was quite a new idea to Alice, and she thought it over a little before she made her next remark. "Then the eleventh day must have been a holiday?"
> "Of course it was," said the Mock Turtle.
> "And how did you manage on the twelfth?"
> —Carroll (1865/1966, pp. 95–96)

INTRODUCTION: PLANNING A LIVED CURRICULUM

Every September, teachers and students gather together in our classroom to learn. Each of us, teacher and child alike, walks through the door bringing experiences and understandings that are ours alone. Yet, each person is also embarking on a journey that he or she will come to share with others. This journey is made anew every year with every class.

Travelers prepare more or less carefully for the adventures they hope to have, but the itineraries, maps, and plans do not in themselves create the voyage. The journey is an experience, lived as just the thing it turns out to be: moment-by-moment, day-by-day, month-by-month. As teachers, we prepare for each year's journey in big ways and in small ways. We make decisions, design plans, and outline key strategies to help us set directions for the coming year. In this chapter, we hope to share some of our decisions, plans, and strategies, therein describing the factors we consider as we prepare for an authentically engaging journey with each new class of children.

Some travelers keep diaries, which we, too, have done, recording actual situations that took place in our classroom from September 1991 to June 1992. In terms of its multiaged, open-area configuration, our class was like others in the primary division of our school. The number of children varied throughout the year, as families moved in and out of the community. At any time, the two of us team-taught between 55 and 58 children in Grades 1 and 2. In many ways, our classroom would be familiar to anyone used to teaching in middle-class neighborhoods. In other ways, however, there are important differences. First of all, the children in our class vary more widely in their abilities, backgrounds, emotional and physical needs than one might expect. In this class, 10 students were second-language learners. One child was in a wheelchair. Several had behavioral problems severe enough to warrant the interventions of social workers, psychologists, and psychiatrists since before the children entered first grade. Some had been identified as gifted, others as learning disabled.

Since the mid-1970s, the school in which we taught had maintained a tradition of multiaged, open-area classrooms as part of its demonstration function for the local university. Because innovative structures and teaching practices are expected and encouraged, we were supported in our request both to teach together and to conduct action research. From the earliest days of our work as a team, everyone knew what we were setting out to do. Never content simply to replicate existing best practices, our school wanted to find out what would happen if we did what teachers at our school, University Elementary School, have always done: question, challenge, and change fundamental assumptions about the education of young children.

Using excerpts from the diaries we kept from 1991–1992, we hope in this chapter to illustrate some of the struggles and successes we encountered. We feel the examples we give suggest a quality of children's thought and work that some may find astounding, given the fact that our students are only 6 and 7 years old. We believe, however, that this is an example of the kind of work and thinking in which *all* children could engage and that all teachers could endeavor to bring forth. We would like to pose serious questions about how teachers can prepare themselves to create situations in which the voices of children genuinely inform the construction of each year's curriculum. For some teachers, administrators, and staff developers, these questions may be uncomfortable to hear because they call into question much of what is currently recognized as sound professional practice. We maintain that many of such current practices stand squarely in the way of the kinds of educational reform our profession needs most urgently to begin.

When schools open each year, one of the first things many teachers do is begin making long-range and unit plans that outline what they hope to accomplish by Christmas or, perhaps, for the whole year. If you are a school administrator reading this chapter, we want to give you some things to think about as you request such plans. If you are a classroom teacher, we would like to give you things to consider before you actually sit down to plan. If you are a teacher of teachers, we would like to give you pause as you prepare student teachers for their work with children. We would like, in short, to add our voices to the conversations aimed at ensuring that lessons do *not* lessen from day to day, from year to year, for children who have no choice but to come to school. We are committed to developing a classroom where teachers and children are passionate, robust learners. This commitment requires something more than new programs or new methods. It calls for what we can only characterize as a fundamentally different idea of what is considered "basic" to education, and a different disposition that permits teachers to live more generously with the children in their care.

We are searching for a school curriculum that acknowledges the importance of the lived experience of children and teachers; that understands growth as more than an interior, private, individual matter of unfolding development; that situates teaching and learning within the context of an educative community; and that asks hard questions about the fuzzy, feel-good legacy of much of what teachers now do in the name of "progressive" practice. Creating such a curriculum is a life's work. Perhaps it is significant, however, that neither of us came to early childhood education as our first career. One of us worked for 5 years as a systems analyst, and the other taught senior high school for 15 years. For different reasons, and on different paths, we had both developed similar concerns about public education long before we met each other. We were worried about the boredom, dropout rates, and general lackluster performance of many students. In that we were not alone; we were part of a growing public concern that young people in North America were not learning as much as they might. Two things were different for us, however. First, we resisted the return to traditional images and practices that seem almost inevitably to accompany criticism of schools. And second, each of us knew (again, long before we met) that attempts to reform schools by concentrating mainly on the attitudes and achievements of secondary students, or on the attitudes and achievements of those being hired to teach in schools, was unlikely to succeed. Each of us had already decided that the most promising place to create genuinely new practices was with the very young.

We endeavored initially to find out something about what a classroom would look like if we called into question some of our profession's most ordinary assumptions about teaching and learning. When we first wrote this chapter in 1992, we had studied, taught, and written together for 4 years. In that time, we learned a great deal, and we fight constantly with the temptation to try to say everything at once. In this chapter, we hope to make a small start by posing three important questions:

How can curriculum remain open to children's unique experiences and contacts with the world they know outside the school?

Why is imaginative experience the best starting place for planning?

What happens when teachers break down the barriers between school knowledge and real knowledge?

DAVID'S STORY: ON KEEPING THINGS CONNECTED

"I would ask you to remember only this one thing," said Badger. "The stories people tell have a way of taking care of them. If stories come to you, care for them. And learn to give them away where they are needed. Sometimes a person needs a story more than food to stay alive; that is why we put these stories in each other's memory. This is how people care for themselves." (Lopez, 1990, p. 48)

We met David and his parents on the first day of school. They had just returned to Canada after spending 7 years in Africa, where they had lived and worked among the Masai. Although he was of European descent, David had been born in Africa. He went to a village kindergarten, and played and tended cattle with the Masai children. No one in our class, including us, knew much about Africa. Although we had listened carefully to what David's parents told us at the beginning of the school year, we remembered embarrassingly little of it because we had been trying to learn about our 54 other children at the same time. So, as we watched David take his first tentative steps in school, we often forgot that the life David had been living until the end of August was radically different from the one he now had to negotiate in our large, complicated, noisy Canadian classroom.

Throughout September and into October, David spoke very little. He would answer direct questions briefly, but never offered to share much of himself. Once, in response to an assignment to tell a personal story, he told a small group of children how he and his family had gone camping, and had woken up to find lions crouching under their truck. The other children acted the story out, growling and shrieking with frightened delight. But aside from this story, we knew little about David. As time went on, David made a friend in class, hooking up with Jason out of mutual need. David was lonely, and he wanted to establish himself in a new country. Jason needed a companion to coerce, command, and bully. This friendship worried David's parents. David had spent all of his life nurtured within a trusting, gentle community, and he approached his friendship with Jason with the same quality of trust. David got into trouble almost daily because of Jason, and David's parents found themselves having to talk to him about the inappropriateness of some people's intentions. They were heartsick, both about what was happening to David and about the ugly lessons about "the real world" that their gentle, naïve son was beginning to absorb.

One day in early October, David arrived at school with a huge book about the Masai and asked if he could show his book to the other children. This was the first time David had ever offered to share part of his life experiences with the whole class, to teach us all what he knew best—life among the Masai. David stood in front of the class with his book. He flipped to a few pictures and spoke softly—so softly that only the children near the front could hear him. We tried to offer a few details about the Masai, but we knew so little. In spite of these difficulties and limitations, the children were entranced. They had so many questions to ask David, so much they wanted to know. This was the second time we had seen the children respond with enthusiasm to David's life in Africa. This time we recognized the power of the invitation that he had offered us. Here was the perfect chance to bring David into the full life of the classroom.

That afternoon, David's mother came to volunteer in the classroom. We asked her if she would speak to us about the Masai. She agreed, took her place in a small chair at the front of the group, and opened David's book. As she spoke, David stood quietly at her shoulder, gently stroking her long hair. He seemed to relax into the memories of that safe, familiar place, trusting the intimacy of his mother's voice and body to secure the connection between here and there.

As our eyes met above the heads of the children, we knew we had been waiting for this all along, without knowing it: waiting for David's life in Africa to come alive for us. Up to now, David had blended in too readily with all the other children. We had had no images to help us understand that this new country, this new classroom, held few connections with the world he had known in Africa.

Our efforts to see all children as contributing members of our classroom community is a kind of standing invitation, but we never know who will take it up, or how they will do it. It appeared that David had decided that *now* was his time, and he made the first essential move. David and his mother shared their life among the Masai with us, and in that sharing helped forge new links between David, his classmates, and us. The class was filled with curiosity, and questions overflowed the hour we spent together. Because of the intensity of the children's interest in David's experiences in Africa and the potential to find, in their pleasure, a new place for David in the classroom, we felt committed to act beyond the delights of that afternoon. We accepted eagerly when David's mother asked if we were interested in using a children's book about the Masai that they had at home.

The next day David brought us *Bringing the Rain to Kapiti Plain* (Aardema, 1981). As we read the story to the class, David sat at the back mouthing every word to himself. Once again we saw David relaxed, smiling, basking in the genuine delight of hearing that well-loved story again, this time in the world of his classroom in Calgary. This book was just the beginning of the stories about Africa, for we found others: *The Orphan Boy, Rhinos for Lunch, Elephants for Supper,* and *A Promise to the Sun.* David brought in other things to share with us, such as elaborate beaded collars and knives used to bleed cattle.

Months later, when the children drew maps of their known worlds, David's map showed his house in Africa, the cheetah park, the camping place where the lions crouched under the truck, a Masai warrior. We sensed then how much of his heart was still there and were honored that he felt safe enough among us to share himself in this way, for as David now tells us, he is "a very private person." We are also keenly aware that we would have known nothing about these places had David not come into our lives. Recently, when we were reading about Mongolian nomads living on animal blood and milk, many children remembered what David had taught them about the Masai. They speculated about why the animals didn't die when they were bled, and looked to David for confirmation that such a thing was, indeed, possible.

We continually ask ourselves: How much of the life that is lived completely outside school is welcomed into the classroom as knowledge and experience that can enrich all those who inhabit a particular classroom? How much of each child gets to come to school? When a child says, "This is me, and I am ready for you to know it," we must try to honor this offering, not shut it out, control it, or hurry to get on with the curriculum. An invitation is more than words. Offered sincerely, invitations create obligations to welcome and to provide. Having extended an invitation to David, we felt compelled to act. David's knowledge and experiences needed to become part of the curriculum, part of the life of the group.

Bringing David into the class in this way opened up new possibilities for him, but it did something just as important for the whole class. All of the children lived the experience of a standing invitation. By observing how we attended to David and to others who also offered *their* stories, the children came to understand the importance of what each of them might bring to the journey our class had embarked on together.

Our curriculum work demands mindful, deliberate improvisation at such moments. It goes far beyond "Show and Share," which can be a perniciously educational practice: "You show me yours and I'll show you mine." Children's sharing is often limited to a slot in the daily agenda. Although such activity is designed to bring home into the school, the activity of sharing can, unfortunately, become an end in itself, requiring no further commitment from the teacher than to provide the opportunity for each child to bring in a favorite object or news event. That is not at all what we mean when we speak of invitations. We mean, rather, that each child's voice can be heard, and that their speaking can make a difference to our curriculum decision making. Improvising on children's responses to our standing invitation demands a commitment to recognizing human relationships as a fundamental source of knowledge. At the beginning of the year we could not plan for these moments, but we were prepared for them because we knew that they would inevitably arise. We knew that the children would give us what we needed to know, as long as we remained open to the possibilities.

Determined to foster continuity between personal and school knowledge, we work in a constant state of watchfulness. Children's authentic offerings are often made tentatively. Unlike David's, they can be subtle and easy to miss, but they are nevertheless vital components of a lived curriculum. We know that when curriculum includes only the plans teachers make to deliver instruction, the child who emerges is usually what we might call a "school child," one who is either compliant with or defiant of the exercise of institutional power. It is our belief that when curriculum is divorced from real life, children often lose connections with their own memories and histories. They lose touch with who they are. They may exist in our eyes more as students than as emerging selves, and we wonder if they continue to learn in any passionate sense of that word.

LEARNING: FROM THE KNOWN TO THE UNKNOWN

Children develop most fully as passionate learners when they—like all of us—are allowed to claim fully their own experience of the world. We are not, however, talking about the type of experience made relevant to children through its commercial appeal or immediate access: Ninja Turtles and Barbies, video games, superheros, or cartoons. Nor are we talking about the immersion in local experience that some call "the belly button curriculum": me and my house, me and my family, me and my neighborhood. Much of early childhood education is grounded in a view of learning as predictable development through ages and stages, from familiar to strange, from concrete to abstract, from (supposedly) simple to complex.

In one sense, we accept these assumptions. After all, David *did* want to share his daily experiences in Africa with his classmates in Canada, and we watched David blossom as he accepted the invitation to connect his life in Africa with life in Canada. In another sense, however, what happened to David is best understood as a starting point for even richer engagement. What intrigued the children was not the sharing of "me and my family." They did not want to talk about *their* daily lives in Calgary in response to David's stories. They wanted, rather, to talk about knives and arrows, about drinking blood and milk, about women who shaved their heads, and about children who tended cattle all day long, far from the gaze of watchful adults. What was familiar and well-known to David called out to the imagination in each of us. Enriched by David's knowledge, we began to experience new worlds together, creating within our classrooms the kinds of imaginative experiences that Egan (1986, 1992) described: those imaginative experiences that engage, intrigue, interest, puzzle, and enchant; those imaginative experiences that call forth sustained and key conversations about freedom, loyalty, responsibility, strength, and human relationships. When we speak of imaginative engagement, we mean the kind of engagement that invites children most fully, most generously, into the club of knowers; not at some unspecified time in the future when they are grown up and able to use their knowledge, but today and each and every day they spend with us.

Egan (1992) invited us to consider that "even the briefest look at children's thinking from this perspective opens profound conflicts with some of the ideas that dominate educational thinking and practice today" (p. 653). When we learn to look at children with new eyes, we can see clearly that, by the time they come to school at age 5, they have already learned about some of the most complex, abstract, and powerful ideas they will ever encounter. Simply by virtue of their humanity, they have experienced joy and fear, love and hate, trust and betrayal, power and oppression, expectation and satisfaction—all, as Egan (1986) noted, before they have even learned how to ride a bicycle (pp. 28–29).

Our study of a familiar fairy tale shows how this view of imaginative experience can challenge dominant educational thinking. Early in 1991, the children in our class listened to *Rumpelstiltskin,* an ordinary experience in a primary classroom. In choosing that story, we were depending on the children's knowledge in important ways. We did *not* assume that they had had direct experience with princes and princesses, much less with malevolent dwarves and alchemic transformations. Indeed, if learning is understood to proceed from concrete to abstract, from familiar to strange, from daily experience to the world of wonders, then *Rumpelstiltskin* should make little sense to children. But they loved the story, debating fiercely about issues such as whether parents, like the miller, have the right to put their children in danger; whether people have the right to ask for help without pledging something in return; whether adults should be allowed to give their children away, and the grief that may follow if they participate in such bad bargains. For children to understand this story, they needed to know about deception, the politics of rescue, false pride, boasting, and the indomitable human spirit.

As Egan (1992) noted, "to teach concrete content untied to powerful abstractions is to starve the imagination" (p. 653). David's story is important to us as teachers because of what it tells us about hearing each child's voice and bringing each child into the life of the classroom. However, it is also important to us because of what it says about children's interest in places far away and times long ago. The great stories of history and literature are as fascinating to the children in our class as David's accounts of Africa. Stories about Leonardo da Vinci, Columbus, Ghengis Khan, Radomes and Aida, Pythagoras, and King Arthur and his court prompted the same kind of lively debate and discussion of big questions about the human condition we saw in their response to *Rumpelstiltskin*. Retellings of *Romeo and Juliet, Beowulf* and parts of Chaucer were as enchanting as readings of *The Lady of Shalott, The Highwayman,* and *The Rime of the Ancient Mariner.* All of these stories have engaged the imagination of generations of adults because of the engagement they demand. We have discovered that these stories touch young children with as much power. They connect both them and us as their teachers with the past, ground us all firmly in the present moment of listening to their rich language and images. They cause us, even compel us, to contemplate together what life holds in store.

Thus, for us, a second important planning issue centers on the "big questions" we offer to and accept from the children we teach. Without those big questions, tied to great literature that engages the imagination, the spirit, the feelings, and the intellect, curriculum is likely to be thin and unsubstantial, fully satisfying to neither teacher nor child. Arising from questions about the human condition that engage each of us because we share the planet together, the curriculum we have created with our children permits them access to intellectual and aesthetic traditions that are thousands of years old. Children often ask some of the same questions the ancients asked, and discover anew, for themselves, the power of learning both to create and to solve important, engaging questions.

We have many, many typed pages of notes we took while the children were discussing stories and films about Columbus, Leonardo da Vinci, Ghengis Khan, the Arthurian saga, outer space, Greek myths, and Chinese legends. These subjects may not be considered the usual fare offered to 6- and 7-year-olds. Indeed, we had no idea in September, when we were writing our plans, the various directions our studies would take. How could we have imagined, for example, that Jason would bring us back again and again to the idea that human knowledge is really a model of how we think things work? He asked us over and over how people know when their models are wrong. And over and over, we thought about that question as a way of understanding what adults have come to call "history," "mathematics," "science," "literature," "ethics," and "education." How do any of us find out if our models are wrong?

How could we have anticipated the amazement of Diana, a child in Grade 1 who could not yet read, when she learned that the ancient Greeks had known the earth was spherical, but that people had subsequently *lost* that knowledge for centuries. They had lost precious knowledge about space, Diana's passion. She was offended by what she considered to be the carelessness of her ancestors, and endlessly intrigued by how that knowledge had been retrieved. Had there been one person, she wondered, who had just stood up and said, "Look, you guys, this is how it is"? Or had there been many people at the same time who figured it out together?

Could we ever have guessed that Edward would lean over to Sharon during a reading of *The Rime of the Ancient Mariner* and whisper, "It feels like the ghost of the ancient mariner is in this room right now. Do you think he's here? Do you?" Until Christmas, Edward had hardly spoken to us. He was so withdrawn from others that he often buried his face in the hood of his kangaroo shirt and rocked back and forth during lessons and class meetings. He seldom wrote, preferring to sit by himself and draw minutely detailed mazes of miniature battle scenes, seemingly obsessed with blood dripping from gaping wounds and vicious swords. On a blustery January day, Coleridge's words had reached across time and space to touch a little boy who wanted, for the very first time, to talk to his teachers about the world inside his head. The next day, he picked up the conversation again. "Do you know," he told us, "that an imagination is a terrible thing? The pictures in my mind really, really scare me." For Edward, the thing that had frightened him most—his ability to conjure detailed, vivid images—became the vehicle through which he was able, for the first time that we could see, to connect with others in the classroom.

Would we ever have expected that, after several weeks of reading, discussion, and project work about human discoveries, dreams, hard work, courage, tenacity, and integrity, the children would have pulled together the following questions about knowledge and work, questions to which they—and we—returned again and again in the months that followed:

Where do you go looking for knowledge?

How do you learn the secrets of the world?

The more you learn, the more you get to know what you have to do. Why?

Why do things come alive when you put yourself into your work?
What do you need to give so you can get knowledge?

The children drove us deeper and further than we could possibly have
gone on our own, demanding more stories, more history, more problems,
more answers. The children stretched our knowledge and our capacity to
hear, in their demands, the next best step to take. We haunted stores and li-
braries, searching for books to bring back to them and for books to help *us*
learn more physics, mathematics, mythology, history, literature. When, for
example, we read the children *I, Columbus*—excerpts from the log Columbus reputedly kept on his journey to learn what he called the secrets of the
world—they asked many questions. Was Columbus the only person who believed that the earth was a sphere? What must it have been like to be Columbus, certain of your own knowledge but wrong in the eyes of many of your
peers? Where did Columbus get his maps from, anyway? How did he navigate once he had passed the boundaries of the known world? Where was
the Sargasso Sea, and was that where the Ancient Mariner had been be-
calmed? Why do people say Columbus discovered America when there were
people living here already?

As teachers, we saw opportunities in these questions to bring in more
and more material about maps and map-making, astronomy, geography,
and history. One child brought in an article from the Manchester *Guardian*
about Renaissance maps. We found stories such as Yolen's *Encounter*, which
raised important issues about the effect of European contact on aboriginal
peoples, and we introduced the children to the fact that the First Nations of
Canada struggle to this very day with the consequences of voyages of so-
called discovery that ended up on shores we now think of as our own.

During each story, lesson, and discussion, we would sit side by side at an
easel at the front of the group. One of us would facilitate the children's conversation, and the other would scribe as quickly as possible, catching wherever we could the actual words of the children, and paraphrasing when the
talk moved too quickly. Earlier in the year we had tried to tape-record these
conversations, but the microphones let us down. First, the conversation was
too complex for a machine to capture properly. Second, capturing key elements of the discussion required a teacher's judgment. Which comments
and questions did we want to formulate for the whole group? Which were
the threads that seemed, even in the moment, to hold real promise of future exploration? Where were the moments that allowed us to make powerful connections between the mandated program of studies and the children's own questions?

At the end of days on which the children had been engaged in such discussions, we would sit at the easel re-reading and organizing what they had

said and asked. We would highlight for ourselves what the next step ought to be. What had the children said that we could most profitably mine? Sometimes we knew exactly what resources we could use. We would go to our class library, the school collection, or to the public library for books and films we already knew about and bring them in for future classes. At other times, we would just go looking. If a question seemed sufficiently promising or intriguing, we would look for material we were certain must exist.

Curriculum planning that takes the voices of children seriously represents a kind of openness. Teachers need to remain open to children's experience in the world and construct curricula that are deeply responsive to and resonant with what each child knows, who each child is. Teachers also need to understand that it is only the big, authentically engaging questions that create openings wide and deep enough to admit all adventurers who wish to enter. Three things are important in this regard. First, when children raise the kinds of questions that capture their attention in our studies of literature, history, and mathematics, it becomes possible for each of them to find compelling ways into the discussion and work that follows. Individuals cannot tell in advance when moments of connection will occur—for themselves or for others. Our experience has shown us time and again that questions about fairness, justice, knowledge, learning, courage, and oppression, sparked by stories of substance and worth, seem to free children to engage with complex aspects of the world and of their own experience.

Second questions are ones that intrigue adults as much as they enchant children. The conversations, the debates, and all of the work that flow out of these questions are deeply engaging for us, as teachers. The children experience our own genuine sense of excitement and commitment to the world of the mind and the spirit as they struggle with us to relive, in the present moment, dilemmas that were equally real to our ancestors. Moreover, when the children see their own questions returned to them as the basis for subsequent work and study, they come to know curriculum as a living, connected experience. Curriculum is not delivered to them through fragmented activities made up by others; it is created with them, inspired by the work of the community of which each of them is a valued member.

Third, the worlds made available to children through stories and philosophizing of this sort form strong links with the complicated, everyday world in which they live. When the dean of the local law school, the mother of one of our students, came into the classroom during our study of *Rumpelstiltskin* and saw a child's comment written on chart paper, she hastened to copy it down: "When parents give their child away for gold, they will regret it later on, when they've had time to think about it." She was about to make a presentation about surrogacy contracts to the legal community, and she was delighted that young children, inspired by this classic tale, had articulated so clearly the dilemma that many legal scholars were now exploring. Thus, teachers must remain open to the power of real literature, real science, real mathematics, real art to touch all of us profoundly—not only the children.

REAL KNOWLEDGE AND SCHOOL KNOWLEDGE: EXAMPLES FROM MATHEMATICS

Coming to know the world as mathematicians or scientists—like becoming a reader and writer—involves authentic engagement in mathematical and scientific experiences, not the busy work that often comes to count in school as mathematics and science or reading and writing. Many school textbooks and workbooks are organized to encourage mindless recitation. Most mathematics curricula are organized to support the notion that accuracy in computation equals excellence in understanding. Even Alberta's new mathematics curriculum, which states that problem solving is at the heart of mathematics, relegates problems to a separate unit. Many curriculum designers seem to think that problem solving means doing word problems. It is also clear that many teachers think that they are teaching mathematics when they are merely covering the textbook or the workbook. Unfortunately, the result often is a student who is schooled in "school mathematics"—a form of mathematics that bears little resemblance to the "real mathematics" that mathematicians, physicists, and engineers experience, or to the mathematics that sparks the imagination and ignites a passion for understanding the world mathematically and scientifically.

We want children to experience mathematics as a powerful language of the imagination that allows them to explore big mathematical ideas like balance, space, time, patterns, and relationships. We have come to see that they enjoy thinking about these matters, exploring, debating, solving problems, and learning together. We have found, too, having taught in many different school settings, that too many school children learn only "school mathematics," a dull, lifeless, scary, and irrelevant round of pluses and minuses that usurps the real, much more engaging, thing.

How might it look in a classroom if teachers set about to make math real? The Alberta science and math curricula both state that children in the primary grades must know certain things about time: They must know how to read both analog and digital clocks, know the days of the week, the months of the year, and something about the seasons and the phases of the moon. When we sat down to talk about how to teach this part of the curriculum, we saw that among our options were activities that would encourage children to think that time resided in a clock or a calendar. Such activities would have satisfied the curriculum objectives, but we wanted more. We wanted children to learn that time is a mysterious and puzzling phenomenon.

We felt that if we restricted an understanding of time to the narrow view of "telling time" contained within most curriculum guides, we would transmit a useful skill, but not much more. Instead, we thought that if we paid attention to what physicists ask about time, we might give children access to what is undeniably one of the secrets of the world.

Here is what Bruce Gregory (1990), the Associate Director of the Harvard–Smithsonian Center for Astrophysics, tells us about the human understanding of time:

> Galileo's accomplishment was made possible by his decision to talk about the world in terms of motion through space and time. These concepts seem so obvious to us that it is difficult to remember that they *are* concepts. Time is normally measured in terms of motion, from the swing of the pendulum of a grandfather's clock to the oscillations of a quartz crystal in a modern watch. Apart from such periodic behaviour, how could we even talk about the uniformity of time? In the words of the contemporary American physicist John Wheeler, "Time is defined so that motion looks simple." Wheeler also said, "Time? The concept did not descend from heaven, but from the mouth of man, an early thinker, his name long lost." Einstein demonstrated the power of talking about space and time as though they were a unity, and in the process he showed that both space and time are human inventions—ways of talking about the world. (p. 70)

To let children in on some of the secrets of this way of talking about the world, we need to let them in on two other big secrets. First of all, they must come to understand that human knowledge is humanly constructed. As a culture, a society, a community—and as a classroom—we make decisions about what will and will not count as knowledge, and those decisions make some understandings of the world possible, as much as they render other perspectives impossible.

If we really want our children to face the challenges of the 21st century with confidence and skill, we need to teach them not only that they can acquire current knowledge, but also that they have voices that can shape what their society comes to accept as knowledge. This philosophy of teaching is exemplified in the following illustrations drawn from a series of lessons and activities about time.

We began one morning by asking the children to talk to us and each other about what they knew about time. Seated on the floor in front of the easel, they began to talk. As they offered examples of how time works, we recorded the following comments:

It's something you have to use.
You need to wear a watch to know what time it is.

You need it—you can be late if you don't know the time.

You can run out of time when you are playing or when people bother you.

Sometimes grown-ups say, "You have two minutes to do something!" They really mean get it done quickly.

You need to know time to know how fast you run in a race. You win when you have the least time.

You can waste time.

It is important to tell time.

People get worried if they think they are running out of time.

A day and a night equals 24 hours.

Time can be fast and slow.

Time lets you know when you should be doing things.

Time goes fast when you're playing. It goes slowly when you're not having fun.

Everyone in the world needs to know what time is the right time. You need to synchronize time with world events, like the Olympics on TV.

Adults are expected to tell time. Children don't have to.

If your house is flooded, it takes a long time to get it out.

When we're doing projects, people always ask, "How much time until lunch?"

You can tell time by counting by fives.

People need to be home on time.

Clearly, this long list shows that the children had many experiences with time. For example, they knew about clocks and strategies about how to read clocks, they knew time was related to astronomical and geographical phenomena, and they knew time experientially. One of the children asked, "How can you tell time without a watch?" This question was to lead to intriguing explorations into the history of time and time-keeping devices and opened the possibility to explore time and its astronomical relationships. When one child recalled that a member of Columbus's crew was charged with the responsibility of turning the hour glass over when it emptied and keeping track of how often this occurred, another remarked that at one time people used sundials. This idea of the sundial caught the children's imagination, and they wanted to know exactly how a sundial told time. Fortunately, the sun cooperated with us and we went outside to begin some preliminary investigations.

In order to understand what happened next, it is important to know something about how our day is structured. We reserve a 2-hour block of time between morning recess and lunch for the integrated study of litera-ture, social studies, science, and mathematics. This time might be devoted on one day to conversations such as the one described earlier, and on an-other it might be used for a lesson and supporting activities. Sometimes we read stories and explore the children's responses; sometimes the children conduct investigations and experiments; sometimes we all listen to a guest speaker who can shed light on a question that has emerged on previous days. Often, the children paint or perform plays.

The flexibility of this long block of time permits us to follow up promis-ing questions and comments like the ones about sundials. On this particu-lar day, we had enough time left before lunch to go outside to explore the daytime astronomy of the sun's light and motion. Before leaving the class-room, we asked the children to observe where their shadows were and to try to make them fall in a different direction. Once outside, they turned and twisted themselves about in the sun, succeeding only in making their shad-ows change shape, not direction. A group of five children called us over to where they were standing. They proudly announced that they had found a way to tell time using the sun and their bodies. The children had positioned themselves in a circle and explained that one of them was at 12, one at 3, one at 6, and one at 9, with the fifth child in the center. They had formed a clock and the direction of the shadow that was cast by the center person in-dicated the time.

Inside again, the children made further observations and asked more questions:

> If you stood in the same place for a whole day you would see your shadow change places because the earth changes position.
>
> Clouds can block the sun's rays so sundials won't work on rainy days.
>
> Can you tell time with one "hand"?
>
> Why is my shadow longer than I am in the evening but shorter than me at noon?
>
> People can't make time go faster because they're not the boss of the world. Even if you change the hands of the clock, you aren't changing time, itself.
>
> How do we know what the real time is?
>
> How did people start to tell time?

By now, 2 hours had passed. What had seemed like a simple beginning had flowered into exciting possibilities for future investigations. From the children's work and conversation, we saw themes on which we could now begin to improvise.

On another day, we asked the children to name all the ways they knew to record time. We learned that they knew about months, hours, and minutes; that 60 minutes equaled an hour; that 120 minutes made up 2 hours; and that 30 minutes was half an hour. Time, some said, could be measured in years, seconds, days, weeks, decades (which we told them meant 10 years), and centuries (which they knew meant 100 years). There were birth years, seasons, milliseconds, generations, and lifetimes (which we all decided together usually lasted from about 70 to about 90 years).

The next question was easy for us to ask: "Which of these measures of time is the longest?"

We even expected an easy answer: centuries. But we didn't account for children like Michael, whose hand shot up at once.

"I know, I know," he said, "it's seasons!"
"Why, Michael? Tell us what you are thinking about."
"Well, you see, seasons keep going on and on. You can have summer and fall and winter and spring. Then you keep having them all over again, and they make a pattern. See?"

And all of a sudden, we did see: not only that we had both locked into a narrow focus when we thought centuries was the best (even the only) answer, but also that Michael understood something important about the concept of relativity: that is, that "right" answers had everything to do with the framework you adopted. We looked at other measurements on the list. We asked if some of *those* could be candidates for "longest" as well. Joseph responded that generations were even better than seasons because generations went on and on with parents and children, and then their children and their children and *their* children. It all ended up in Heaven, he added, where time went on forever and ever. This idea of generations set another conversation in motion. To how many generations could each of us belong in a lifetime? Could they ever be in the same generation as their parents? As the children they would come to have? Would they *want* to be?

And so it went—from topic to topic, question to question, insight to insight. By the end of yet another discussion, we reached a conclusion to which everyone agreed: When you talk about days, seasons, or whatever in a general way, many units of measurement could be considered "longest" because they repeat themselves in a patterned way. As Michael's and Joseph's comments indicate, duration can also be understood as cycles—a fundamentally different framework from a linear one. Moreover, the children spoke of freezing time. They gave the example of designating a time—say, Friday, June 5, 1992, 11:48 A.M.—which is the precise time we had this part of the conversation. That moment will never repeat itself, they reminded us. The instant it passes, it becomes part of history. You can never, ever go back and do *that* time again the way you can repeat summers, year after year.

As the discussion continued, thoughtful and excited murmurs passed through the group like a wave.

> "You mean, if we just waste that time we can't ever get it back?"
> "Like, if we just were fooling around right now, we wouldn't get to come back to 11:48 because it was gone forever?"
> "No, not gone forever, because tomorrow there will be another 11:48. But *this 11:48 can't come back.*"

We pushed them by asking: "How precisely do you have to indicate a time before you know that that particular moment would never repeat itself?" Clearly, every day had 11:48s in it (and Maria reminded us that there was an 11:48 for the morning and one for the night time because there were always two 12:00s in every day). Fridays would repeat themselves, and so would Junes. But the Friday that occurred on the fifth day of June in 1992—not 1993 or some other year—was the one that would not come back. The 11:48 that belonged to only that Friday was the moment that was now part of our collective history.

This discussion was in June; we had worked hard since September to create an intellectual community. We were witnessing the work and dispositions that we had nurtured throughout the year bearing fruit. The next time the children gathered to talk about time, their observations bore the mark not only of their individual experiences of time outside the classroom, but also of the hours we had spent in exploration together. We decided to ask them what we thought was a harder question: "What is time?" This is what the children told us:

> Time is something that keeps on going.
> It helps you keep track of the events in a day and also of the day.
> It's not in a clock—it's everywhere.
> It's something we use.
> It's invisible—like air.
> It's part of our lives.
> We can't hear it, we can't see it, but we can use it and waste it.
> We live time, we make it.
> You can't speed it up or slow it down.
> Planets use time to travel around the sun.

It's a different time in every country. When we have morning other countries have night.

If everything stopped, we would float quickly off to the sun—like a very fast airplane ride.

The clocks we use can be wrong—but time itself can't be wrong.

The sun uses time—it takes Mercury less time than any other planet to go around the sun. Pluto takes much more time to orbit the sun.

If we didn't have any time we would be dead. We wouldn't have any time to be born or to live.

Time was in the past and it is still part of the world.

They were also left with questions:

How do we know if our clock is wrong?

When was math invented?

Was there time before there was a universe? Did time exist before the Big Bang?

Where would stars and planets "go" if time stopped?

How did time get started?

As we went over the list, we noticed that much of what they discussed referred to the solar system. We recalled that, for a number of weeks, a group of children had worked together to create an elaborate, scaled model of the sun and the planets with all 60 of their respective moons. All of us had been involved in lively discussions about outer space, gravity, density, and light. The children brought forward into this current conversation on time some of the questions and issues they had visited before. We hadn't planned to integrate or summarize their experiences, but then Scott looked pensively at the ceiling and said, "Time is the whole universe. If there was not time everywhere, there would be no time. The only way time could stop is if the universe stopped." He formulated for all of us an understanding made possible by the history we shared together.

We were excited and honored to have been part of this conversation. These children were pursuing knowledge, making conjectures, reasoning with each other. They were asking the kinds of questions that Einstein, Feynman, Sagan, and Hawkings ask. They were coming to understand that mathematics is a way of speaking. It is a language that permits those using it to experience the world in particular ways. It is a tool that allows the exploration of other, larger ideas. The ability to think mathematically is not simply the ability to produce number facts. It is not even the ability to solve word problems. If we want to nurture children who are passionate about science and mathematics, we have to start right (in both senses of the word) from the beginning:

> Because the discourse of the math class reflects messages about what it means to know math, what makes something true or reasonable, and what doing math entails, it is central to both what students learn about math as well as how they learn it. Therefore the discourse of the math class should be founded on math ways of knowing and ways of communicating. (*Professional Standards*, 1991, p. 54)

Did the children ever learn to tell time? Absolutely. It took only 1 hour for 50 of them and an additional 30 minutes for the other five to learn *that* kind of math language, too. Many of the Grade 1s and all of the Grade 2s could tell time to the quarter hour, and a substantial number mastered the Grade 3 objective: They could tell time to the minute. As for problem solving, a group of children created, and then set about solving, their own problems. Nathan, for example, wanted to know how many seconds were in an hour. A group of five children who had already completed the required exercises on telling time and who were interested in solving Nathan's problem gathered around him. While the rest of the class worked in small groups with clocks and question sheets, Nathan and his friends figured out what they thought they would need to know in order to solve the problem and then set about doing the computation. This was no mean feat, considering that none of them knew how to multiply. But they *did* know that mathematics is about patterns and relationships, so they were able to draw on what they knew about addition, set organization, and place value to solve this real and interesting problem.

There is more to our story of time. The children's questions about the beginnings of clocks led the class to ancient Egypt and Stonehenge, to early calendars and struggles to align solar and lunar years, to the mythological sources naming months and weekdays.

Unfortunately, like the sands in an hourglass, we ran out of time. But we were left with a wonderful and exciting starting place for the following September. We were going to teach these same children again the next year.

CONCLUSION

These are not easy times for public education. Beset on all sides by calls to do better work on behalf of children, it is difficult not to feel defensive or defeated when others far from the daily life of a classroom call for school reform. For a long time, teachers have been charged with implementing the-

ories developed by others. Those who have been teaching for a long time
have seen many theories come and go, and have worked hard to keep up
with what was expected of teachers because of such changes. Increasing
numbers of teachers have, however, begun to sense that the educational
conversation is changing in important ways. Often excluded in the past, the
voices of teachers and children are being welcomed as ones that can inform
both theory and practice in unique ways. For it is teachers who spend their
daily lives in the presence of children; teachers who are better placed than
anyone to see what can happen when they begin to think differently about
their work with children.

In our daily work, our reflection, and our writing, the two of us have
taken seriously the challenge of thinking about education differently. We
began our work together knowing *that* we wanted to challenge basic assumptions about primary practice. As our research proceeded, we began
also to be able to talk about *how* we thought changes in teaching practice
might come about. First, we came to see, in the relationships that we established with each child in our care, the importance of offering invitations to
connect the life each child lived fully and completely outside the school
with the life we were offering inside its doors. For us, David's story was perhaps the most dramatic and obvious of 54 other stories we could have told.
As we sat together at the end of the school year thinking about the children
and the journey on which each had embarked with us, we understood for
ourselves that the successes—and the failures—of our attempts to connect
with each child marked the successes—and the failures—of our ability to
work with each in pedagogically fruitful ways..

We do not think that observation will come as any great surprise to good
teachers. Nor will it come as a surprise to anyone when we say that living out
the implications of this understanding is an awesome responsibility. What
did come as more of a surprise to us was to see, in our relationships with the
children, the power of imagination to build connections that were not only
personally gratifying, but also educationally profound. Imaginative engagement in questions and issues that were big enough to enchant each person
in class, child and adult alike, created the space within which each child
could move with strength and freedom. Each found his or her own ways
into the conversations and the work throughout the year, and each voice
contributed uniquely to how the school year turned out for all concerned.

Perhaps what is most unexpected about what we found as we began to
explore the world with children in the ways we have described here is the
extent to which they learned more than we had ever imagined possible. We
heard some of them recite parts of Tennyson by heart on the playground,
loving *The Lady of Shalott* as much as David had loved *Bringing the Rain to
Kapiti Plain*. We did physics experiments with some, and investigated ancient number systems with others. Together, we and the children built

models of the solar system, medieval castles, and the Great Wall of China. We thrilled in their re-tellings of ancient Chinese legends and plots of Italian operas. With each and every study, the children kept pushing: Tell us more. Given access to real science, real mathematics, real literature, and art of substance and merit, they seemed insatiable.

We began this chapter with a quotation from *Alice in Wonderland.* Like many teachers, we are fond of Alice. Indeed, there are days when we find ourselves, like her, wandering around asking foolish questions about matters that seem quite settled to others. The Mock Turtle and the Gryphon listen patiently to Alice's bewildered inability to understand what schools are for, and we wonder what, if anything, they made of her question, "And how did you manage on the twelfth?" We wonder if they clucked their beaks, rolled their eyes, and wished she would just go away.

Having begun to create for ourselves a completely different framework from the one presented by the Turtle and the Gryphon, however, we are no longer left to resolve the beastly paradox that so bedevilled Alice. Lessons need *not* lessen from day to day, month to month, year to year. Children and teachers *can* find new and powerful ways to come to know each other through real work that engages their minds, hearts, and spirits.

We can all, in fact, manage quite nicely on the twelfth.

Preamble 2

A fascinating and important response that we received to the following chapter was that, by using the figure of Coyote-as-Trickster in the classroom and, worse yet, using this incident for a book chapter, we were involved in a form of inappropriate "cultural appropriation." One of the dilemmas we faced in facing this accusation was this: Given (and, of course, this given can and must itself be debated) that "studying native cultures" is a mandated and therefore unavoidable topic in the social studies curriculum in Alberta, what would it mean, given an interpretive understanding of "the basics," to treat this topic well, with some care and attention and seriousness? What would it mean to avoid the basics-as-breakdown "celebrating other cultures" version of such matters, where native histories and lives and tales are treated as the "myths and stories" of exotic "others." What if we were rattled and a bit bewildered by the fact that the Alberta social studies curriculum guides now define native cultures as "special communities"? Calling native cultures "special communities" threatens to simply reinforce an unquestioned sense of normalcy and makes it unnecessary, perhaps even impossible, to take Coyote seriously. Under this rubric, the accusation of cultural appropriation seems apt.

What if, instead, we tried to take Coyote stories seriously as somehow *true* of something, as somehow *telling* of some things in the lives of these teachers and students, here, in this place? What if we understood the social studies curriculum guide mandate generously, thus: We are going to learn about native cultures, not just to learn about *them*, but to learn about what they have to say about the taken-for-granted—taken as "normal"—assumptions at work in the life of the classroom.

This way of proceeding is a major premise of contemporary hermeneutics. As Gadamer (1989) pointed out, interpretively understood, "it is only when the attempt to accept what is said as true *fails* that we try to 'understand' the text psychologically or historically, as another's opinion" (p. 294). If the reader of a Coyote story does not allow that story to *address* him or herself as somehow potentially telling of *his or her* life (and not just telling about Coyote and native life), these stories and the images they present (of the outsider, the trickster, the teacher, the reminder, the screw-up, the clown, the one who can sit still, the one who provides a lesson but never learns, the one that teaches the children by having his tales told) are kept at a safe distance. We act, therefore, as if native stories are simply "another's opinion" and the taken-for-granted stories of, say, a troubled child, somehow name "the way things really are."

Exploring Coyote stories interpretively requires that we let them speak to us of ourselves and what we believe and do *as well as* speaking to us of "native cultures." It is only in such conversations that "understanding" is possible. Only in such conversations can we actually attempt to face and engage in the living, ongoing, contested topography that is named by the school-topic native culture.

One of the things documented in the following chapter is how a young girl, by taking Coyote seriously, was able to help us, as teachers and researchers, to see how taken-for-granted stories about troublesome children (such as Attention Deficit Disorder, Oppositional Defiance Disorder, and so on) are, just like Coyote stories, ways of treating trouble. This chapter is an exploration of how we might take seriously the bloodlines and ancestries that underwrite some of the topics entrusted to students and teachers in school. Just as we suggested about mathematics in the introduction, and about time and place in chapter 1, here, again, is an attempt to understand "the basics" as having to do with all the indigenous, living relations of these places we take our children in teaching them. It explores how we might understand "the difficult, abnormal, troubled children who haunt the margins of educational practice and theory" in ways that allow their troubles to question what we have heretofore taken to be "normal." So often in schools, the troublesome child is understood only pathologically. They are rarely taken to be a commentary on *us* and what we and our curriculum guides and our institutions have presumed. It is this situation that this chapter attempts to breach.

Finding this sort of disruptive classroom event compelling is to be expected from interpretive work. The god Hermes, from which hermeneutics gets its name, was a go-between figure, working borders and boundaries and opening up what seemed previously closed, stirring up what seemed previously settled, questioning what seemed obvious, stealing away with what seemed secure. And, more than this, the mythological figure of Hermes was "a young god, always" (Smith, 1999).

There is a lovely underground stream of implications here: Interpretive work often involves the image of "the young," "the new," as necessarily involved in the possibility of understanding, reading back to us what we have come to take for granted in ways that we could have not done alone. As with that young Grade 2 girl of our introduction, or the children's queries explored in chapter 1, such "reading back," although inevitably troublesome, is not a problem that needs to be fixed, but a portend that we must learn to live with, perhaps to love if we are to pursue an interpretive version of "the basics."

More of this in Preamble 3.

Chapter 2

"Whatever Happens to Him Happens to Us": Reading Coyote Reading the World

Patricia Clifford
Sharon Friesen
David W. Jardine

PATHOLOGIZING DIFFERENCE

When Robert Coles was a resident psychiatrist, one of his professors kept insisting that he tell stories, not clinical synopses, of the patients with whom he was working. He would say to Coles (1989, p. 28), "At times I feel you're explaining *away* those people—and I know you don't want to do so; I know you are a friend of theirs, and they are friends of yours." Today, we propose to tell the story of one child whom we will call Manuel, a child who came to us 3 years ago full of problems. Grounded in the "stubborn particularity" (Jardine, 1995b; Wallace, 1987) of one child, we offer his story not to explain him away, but instead to offer ways of reading differently the difficult, "abnormal," troubled children who haunt the margins of educational practice and theorizing.

What we propose is, in some sense, quite radical, for we call into question the pathologizing of difference that underpins so much of the way education understands children, their lives, their experience, and their reading and writing of the world. We question the usual understanding of classrooms as collections of individuals whose separate worlds connect from time to time and who come together simply so that each can mind their own business (Dressman, 1993). We want to interrogate the very idea that difference can be merely "known" and thereby, if teachers and researchers are diligent enough, eradicated as a problem of practice, and we want to challenge what is, sometimes, education's neurotic compulsion (Evetts-

41

Secker, 1994) to tame and understand the exotic "other." Instead, we believe, the intractable, irreducible differences of individuals can form the ground of true freedom, for in:

> coming together in their pluralities and their differences, . . . [students] may finally articulate how they are choosing themselves and what the projects are by means of which they can identify themselves. We all need to recognize each other in our striving, our becoming, our inventing of the possible. And yes, it is a question of acting in the light of a vision of what might be a vision that enables people to perceive the voids, take heed of the violations, and move (if they can) to repair. Such a vision . . . can be enlarged and enriched by those on the margins, whoever they are. (Greene, 1993, pp. 219–220)

Manuel came to us in Grade 1 already wearing almost every one of the flattening, professional pseudonyms available for troubled children. He was "physically challenged," "severely disabled." He possessed, we were told, "a file this thick" documenting his "behavioral difficulties" (this file, it turned out, did not exist). He could not count reliably, could not print between the lines, could not sit still, could not resist touching his classmates or calling out in lessons. Unable, it seemed, even to *recognize* any given task at hand, Manuel certainly had problems devoting time to the classroom agenda. Sometimes he would wander like a lost soul, apparently unconnected to anyone or anything around him. At other times, the mere prospect of a day at school with his friends made him so happy, so excited he would have a coughing fit and his breakfast would slide out on the floor. Manuel was a puzzle. Of that we were certain. In him, we saw the puzzle of difference constructed as either remediable or irremediable deficiency by the institutions that had already labeled him for us. The walls had gone up, and Manuel had already been offered two choices: Learn to be more normal, more ordinary, or face exile forever beyond the pale. Meanwhile, he bore the brunt of feigned clarity that comes from this odd, harsh-edged, school board version of educational psychology.

Manuel's parents had felt compelled to leave their homeland to come to Canada because the only classroom that could be made available for such an unusual child was one that already contained 19 autistic children. That's how it started for Manuel in kindergarten in his own country, half a world away. His parents were afraid, almost literally, for his life when they moved to Canada.

And his welcome, here, was that the very first teachers who took him in kept him for only one day and asked that another placement be found for him because they already felt themselves overwhelmed by the number of problem children in their charge. All three of us recognized, in Manuel's arrival, a scenario we had played out with other children: The principal appeared at our door early one morning.

"Will you take him? No one knows quite what to do with him."

And of course we took him in, for we knew what leaving him outside the door, outside the walls of our classroom might mean. Unable to find a home, exiled from his own life, Manuel might well have become a latter-day Caliban, a monster child labeled and enslaved by the malefic generosity (Greene, 1978) of school—a child confined to its margins.

The margins of the institution are not places anyone would necessarily self-select. Certainly, there exist boundaries that are full of adventure and the possibility of transgression, transformation, and movement (see chap. 9). But there are also boundaries that imprison and demand either inclusion or exclusion, either normality or pathology—and those were the boundaries that had already begun to close around Manuel.

Not without care, not without concern for his difference, of course. The impulse behind institutional labeling and classification, however toxic the effects, may well have generous roots in professionals' wanting to help, wanting to do well by the child—wanting to fix his wounds and put an end to everyone's suffering. But fixing is such dangerous enterprise. It seeks to eradicate difference; but it also eliminates openings and possibilities, especially the unhesitant, grotesquely self-certain fixing we have come to expect from many educational psychologists in our respective professions. "Fixing" has a dark, colonial shadow that educators do not always acknowledge— outsiders stream in to classrooms, find an ambiguous and difficult child like Manuel, and proceed, with clarity and confidence to order us around, all, of course, "for [our] own good" (Miller, 1989).

As *Coyote Columbus* incites, too often "they act like they got no relations" (King, 1992).

Children like Manuel can sometimes show that what is often dismissed as in need of identification, naming, intervention, and eventual transformation by the institution may become understood in a totally different way. Monster derives from the Latin *monere*, the word for portent, for warning (Jardine, 1994a; Werner, 1994). Manuel and marginal children like him can sometimes offer warnings or demonstrations to the clear and confident centers of normality in the classroom, and the ordinary, taken-for-granted course of things that classrooms often portray and defend. Such children can bring about the transformation and renewal of the center, providing that center can remain vulnerable and open to their arrival—provided, that is, that those at the center are able and willing to read their arrival more generously than the institutionalized discourses of marginality and normality have often allowed. The troubles that Manuel brings may thus be understood as what James Hillman (1979a) calls lacunae, weak places which can give opportunity:

Perception of opportunities requires a sensitivity given through one's own wounds. Here, weakness provides the kind of hermetic, secret perception critical for adaptation to situations. The weak place serves to open us to what is in the air. We feel through our pores which way the wind blows. We turn with the wind; trimmers. An opportunity requires . . . a sense . . . which reveals the daimon of a situation. The daimon of a place in antiquity supposedly revealed what the place was good for, its special qualities and dangers. The daimon was thought to be a *familiaris* of the place. To know a situation, one needs to sense what lurks in it. (p. 161)

COYOTE STORIES AND THE WORK OF THE IMAGINATION

At one point in the year we taught Manuel, we began reading stories about the native trickster figure, Coyote, a creature from the boundaries and margins, whose wild energy and tricky ways were enchanting. We read picture books together; listened to told stories; drew pictures; studied the art of native illustrators and of artists like George Littlechild. Because we, as teachers and as researchers, had become fascinated with what we were now calling "borders work," the interrogation of taken-for-granted protocols under which we live, we offered the children the heady opportunity to inhabit some of the spaces that a character like Coyote offers. Although nominally attached to curriculum requirements that we study native people in Alberta, the Coyote stories took us far away from the rampant literalism of the prescribed program of studies. And we could never avoid the coincidence: Coyote himself, in such stories, always reaching out beyond prescription and teaching thereby.

The possibility of creating a world that is different from the world as taken-for-granted-as-normal is the work of the imagination (Bogdan, 1992; Coles, 1989; Hillman, 1983). The possibility that things might be otherwise than they seem can be apprehended only in the imagination, and the strategies for resistance and for unnaming (LeGuin 1989), reshaping, and renaming the world come only from imagination as well. It is no wonder, then, that these teachers and students loved Coyote so much, for Coyote, both fool and savant, was given the power to create anything he could imagine. Calling to each person from the boundaries of their world of normal experiences, Coyote howls holes in the taken-for-granted, the assumed, the unuttered, and the unutterable. But he does not simply howl such holes: he incites those who meet him "in" through such openings, such opportunities for understanding, with his silly grin and his all-too-human foibles and the energy and foolish wisdom he exudes.

That is, he teaches. And he teaches by teaching us the limits of the world. And he teaches such limits through their violation, through "keeping the world open" (Eliade, 1968, p. 139) so that the lessons of balance and respect can be learned once again, here, by this child that:

child, the owl, too has young,
tiny hearts and warmth of down. (in Snyder, 1977, p. 56)

Like almost every child in the class, Sinead decided to write Coyote stories. We never asked the children to do this; never required or even suggested that they take up Coyote for themselves. They just did it anyway, so fully had this ratty creature captured their hearts. Through one of Sinead's stories (and, we suggest, also through the feral agency of Coyote herself), Manuel the monster child is welcomed in from the margins and given a home. A close reading of Sinead's story will show something of how one of the children in Manuel's class did the generous, generative work that was so difficult for many adults in Manuel's life to accomplish.

COYOTE AT THE CHRISTMAS CONCERT
by Sinead O'Brien

Sinead, Robert, and Manuel were helping Ms. Patrick and Ms. Charleston decorate the gym for their Christmas concert. Sinead asked Manuel, "Is your dad coming to the concert tonight?"

"Yes. Bah humbug," said Manuel, fake-laughing and throwing his head back.

"Oh really," thought Sinead to herself.

"Come help me lift this," yelled Robert.

"I'll be there in a second," replied Cheryl, who had just come back from gym.

. . . . .

"We come as clouds, the . . ." the class recited together, practising for the evening's performance.

"WE COME AS CLOUD," yelled Manuel, walking into the classroom. Sinead rolled her eyes.

"Guess what? We're going to read The Christmas Carol," said Joanie as she came over to Cheryl and Robert.

"YES!" yelled Robert.

"YES!" yelled Manuel, jumping up and down.

"I already knew that," said Cheryl.

Just then, Mrs. Smith came on the speaker. "Boys and girls, may I have your attention."

"No you can't," thought Sinead.

"Students in the gym, may I have your attention."

"I'm not in the gym, so I don't HAVE to pay attention," thought Sinead again.

"Remember to have your best manners on tonight and great voices. We want our parents to be impressed, don't we? Of course we do."

"Not me," thought Sinead to herself."

"Good afternoon."

RRRRRRRRRRRRIIIIIIIIIIIINNNNNNNNNNNNGGGGGGGGGGG. The bell rang.

"Try to wear something nice tonight," said Mrs. Cliffrie.

. . . . .

"Ayeeeya aeeeeya," sang the choir, beginning a native song.

Coyote, coming in the door, heard the wonderful singing. After his hard day with Grandfather Rock, he sure did feel like singing—especially when they got to the part with the "Harpoooooooooooooooooooooooon him?" That tricky Coyote, he started singing along with the choir. OOOOOOOOOOOOO. OOOOOOO. OOOOOOOOOOOO OOOOOOOOOOOOOOOOOOO. OOOOOOOOOO.

"What fun," thought Coyote to himself.

But not very many parents in the audience thought that listening to OOOOOOOOOOOOOOOOOOOOOOOOOOOOOOOOOO was the most pleasant way to spend the Christmas concert.

"Who's making that racket?" someone whispered to Zoe's dad.

"I don't know," said Don under his breath, "but it certainly isn't Zoe or Jeremy.

Robert's mum turned to look. "Oh no, Don. I can't believe it. That's not a child at all. It's a big dog or something.

"Oh don't be ridiculous, Pam. There can't be a dog in here. It must be someone's child." and he turned around to see whether it was anybody he knew.

"Oh NO! It's a coyote. A coyote! COYOTE AT THE CHRISTMAS CONCERT!" And he fainted dead away.

Suddenly, from the other side of the gym, a sound started to build. It was Coyote number two, Manuel the Magnificent. He wanted to sing, and he did. And guess what? Everyone else started singing and even Sinead was happy and they had the best Christmas concert ever—at least for that year.

IMAGINARY FIGURES AND THE REAL WORLD

The voyage out of the (known) self and back into the (unknown) self sometimes takes the wanderer far away to a motley place where everything safe and sound seems to waver while the essence of language is placed in doubt and profoundly destabilized. Traveling can thus turn out to be a process whereby the self loses its fixed boundaries—a disturbing yet potentially empowering practice of difference. (Minh-Ha, 1994, p. 23)

Sinead's reading of Coyote stories is a reading that touches the very world we live in, that makes the world "waver and tremble" (Caputo, 1987, p. 7) and, as a result, makes the world become more multivocal, complex, ambiguous, and alluring than it was before. Such readings do not simply add stockpiles of "images" or "concepts" to the one doing the reading. They reveal layers of the living world, add meaning to the creases on the faces. They are readings that, in other places, we have called "edgy readings" (Jar-

dine, 1995a; Jardine, Clifford, & Friesen, 1995a), the sense of which is elo-
quently captured by bell hooks (cited in Greene, 1993, p. 220):

> Living as we did—on the edge—we developed a particular way of seeing real-
> ity. We looked from the outside in and from the inside out. We focussed our
> attention on the centre as well as on the margin. We understood both. This
> mode of seeing reminded us of the existence of a whole universe, a main body
> made up of both margin and center.

And, of course, it is especially Coyote (not unlike Hermes) who tracks the
passages and openings in between inside and outside, between center and
margin. One could add, between young and old, between new and established, between teacher and learner, since Coyote is a figure who most often appears in the elders stories to and for and about the young and their
ways in the world.

As we considered the text of Sinead's story, it became clear that Coyote
was not just a "concept" or an image or a literary figure housed inside this
and other writings and readings we had done. Reading Coyote stories did
not mean simply decoding the literal meaning of what she heard or read,
nor did it mean instrumentally using Coyote simply as a "metaphor" for
what was somehow "in fact" an otherwise literal, "real" world of "children
with Attention Deficit Disorder (ADD)" (again reinforcing the boundary
between "the normal" and "the special"). Rather, the living figure of Coyote
became part of her living world, re-figuring that world, adding to it and
transforming its multiple relations. Reading *texts* about Coyote pulling
tricks, getting into trouble, and teaching lessons thereby, and reading the
world of the upcoming Christmas concert became strangely akin. The
boundary between text and world gave way. Coyote became part of the
text(ure) of the real world, not simply a figure within various written texts
within that world.

In Sinead's story, Coyote is not just the wild animal with which we are all
familiar. Neither is he just a figure in a wide open range of stories presented
to children. Through Sinead's reading and writing, Coyote has somehow
escaped the orbit of such literalism. He may be understood, through
Sinead's own work, to be a living, breathing figure that haunts the living,
breathing world—and not just "Sinead's world," as might go the individualistic, psychologistic formulation. As Native tales show, Coyote does not live
inside people's heads. His tracks are real tracks, if only one knows how to
"read" the world for them. He is, to reiterate Hillman, "the daimon of . . .
[the] place, . . . [revealing] what the place is good for, its special qualities
and dangers":

> While laughing at Coyote with their friends and family, native children learn
> how to behave and how not to behave. This is why Coyote is a sacred fool. This

clown gives us a way to know and accept ourselves. His foolish mistakes and
his heroic imagination teach about balance and respect. This is the balance in
ourselves and in our interrelationships with all life-forms.
                        —Anges Vanderburg, Flathead Indian Elder

In Sinead's story, it is not only Coyote who becomes de-literalized.
Manuel, the classroom, the Christmas concert, parents and their concerns
and embarrassments, school administration, interruptions, teachers—all of
these become *readable* beyond their mundane, taken-for-granted, literal,
surface features. They take on a spacious, generous, imaginative character.
The "real" world of the Christmas concert is no longer a mere actuality. It
opens up into the ephemeral temporality of "in-between"; into a world constituted by *possibilities of interpretation,* a world that could, therefore, be read
otherwise than the protocols of everyday life might allow. Manuel, therefore, is not "really" a child with ADD who can incidentally be read-as-
Coyote; neither is he literally Coyote (as if we can overcome the strangu-
lations of educational psychological discourse by simply appropriating
another, more exotic discourse with the same literal-mindedness). *Both*
Coyote and ADD become possible ways to read a real child who exists in the
cracks and edges between these (and many other) readings.

Reading in this edge sense opens up to a world of meaning, attachment,
and consequence; a world that, if deeply understood, generously counter-
poses the world as taken-for-granted, putting that world, the "normal"
world, into perspective. It makes horizons of action, belief, and hope visible
as not simply "the way things are," but as readings that *could have been read
otherwise.* Instead of a world in which margin and center are at odds, margin
and center might only make sense only in relation to each other. Coyote
stories show how those living together in a classroom might get along well,
with some sense of balance and respect, not *in spite of* figures like Coyote
but *because of them.*

Teachers and the disciplines they teach, in an odd way, owe their lives to
such figures. Such figures herald places of movement, of difference, of
openness and transformation, or regeneration and the "original difficulty"
(Caputo, 1987, p. 1) entailed in having "life itself" (Smith, 1999) erupt
right in the midst of multiple shared and contested worlds.

Reading in this way thus de-literalizes the professionalized understanding of real-world, upper-case events like Attention Deficit Disorder, Hyperactivity, Learning Disabilities, Developmental Delays, all of which had been
attributed to Manuel. It opens up the possibility that these "disabilities" can
be understood otherwise. Horizons of meaning are not fixed; educational
categories and typifications that freeze children into codes and into terse
objectifications, just might thaw and release under Coyote's address;
boundaries might flutter and shift, holes and spaces open. And through
those holes would pour children like Manuel, now with proper names and

obligations (Caputo, 1993), with bodies and hearts and minds that we might know otherwise.

RECOGNIZING OURSELVES IN THE MESS
OF THE WORLD

Interpretive readings set Coyote loose. Coyote, the trickster who loosens and violates boundaries, works in Sinead's story to blend and blur two "realms": the "real" world of the concert at which there was a "real" disruption and "fictional" tales of Coyote as a disruptive character. Through Coyote stories, Sinead makes the world in which she and Manuel live *readable* again beyond its surface actualities. The "real" world becomes an imaginative space readable in its possibilities, containing both the discourse of ADD and the goofiness of Coyote. The "real world," interpretively understood, thus becomes a place in which we must decide what reading might be best here, now, in these circumstances. Reading becomes a deeply ethical and pedagogical act. What way of proceeding would best evoke balance and respect in the circumstances faced by teachers and children in a classroom where "native life" is a mandated curriculum responsibility? Because of Coyote, Sinead makes visible, just for a moment, all the parental concerns and pretense, all the rhetoric of school announcements and protocols, all the howls of children full of excitement. We can now "recognize ourselves in the mess of the world" (Hillman, 1983, p. 49). Coyote stories are about us, about this real world and these real children.

Which is not necessarily to say that this news is good news for everyone. The pedagogical context in which such edgy readings are accomplished is crucial, for:

> this fluidity of boundaries between self and the world, ordinary existence and
> imaginative experience, consciousness and repression of consciousness, iden-
> tity and loss of identify—makes the reading experience fraught with the po-
> tential for the kind of destabilizing that student readers may neither expect
> nor welcome, depending on where they might be in terms of feeling, power,
> and location, especially in a classroom. (Bogdan, 1992, p. 192)

Sinead's reading of the Christmas concert could have exploded like a bomb in the middle of a classroom where protocols were never read, never challenged, never really understood or understandable as living decisions made in response to a living world. Sinead, herself, might have become problematic: the wilful girl-child who lacks respect for her elders and betters. Or her story could simply have disappeared, mis-read, beneath the weight of the everyday crush of events in a busy school. "That's nice, Sinead. Thank you for sharing your story with us," someone might have said as they plunked her into Author's Chair (Calkins, 1986) and unleashed a barrage of profound illiteracies:

> "How long did it take you to write?"
> "Where did you get your ideas from?"
> "I like the part with the howling. What part did *you* like the best?"

Sinead's story allows for the possibility of reading the howling of the Christmas concert as a lesson badly in need of learning. Reading and retelling Coyote stories helped Sinead, and can help anyone charged with Manuel's education, to "read" the stories of children like Manuel in ways that are more generous, more open, more forgiving than the flattening, psychologizing discourse of education generally allows. And she demanded from her teachers a response to her writing that was deeper and more difficult than the well-intended niceties of "tell me about your writing." As her teachers, we were *addressed*, we were directly *claimed* by her work. Through it, we were helped to "read" like children like Manuel not as deficient and in need of fixing, but, like Coyote, as bumping into the limits of the world, opening them again, making them newly visible, audible, readable, understandable.

But there is a deeper, more urgent claim at work here: By way of Coyote's lessons, Manuel, this real, difficult child, this wild thing whom others would not, could not allow in the world of their classroom, *became one of us*, that one, Coyote-like. As remembered in Sinead's story, Manuel becomes understandable in the sense of livable, bearable, here, with us. He became a child who once bore a tale of suspicion and isolation, and who now bears as well the possibility of a more generous tale of tolerance and necessity and relation and community. He came to have a place in the classroom uniquely his own, one without which the classroom would have been a very different environment, lacking the sharp-edged reminder of the protocols of the world we so comfortably assume. And Manuel was often protected by other children in the classroom when outsiders arrived with their clinical gazes and tightly gripped clipboards. They helped him "do normal" until the troubles passed. In this way, just as surely as Manuel became one of us through Coyote, this "us" *became different because of him.*

DE-ROMANTICIZING COYOTE

Of course, we cannot romanticize here. Coyote would be difficult to be around as often as he would be wonderful to be around. He is a playful trickster and a greedy, arrogant, self-centered fool who never, ever learns and who often falls out of trees at exactly the wrong time and ends up dying, rotting, and smelling up the place.

Reading Coyote stories as a reading of the world of the classroom does not simply dispel the negative characteristics of Manuel. He was not always and everywhere a joy and wonderful to be around. Sometimes his openings of boundaries and his violations of protocols are tolerable and revealing. Sometimes they are most decidedly not. The issue becomes not only pedagogical. It is an ecological and ethical one as well: How much disruption can a living community of relations *sustain?* What course of action is best in the circumstances we individually and collectively suffer? And how does Sinead's story help us address this question in better ways than we might otherwise have done? Her story does not necessarily help us tell which openings are tolerable and sustainable and which are not. It does remind us that there is a *difference,* and there can be a lesson of balance and respect to be learned through Coyote's ways.

The question about disruption can never be answered in advance or alone. What Coyote does, however, is teach us about the issues of balance and respect from which an answer might come, here, today, this time around, in this place and at this time with these children, about this bit of wisdom of the world. Coyote puts the difficult child (and the difficult work of pedagogy) back into perspective, back into "place," back with all his relations. The opening up of boundaries is thus both good news and bad news and sometimes both at once. And the point may be that we have to learn to take the good with the bad and tolerate disruption in the classroom if it can help us read our world more generously and help us treat children on the margins more generously as well: more like one of us, with more humor and forgiveness and protection. Again, the lesson of balance and respect. Coyote loose again.

Through interpretive readings, we can perhaps resist pathologizing the figures who disrupt our complacency. Through interpretive readings we might come, in however grudging a way, to honor those who live on the margins as essential to the life and vigor at the center. We owe such figures a debt of gratitude for the lessons they might teach us. Such figures might teach us about the character of pedagogy as boundary work. The portals they open for us provide opportunities, images, and the will we need "to name the impossible space we inhabit" (Bogdan, 1992, p. 218). Understanding, seeing from below and from the edges, we learn to converse with "the world as coding trickster" (Haraway, quoted in Bogdan, 1992, p. 218).

Embodied, irretrievably grounded in partial perspectives and located in "the tangibly real world that makes claims on people's lives in the infinite playing out of the creative imagination" (Bogdan, 1992, p. 219). But we should not leave with unwarranted optimism, for Sinead's story also leaves us with a disturbing picture of what might become of Manuel. Our classroom opened a space for Manuel that was large enough to house his special ways in the world and Manuel himself helped make that opening possible and transformed us and the classroom and the work we pursued in the process. We refused either to cut him loose or to abandon him to psychological isolation and caricature. We refused to pin him down, for:

> the symbol which Trickster embodies is not a static one. It contains within itself the promise of differentiation, the promise of god and man. For this reason every generation occupies itself with interpreting Trickster anew. No generation understands him full, but no generation can do without him. And so he became and remained everything to every man—god, animal, human being, hero, buffoon, he who was before good and evil, denier, affirmer, destroyer, and creator. If we laugh at him, he grins at us. Whatever happens to him happens to us. (Radin, cited in Bright, 1993, p. 183)

We might well ponder how best to deal with those who know beyond a shadow of a doubt that Coyote is but a fiction and that Manuel, undoubtedly, is just a child with ADD.

Coyote reminds: Whatever happens to him happens to us.

Preamble 3

An interpretive understanding of "the basics" begins by imaging the disciplines teachers and students face in schools, not as objects to be broken down and then doled out in ways that can be controlled, predicted, manipulated. Rather, an interpretive understanding of the basics entails that these matters be considered more in the manner of shared and contested and living and troublesome *inheritances* (Gadamer, 1994, p. 191). Addition, subtraction and their belonging together, Coyote tales and his kinship with an ancient Greek god, Hermes, the geographies that children are raised in and the stories they bring with them to school, age-old questions of time and its telling—all these things have been *handed to us* or, more oddly put, we have been, so to speak, handed to them. We *find ourselves* faced with, surrounded by, in the middle of, and living with these matters. In multiple, often contradictory ways, these topics are being lived out. These topics, interpretively understood, *already define us* (through upbringing, language, cultural background, gender, geography, age, interest, decision, imposition, default, or choice) *before* and sometimes *in spite of* the work of formal schooling.

A pedagogical consequence of this is that keeping the conversation going (Smith, 1999) and keeping the conversation open about such inherited topics is not pursued because it is nice to talk and value other people's opinions. Rather, interpretively understood as inheritances, things like addition and subtraction, or quandaries about time, or trickster tales, interpretively speaking, *are* all the ways that they have been handed down, all the writing and talking and quarreling and forgetting and remembering and teaching and learning. "Only in the multifariousness of such voices" (Gadamer 1989, p. 295) do these things actually exist *as* living inheritances. To understand addition and subtraction, interpretively speaking is, therefore, to try to *get in on this conversation*, this multivocal, interweaving "conversation that we ourselves *are*" (Gadamer 1989, p. 378).

Therefore, as part of an interpretive understand of what is "basic" to the living disciplines of our human inheritance is "keep[ing them] open for the future" (Gadamer 1989, p. 340), keeping them open, that is, to being taken up differently than could have been imagined. We must "accept the fact that future generations will understand differently" and that this difference is precisely what defines the *living* character of such matters. To attempt to simply control, predict, and manipulate such matters works against their living character and forecloses on the future. It could be claimed, therefore, that "basics-as-breakdown," which entails such foreclosure, works against our children, finding their arrival always and only a problem to be outrun.

This third chapter is, in part, an exploration of the nature of interpretive inquiry in general and an interpretive exploration of an affinity between such interpretive or hermeneutic work and the work of education itself. As mentioned in Preamble 2, interpretive work often involves the image of the young, the new, as deeply involved in the possibility of understanding and in the possibility of maintaining the living character of the disciplines education has inherited. In the work of education, this phenomenon appears in the amazingly frequent invocation of the idea of regeneration and "new blood" as a commonplace descriptor of the arrival of new children, new teachers, new ideas. Once treated interpretively, these ideas and images of our relationship to new blood arrives full force. Interpretively understood, curricular inheritances *require* the arrival of the young if they are to remain inheritances and not become mere dead objects. Our children's taking up of these inheritances, attempting to get in on the conversation, are thus understood as *necessary to the well being of such inheritances*. Our children's questions, like that Grade 2 girl mulling over addition and subtraction, or Sinead's recasting of the classroom "outsider," are not *problems to be fixed*. They are, rather, moments where what seemed like a given was "set right anew" (Arendt, 1969, p. 192) by being set back into its living movement as a living question of human inheritance.

Chapter 3

The Profession Needs New Blood

David W. Jardine

The blood is the life.

—Deuteronomy (12:23)

INTIMATE RELATIONS: ON EDUCATION AND INTERPRETATION AND THE IMAGE OF "NEW BLOOD"

> I enjoy having student–teachers in the school. It keeps things lively, keeps us on our toes. And anyway, it's our responsibility. The profession needs new blood.

These words of an elementary school principal are, on the face of it, rather commonplace and familiar. We all know what he means in some colloquial sense in that we can all recognize these lived features of the community of teaching and the wonders and difficulties of student-teaching they bespeak. This commonplace, lived familiarity is a fascinating phenomenon because it suggests that, prior to any deliberate and methodical "educational inquiry," we find ourselves somehow already in relation to this principal, already sharing in a complex, ambiguous, often unvoiced understanding of the constitution of the community of teaching. This realm of ambiguous, lived familiarity and the evocations of sense and significance enfolded within it defines the field of study for interpretive inquiry.

If playfully allowed to "expand to their full breadth of illuminative meaning," (Norris-Clarke, 1976, p. 188) this principal's words echo down into a
rich "implicate order" (Bohm, 1983) of metaphors, mythologies, and traditions. They contain images of education's relation to and responsibility for
the young, as well as images of the mysterious "liminal period" (Turner,
1969, 1987) indicated by the hyphenation "student–teacher." The movement through such "threshold times" (Mahdi, Foster, & Little, 1987, p. ix)
is full of "ambiguity and paradox, a confusion of all customary categories"
(Turner, 1987, p. 7) and as such, the tales told of such times lend themselves to a discourse that is itself "incurably figurative and polysemous"
(Clifford, 1986, p. 5). In this sense, such tales lend themselves to interpretive work; they call for a reading which does not take them literally but
rather figuratively, full of haunting figures and forms that stalk our profession and give it its life and its vigor.

These phenomena of liminality and transition and thresholds and passage are nothing new. The entrance of the young into the community, our
responsibility for them, and the initiatory movement from student to
teacher, all these bear a "family resemblance" (Wittgenstein, 1968, p. 32) or
"kinship" (p. 34) to long-standing tales told in many cultures and in many
communities. Most pointedly, the graphic notion of "needing new blood"
suggests archaic images of fleshy vitality, regeneration, transfusion, fertility–fecundity, reproduction, blood sacrifice, menstruation, child bearing,
renewal, healing–wounding, transformation, and the whole cascade of
bloody events surrounding the Christian worship of the consuming of flesh
and blood and its intimate coupling with crucifixion and resurrection.

Needing new blood also suggests a deeply ecological and ethical impera-
tive that the Earth (ecos)–the community (ethos) somehow *needs* the
young, the initiate, for its own sustenance, continuance, and renewal.

These commonplace words of an elementary school principal are, in this
sense, not so commonplace. "In this short passage, we have an embarrass-
ment of symbolic riches" (Turner, 1987, p. 18)—multiple meanings, "interweaving and criss-crossing" (Wittgenstein, 1968, p. 32) (*textus* originally
means "to weave," like textiles). These words are thus clearly not simply an
autobiographical titbit and to treat them as such would serve a dual abandonment. We would abandon this principal to the isolation of "personal knowledge" (where we "become stuck in the case without a vision of its soul" [Hill-
man 1983, p. 23]) and we would equally abandon the interweaves of
tradition and language and the mythologies that house our profession to remaining uninvigorated by this suggestive rebirth of an age-old tale.

It is vital to note here that such a dual abandonment leaves both sides at
work in their worst aspects. The young–new case–individual is left unable to
find itself a voice in the midst of the established–long-standing, and thus appears pathetic (the etymological opposite of *ethos* is *pathos*—the one with no

home). This is the potentially pathetic character of "teacher narratives" when these are left as simple self-announcements of teachers who have been abandoned to the isolation of the classroom. Clearly, we must overcome the hegemonies that have silenced and isolated such teachers. However, when these "narratives" are left unread out into the world, teachers are re-abandoned and re-isolated to the pathos of "my own story," which can only be "shared" with others in equally pathetic situations. In this way, the re-invigoration that the young–the new case could have provided the world is forgone in favor of merely puerile self-annunciation.

And, conversely, once the new case refuses to read itself out into the world, the old–established closes in on itself and is no longer visible as the senatorial, accumulated wisdoms of age and experience, able to provide comfort to the young (i.e., common fortitude, strength). Bereft of new blood, the senatorial becomes merely senile.

Contrary to this dual abandonment, an interpretive understanding suggests that the words of this principal are not only expressions of this principal's personal experiences, feelings, beliefs, images, and the like (although they are certainly all of these in some sense). These words are *the new, unanticipated* (and most likely *unintended*) *re-voicing of a world*, a world full of multiple tales that are folds of the same cloth (the same weave). This principal is, however unwittingly, folded in to a world—implicated in it—a world full of blood relations. Such implication does not mean that his words are identical to that world (so we can simply explore that world and tell this principal what he means). But neither are they simply different. His words bear a "family resemblance" to tales we have heard before but now, having heard this principal's tale, we will never hear those old tales quite the same way again. Differently put, this principal has "kin" even though he may not know it or experience it. This is why, interpretively speaking, simple reflection on experiences is not necessarily enough. The inverse of this is also true. Citing authoritative and established texts on "blood mythology" is *also* not enough, interpretively speaking, since this fecund new case rips open those texts (itself a bloody-minded metaphor) and makes them *readable* again by re-enlivening them, re-living them. It is the old and the young, the established and the new *together* that make interpretation possible.

This is the hermeneutic dance of part (new–young) and whole (established–old), where the new tale (just like new blood) is not simply additive to the whole but restorative and thereby transformative of it and where, because of the generous arrival of new case, "the whole" is never a *given* that could be simply described. Thus, interpretively understood, what new blood *means* cannot be stated once and for all as if it were an object: What it means is always in a state of "interpretive suspense" (Jardine, 1992c) always "yet to be decided" (Gadamer, 1989, p. 361). For example, having heard a principal of a school full of young children speak of "needing new blood,"

Christ's role as a teacher and his summoning of the "little children" (Matthew 18:3) (which we may have heretofore considered ourselves to have "understood") begins to "waver and tremble" (Caputo, 1987, p. 7) with new, unanticipated interpretive potency and power. Christ's summoning of the "new blood" and his saying that we must become like these children if the gates of heaven are to be open to us—this merges with images of Hermes as himself a young boy (the young as the portend of a hermeneutic-interpretive life—Hermes was also "a phallic god and a god of fertility" [Crapazano, 1986, p. 52]), but also as a guardian and opener of the portals, the gates (which itself bespeaks images of open, bleeding wounds as mythological signs of vulnerability and sensitivity and openness to the world [Jardine, 1992e]: precisely the vulnerability and sensitivity and openness that we see in those student–teachers that provide the school with new blood).

From this admittedly overextended interpretive spinning, we see that this principal (of a Catholic school, I might add) is "in" a living world full of its own histories and ways and we, too, are "in" this world along with him, and our knowing of its ways is attested to by the original familiarity of the tale he has told, and the spins of significance and sense enfolded within that familiarity–family resemblance:

> Language itself contains sedimented layers of emotionally resonant metaphors, knowledge, and associations, which when paid attention to can be experienced as discoveries and revelations. . . . [The interpretive task] is to inquire into what is hidden in language, what is deferred by signs, what is pointed to, what is repressed, implicit, or mediated. What thus seem initially to be individualistic autobiographical searchings turn out to be revelations of traditions, re-collections of disseminated identities. . . . (Fischer, 1986, p. 198)

As we have been witnessing, "stories [like this principal's tale] never live alone: they are branches of a family" (Calusso, 1992, p. 9), and a telling story bespeaks a family (a "familiarity," if you will) to which we already somehow belong. This is why interpretation is often equated with a form of recollection, a sort of family gathering (a gathering of blood lines), where "gathering" takes on anew that archaic sense of a way of deeply *knowing*.

It is becoming obvious that this particular phenomenon of new blood has a more intimate relation to interpretation than being just another possible topic of investigation.

Generativity, renewal and the need for new blood can be read as evocative descriptions *of the nature of interpretation itself* in its concern for the delicate interplays between tradition–community and the "fecundity of the individual case" (Gadamer, 1989, p. 38; Jardine, 1992b). Interpretation is caught, in a fashion similar to education itself, in the ongoing, living tension (one might say, the blood relations) between the old and the young, between the established and the new. As with education itself, the interpretive task is not to *cure* this tension, but to care for it, nurture it and protect it—to *read* it for its most generous possibilities. Because it does not aim to cure but rather to care for and attend to the living ambiguities and tensions that inform our lives, interpretation has been described as "restoring life to its original difficulty" (Caputo, 1987).

In this way, interpretation is not simply a "method" that can have the tales of student-teacher initiation and their parallels to philosophical and mythological literature simply as its *topic.* Interpretation is also "akin" to that of which it speaks—interpretive activity itself bears a "family resemblance" to the notion of needing new blood. Thus, the earlier tale from a school principal is as telling of interpretive inquiry as interpretive inquiry might be telling of it. This is vital to understanding the conduct of interpretive work (and it recapitulates Wittgenstein's images of family resemblance): "The practice of understanding is the expression of the affinity of the one who understands to the one whom he understands and to that which he understands" (Gadamer, 1983 p. 48).

Interpretation seeks out its affinity to its "topic." One does not have "interpretation" in hand as a method and *then* go out looking for a topic—scouring transcripts, for example, and "doing" an interpretation of them. Rather, something *becomes* a topic only when its interpretive potency strikes or addresses the one doing the interpretation. The words of a school principal cited in this chapter form a small fragment of countless conversations. I did not *select* it as an "interesting" topic and then "do" an interpretation of it. Interpretation does not begin with *me.* It only begins when something *happens to me* in my reading of a text, when something *strikes* me, tears me open, "wounds" me and leaves me vulnerable and open to the world, like the sensitivities of open flesh. Through such sensitivities, a world begins to open around these words, and the interpretive task is to use sniff out this new blood, "to put a finger on the wound" (Grossman, 1988, p. v) and from/through this "opening," to re-enchant and re-awaken that world. As such, these words themselves became echoes of the process of interpretation itself. Not only did they become interpretive "portals" into a whole world of mythologies and symbols—"needing new blood" is itself *about* interpretive portals. Interpretation thus "finds itself" in its topic. Differently put, only in and through the topography of the world can interpretation "come to" and realize its place and limits.

There is a further convolution in this kinship between new blood, interpretive inquiry and student–teacher education. Education has long suffered under the auspices of our Enlightenment legacy which suggests that separation, isolation, and the severance of ambiguous kinships, family resemblances, and relationships are the route to secure a solid foundation of understanding (Jardine 1990, 1992c). We have, in the name of such security, subdivided the ambiguous, texts–weaves of the tales of student–teacher education into a babble of individual skills and techniques and objective checklists of separate competencies and the like, all of which has torn apart the ambiguous, living fabric of the community of education in the name of clarity and manageability. Educators, like much of North American culture, have suffered the alienation and loss of meaning that results from having our lives dissected into the bits and pieces requisite of experimental design. One could consider, for example, how the principal's words would not count if we were pursuing an objective account of student-teaching: His words are too fluid, too evocative, too "poetic" and slippery and wet, too subject to multiple, generative responses.

Under the auspices of our Enlightenment legacy, many educational studies would "marginalize and instrumentalize [his words] into a rhetorical figure called metaphor" (Gadamer 1989, p. 432) which, because of its ambiguous and evocative character, is not considered to be "true." Since student-teaching, under such a legacy, is considered to be an univocal, unambiguous, and objective state of affairs, multivocal and ambiguous language such as "needing new blood" can not possibly correspond to this state of affairs without blurring and "subjectivizing" what is (following the Enlightenment presumption) "in reality" clear and distinct and objective.

One of the aims of interpretive work is to recover the narrative–metaphoric interrelations and kinship systems that give human life meaning and to work against the legacy of severance and its consequences. Interpretive work thus wishes to read this principal's tale for its *truth*, but truth in such a case no longer means unambiguous correspondence to an objective state of affairs. Rather, the interpretive truth of this tale lies in whether it can be read in a way that might help us more openly and generously understand the lives we are already living, that is, whether it can be read in a way that provides us with the re-invigoration of new blood.

Differently put, the truth of an interpretation lies not simply in the fact that a tale has been told (although this, of itself, is often difficult enough, being able to finally tell *at all*) but in how and whether this tale can be made *telling*.

A sure sign of the interpretive truth of such a tale is whether it provokes those who hear it to speak (i.e., whether it provokes generative, creative participation). In presenting such work to teachers, student–teachers, and colleagues I have found, over and over again, that hearing such tales provokes others to themselves tell a tale that bears a family resemblance to the ones I have offered—"have you read Alice Walker's *The Temple of my Familiar?*," "what about D. H. Lawrence? He's full of blood," "as soon as you started talking about blood, I remembered my student–teacher talking about feeling drained," "this talk frightens me. It reminds me of lambs to the slaughter. We don't do that. We *don't*." Interpretive telling thus opens up a haunted space full of tell-tale familiarities that bind Earthly lives together, kinship systems, blood relations whose "truth" is not a given state of affairs but is always yet-to-be-decided by *this* reader's or *that* reader's giving of new blood to what is written. Interpretation thus requires active, creative, risk-laden participation, not distanced, objective, methodological documentation, nor a pathetic, pathological withdrawal into "my story." *Both* of these are refusals to read the deep kinships that bind our lives together. Both of these are forms of institutionalized illiteracy which orbit each other and which assume the severance of blood relations that interpretation is wont to heal.

This puts a peculiar demand on those who *read* an interpretive study. An interpretive study does not center around the presentation of *facts* (the past participle of *facere*—"to make"), as if the phenomenon of "new blood" were simply a given object whose characteristics could be documented and simply handed over to a reader or as if it were "my story," which I could simply tell. Rather, needing new blood is a nest of ambiguous signs that need to be *read* and *re-read* to be understood. Interpretation thus centers around a movement from what initially appears to be merely literal–factual (the *fact* that this is what this principal said—these literal words—or the *fact* that similar words appear frequently over the transcripts of several principals) down into the "make up" or "forming" or "fashioning" of these facts, down, that is, into the generous possibilities of meaning that they embody. Interpretation is thus a movement from the past participle toward the (re-)generative case: It "opens" what has been made (what presents itself as "facts") out into its "makings." This not only allows "the making" to become visible to the reader and thus allows the sedimented layers of meaning encrusted in "the facts" to be subject anew to transformation, healing, and change. Interpretation also necessitates that the reader him or herself must somehow *participate in the making.* To read an interpretive study is to bring forward the ways in which what is being addressed is part of my living "make up." I must attempt to "make" something out of what I read *and* I must read my life into the words. I must both make these words mine *and* I must explore how these words *make a claim on me* and reflect back to me "kinships" of which I might not have been aware. This principal has "kin" *whether he likes it or not, whether he knows it or not.* So it is not enough, in attempting to understand this principal's words, to simply explore what *he* thinks new blood means, as if he *owns* the kinship system of which new blood is a part. "Stories never live alone," and to make them live this way in the name of voice and individuality and empowerment is to do ecological, spiritual, and ethical violence.

In this sense, interpretation is a form of *fiction* (the generative case of "to form" or "to fashion" which nuzzles up close to *facere*) that moves to re-imagine and re-enchant the world that has fallen prey to the degenerate closures of factuality and literalism. Such closures have no room left for the young—the new blood is not summoned and welcomed but shut out. However, to use Wittgenstein's metaphors, "family resemblances" and "kinships" cannot go on without the new ones entering into the flesh of the family ("the familiar") and making it new: The "family resemblances" evoked in this chapter cannot go on with out the reader's entrance into the haunted spaces between the lines. Without such entrance, interpretive work looks like little more than clever textual trickery.

Moving against this mathematical dismemberment of the Enlightenment legacy (*and* against the ways that teacher narrative leaves this dismemberment in place but simply rejects the mathematics) toward re-membering makes interpretive work a profoundly *ecological* enterprise. It cares not simply for the fecundity of the individual case (without which the world would not be renewed, without which the story will not be remembered), but cares also for the openness and generosity of the world (without which the new case could not enter and could therefore not provide re-membering and re-generation to the world). It attempts, therefore, *to make the individual case readable* by opening it out into the world, and it attempts *to make the world readable* anew by introducing into that world this new case.

Interpretation works against the dual consequences of this dissection of blood relations—against *both* our relentless focus on objective documentation (where we cannot read our lives out into the world with its brutal, closed, objective, literal surfaces) and against its dark twin, the potential isolation inherent in "everybody telling their own story" when such stories are left *unread* in any strong sense except as "mine." To play with Wittgenstein's metaphors again, interpretation works against *both* the brutal patriarchal father who silences all his kin in favor of a singular voice. And it works, too, against the abandoned, isolated, self-affirming child who can bear no comfort from the world. Interpretation is focused, rather, *both* on the entrance of the young/the initiate into the world *and* upon the restoration and renewal of the world that can ensue from such entrance. As with the figure of Hermes, interpretation stands at this portal, constituted by "a consciousness that must leave the door ajar" (Hillman, 1979a, p. 154), ready for the arrival of the "new blood" (the next teacher's/principal's/child's/student–teacher's tale) that will not be left to its own devices, but will help transform the world and make it new.

AN ADMISSION OF OUR NEED

> *We keep hearing from principals that some of the best people are the new, young, fresh blood in the system.*
> —Jon Ed, Human Resources Superintendent,
> Calgary Board of Education (*Calgary Herald*, March 23, 1993, p. B1)

We see in [images of new blood and bleeding] inflation and enthusiasm. The vitality of the [young] spreads and stains like the red tincture of the alchemist's lapis. *His bleeding is* multiplicatio, *the infectious giving out of essence for the sake of transforming the world.*

—Hillman (1979a, p. 154)

The passage of the initiate into the community of education and the "original difficulties" that ensue is a phenomenon that defines that community at many levels. Education is constituted, first and foremost, by the arrival of the young (the arrival of new blood), year after year, and this cycle of arrival and its consequent images of inflation and enthusiasm (one could think of the bounties of the new growth of spring, for example, which are themselves iterated in Easter ceremonies of life resurrected and, at a more mundane level, the "bunnies and chicks and eggs" of this celebration—a wonderful pagan underbelly of the Christian legacy) reiterates many other cycles in our lives as well as Earthly cycles of season and planting and growth and harvest. The images of the arrival of new blood thus suggests an image of pedagogy itself. This arrival is full of possibility and full of hope for a re-invigoration of the course (*currere*) of our human inheritance. Differently put, with the image of new blood, it will not do to imagine that our course (our curriculum) is simply fixed and given. Our course—what will come of us and our preciously held ideas and ideals and learning objectives and the like—is always available to us only in a state of interpretive suspense, yet to be decided in relation to the arrival of this child, and this. Education thus sits at an irresolvable point. It must prepare our course for the arrival of the young (so it must understand that course openly and generously), and it must prepare the young to enter our course (so it must understand the young as new blood for our course). It must cradle *both* the child and the world in nursing *caritas*.

Education is also concerned after the arrival of "the young" in the sense of the arrival of new teachers into the profession.

The initiation of new teachers into the community of education is full of "pedagogic intent" (Turner 1987, p. 15). It is a time wherein prospective teachers become "vividly and rapidly aware of what may be called the 'factors' of their culture." (p. 14) However, the lessons learned by student–teachers in their initiatory travails crack open beyond mere *epistemology*—beyond "teacher knowledge." The initiation of new blood into the community of education is not simply a matter of what the initiate explicitly or implicitly *knows*. The smooth transmission of "cultural knowledge about teaching" (White, 1989) is not the sole, center point of initiatory phenomena. Rather:

The term initiation in the most general sense denotes a body of rites and oral teachings whose purpose is to produce a radical modification . . . of the per-

son to be initiated. Initiation is equivalent to an ontological mutation of the
existential condition. The novice emerges from his ordeal a totally different
being: [s]he has become *another*. (Eliade, 1975, p. 112)

Underlying the potentially bloodless passing on of knowledge is a
deeper, more bloody mystery wound up in the entrance of student–teachers into the community of education. It has to do with *ontological* transformations in who the student–teacher *is*, not simply *epistemological* transformations in what they *know*. Through the rites of passage and initiation,
student–teachers not only can claim to know things they did not know before. They *are* something they were not before: they *are* new blood for the
community of teaching. They *are* (be-coming) teachers.

This deeper and more bloody mystery hints at a terrible fact we hardly
ever raise in our teacher preparation programs: *the fact of natality*—that pedagogy is premised on the inevitable, continual arrival of the young (Arendt,
1969)—and its dark twin, *the fact of the mortality of the world*:

> We are always educating for a world that is or is becoming out of joint, for this
> is the basic human situation, in which the world is created by mortal hands to
> serve mortals for a limited time as home. Because the world is made by mor-
> tals, it wears out; and because it continuously changes its inhabitants, it runs
> the risk of becoming as mortal as they. To preserve the world against the mor-
> tality of its creators and inhabitants it must be constantly set right anew. . . .
> Our hope always hangs on the new which every generation brings. (Arendt,
> 1969, p. 192)

Or, linked more directly with anthropological and mythological tales:

> Through its own duration, the World degenerates and wears out; this is why it
> must be symbolically re-created every year. [But note how, with the arrival of
> new children in my Grade 1 class, it is not simply *symbolically* re-created every
> year]. (Eliade, 1968, p. 76)

> It is a living world—inhabited and used by creatures of flesh and blood, sub-
> ject to the law of becoming, of old age and death. Hence it requires a periodic
> renewing. (Eliade, 1968, p. 45)

So, just as the initiate brings renewal, he or she also brings a vision of the
need for renewal and therefore a vision of the mortality, fragility, and dependency of the community of which we are all a part. Our "course," our
"community," is not a given that can be simply documented and detailed. It
is not a given because the entrance of the young, fresh blood makes that
community different than it would have been without them. Moreover, that
the arrival of new blood is *also* not a given that can simply be taken for

granted. There is something miraculous about this fact of natality. The arrival of the renewal of the young simply *happens.*

Through the image of new blood, what we often assume to be relations of (inter)dependency are strangely reversed. We are so accustomed to identifying "the young" or "the new ones" with being (our) *dependents.* Now we can begin to see *our own dependency.* We can begin to see how our hope hangs upon the young and their ability to open up what has become closed, to re-new what has become no longer workable—to find the portals, the openings, the life in what we do.

Because of the inherent mortality of the community of education, the strength and stability of that community cannot be established through its calcification and closure. It will simply "wear out" if it remains closed. Stability and strength can be achieved only through an open and generous relation to the young. More strongly put, it can be achieved only through an admission of our need.

This admission is strangely absent from the literature on teacher education. We speak so often about how the student–teacher needs and depends on the cooperating school, the cooperating teacher, the administration of their practicum school, the University, the curriculum guides, the lists of teaching techniques or classroom management techniques, or the educational theories and so on. Rarely do we admit how the community of education needs new blood. Simply put, without new initiates entering in the community of education—without the continual arrival of new children, new teachers, new knowledge, new worldly circumstances—that community itself would cease to be. The community of education is not only a haven for our dependents. That community itself *depends.*

The profession *needs* new blood.

NEW BLOOD AND THE HEALING RETURN
TO THE ORIGINS

> *Our blood will water the dry, tired surface of the Earth*
> *We will bleed. We will bleed. We will*
> *bleed until we bathe her in our blood and she turns*
> *slippery like a new baby birthing.*
> —Bass (1989, p. 53)

> *The creation of the world was no single, irrevocable act. If the world and its seasons are to continue, the original drama has to be re-enacted every year.*
> —Tannahill (1975, p. 33)

"The profession *needs* new blood." This evokes a dark memory of the mortality of the world and an equally dark memory of our own dependency. It foreshadows a memory of the original making of the world (a memory of its *interpretability*) and of our own dependency on the fact of natality as figuring in that origination (as interpretation recalls its own dependency on the fecundity of the individual case). New blood thus provides an image of the *return to [our] origins*.

The initiate represents that which is first, that which is "initial." The initiation of student–teachers into the community of education thus keeps us oriented to what is first, what is originary in what we do.

This notion of originariness can be understood in two interrelated senses:

1. Education requires an orientation to what is chronologically first. Education entails a relation to the young, the vulnerable, the new. Going back to what is first for the community is going back to what is at its heart: the fact of natality, the fact that children are born into the world and that the community can go on only through its concerted attention to this arrival and to the conditions under which such arrival can be generously sustained. With such a return, hope is renewed that things might be different this time, that things can start again from the beginning, that things can be set right, that things can be put back on course. One can think, for example, of how September can often figure in the imagination of a teacher: a fresh start, a new beginning, starting again.

Here we have a wonderful cross-over effect: the entrance of the initiate into the community of education bears an affinity to the entrance of the child into the world. Both are the new ones and both figure in the "new blood" entrails of "starting again." Hence the powerful images of a student–teacher's description of entering her first practicum school:

> When I went to my practicum school the first day, I felt about this high, like a little kid again, going to school for the first time, beginning all over again, right from the beginning. And my cooperating teacher was, like, my teacher and I was a little kid in Grade 1.

2. A return to the origin can also be understood as a return to what is foremost, what is foundational what is "originary" and "initial" in the sense of what is long-standing, what persists, what pertains. To the extent that initiates return us to the origin in *this* sense, initiation ceremonies are often described as the re-laying of the foundations of the world (Eliade, 1975, p. 175). Or, in the words of a cooperating teacher:

> Having student–teachers in my class makes me go back to what I thought I knew and question it again: "Why do I do that in my math lessons?" They make me ask the questions I have forgotten to ask. They make me say what I know. They help me clear away the crap.

Thus, the arrival of new blood is an event that potentially "washes away the sins of the world." That is to say, the arrival of the young requires that we sort out what is necessary to our world, what is most true and sustainable and generous about it. It is a cyclical, repeated gesture that is restorative and healing (Eliade, 1968, p. 79). It invokes the cleaning away of the unnecessary accretions of time and a re-invoking and remembering (i.e., not only bringing back to memory, but gaining new members the initiate, as the new one, re-members the community by becoming a new member of it) what has been forgotten. This is what the innocent question of the new student–teacher can evoke: "keep[ing] us on our toes" and requiring that what has become mute habit be uttered. "They make me *say* what I know." Not only must I re-think what is vital to this community through the initiates questioning. I must *profess* what is vital to the very symbol of vitality that stands before me.

THE SHADOW-SIDE OF THE NEED FOR NEW BLOOD

> What are we to make of the red symbolism which, in its archetypical form in the initiation rites, is represented by the intersection of two "rivers of blood"? This duality, this ambivalence, this simultaneous possession of two contrary values or qualities is quite characteristic of redness in the Ndembu view. As they say, "redness acts for both good and ill."
>
> —From Victor Turner, *The Forest of Symbols*, cited in Tannahill, 1975, p. 77)

> With the entrance of the initiate] there is a "return to the origin" in the literal sense, that is, a relapse of the Cosmos to the amorphous, chaotic state, followed by a new cosmogony.
>
> —Eliade (1968, p. 52)

A relapse into such originary chaos can be considered as healing and restorative. But this relapse, for all its fecundity and regenerative, also portends something dark and dangerous, akin to the day between the crucifixion and the resurrection (itself a perfect example of "interpretive suspense"). This is the "fallow chaos" (Van Gennup, 1960) of the liminal, initiatory period (like the "–" in "student–teacher").

The old needs not only the renewal that the young bring: "[the] redness [of new blood] acts for both good and ill." The old needs *protection* from the young and, strangely enough, *the young need protection from themselves.*

New blood portrays more than simple renewal. It also suggests wildness, chaos, things being out of control, torn apart, growth that is out of control, cancerousness, overstimulation. The "opportunity" that the young provide also opens a portal to a potentially dangerous "chaos of possibilities" (Hillman 1979a, p. 157). In short, there is a shadow side to the re-generativity that new blood portends.

We suggested earlier that the strength and stability of the community of education can be achieved only through an open and generous relation to the young. But this cannot mean a limitless free-for-all, as if *anything* will do in the constitution of the community of education. Here is the rub: We must open that community to the new ones while, at the same time, preventing simple licentiousness, simply spilling blood without any orientation to what we are spilling it *for*.

So the shadow awakes and it has a dual aspect. The notion of new blood signals a danger to the community. But it also signals a danger to the initiate him- or herself:

1. "I just got the kids settled down and now this new face arrives"—the arrival of new blood is also the arrival of the disruption of what has been settled, the violation of boundaries that have been set, the re-opening of issues that had been closed. There is a delicate matter involved here. Not wanting the new face to arrive can signal calcification and closure as much as it can signal a healthy desire for stability, order, continuity, memory, community, and the like. The continuous, uncurbed, unprepared arrival of new blood is not necessarily sustainable. With such an arrival, new blood is no longer regenerative of the community: it simply becomes what Arendt (1969) named an "onslaught." Sustaining the arrival of new blood requires time and attention and care. It requires preparing the soil, so to speak. It requires sometimes *refusing* the arrival of new blood on behalf of sustaining the fertility of the soil and not overworking, overstimulating or overquestioning what has been established and settled.

The notion of new blood thus signals a potential danger to the community: the danger of a relentless, unbridled onslaught of change.

2. James Hillman (1979b, p. 33) described the young as "afflicted by openness." The danger here is that, "through his[/her] own wounds, [the initiate] may feed others, but may himself [/herself] be drained thereby" (1979a, p. 154). Here lies the possibility that the initiate may "burn themselves out" by giving too much, too quickly, taking on the task of "reinventing the wheel" at every turn, feeling responsible for every happenstance. The vulnerability and openness and sensitivity that new blood provides can suggest that the initiate is *too* vulnerable, *too* sensitive, *too* open: In the desire to love all the children all the time, and provide perfect, stimulating, life-changing lessons coupled with perfect classroom management etc., the initiate can easily twirl out of control, endangering not only the community but themselves.

Lurking here too is the possibility that the old may take advantage of the young and "bleed them dry." Student–teachers are sometimes given the tasks that no one else wants or are overburdened with too much planning, too much teaching too early.

This is perhaps why "myths show divine-child figures each with special nursing attendants" (Hillman, 1979b, p. 49) who have a dual function: They not only protect the child from giving too much; they protect the world from being overrun by the growth the child portends. Coupled together, this is an image of our role as those involved in initiating student–teachers into the community of education: opening both the world and the initiate to the convolutions involved in the fact that "the profession needs new blood," and protecting the world and the initiate from the dangers found in such convolutions.

There is, as we have come to expect, a parallel in the work of interpretive inquiry. Once things start to "happen"—as with this topic of new blood—it is very difficult to get such happenstances to stop. In producing this chapter, how can I refuse the cascade of new instances that continually arrive: Yeats' notion of blood memory? the coincidence of our cultural severances of blood relations through empowerment of the individual and the fact of AIDS and the potential deadliness of blood relations? the rush of children in the halls between classrooms as blood pulsing between the "vital organs" (the science classroom, the library, each of which represent "organons" of knowledge and each which need the new blood's arrival)?

Stop.

As with the arrival of new blood itself, there is no set of rules regarding when enough is enough. All of this has to be worked out in the particular, living case, and it has to be worked out in a way that is full of "interpretive suspense." As with education, so too for interpretive inquiry: There is no set of rules that save us from the agonies of deciding anew, in *this* case, the delicate balance between our responsibility for the world and our responsibility for the young. As with education, so too for interpretive inquiry: One learns that an open and generous (but not licentious and chaotic) relation to "new blood" is an irresolvable, "original difficulty" that we can only learn to live with well.

CONCLUDING REMARKS: NEW BLOOD
AND THE INTERPRETABILITY OF THE WORLD

> *The arrival of new blood bespeaks the possibility of "keeping the world open."*
> —Eliade (1968, p. 139).

The arrival of the fecund new case bespeaks the possibility of keeping the world *interpretable:* full of portals, openings, through which the initiate may enter.

"The profession needs new blood": The profession of teaching must not take itself or its tasks literally. The curriculum must needs be *interpretable*—enterable.

"New blood" bespeaks the interpretability of the world: not only the possibility but the *necessity* of renewal.

Interpretation, as a relation between the old or established and the young or new case, is an intimately pedagogic activity. (Thus, as literalism is the enemy of interpretation, literalism is the enemy of pedagogy).

Education, as a relation between the old or established and the young or new case, is an intimately interpretive activity.

"Stories never live alone: They are branches of a family."

End.

Preamble 4

The prevailing economy of exchange within which things have been inserted condemns them to the status of faceless entities to be offered in payment, compensation and reward, as if they were quantified and quantifiable currency to be tendered among humans. . . .

This involves the deliberate denial of the depth of things, which become the objects of an endless reproduction and a confirmation of the manipulative abilities of the subject.

—Benso (2000, pp. xxxi, xxxiii)

Much of this next chapter was originally written in the heyday of "whole language." It involves a meditation upon and a critique of the relentlessness with which elementary school children were being asked to write about their experiences and explores the possible linkages between such relentless writing and the school's desire to "keep track" of children's lives and work.

Again, as is common in interpretive work, this chapter had its origins in a disruptive incident, a simple act of a child asking the teacher, "Are we going to have to write about this?" We ended up taking up this incident as an invitation, an opening into the great and often unnamed presumptions of elementary schooling practice and then-contemporary writings on "whole language." What is most fascinating here is that the question of writing in elementary schools, seemingly so simple and only a matter of the "how-to"s of practice, hides many ancestors: writing's place in relation to the formation of memory and character, "the helplessness of the written word" in the face of the possibility of misinterpretation, writing and the expression and/ or interruption of immediate experience, writing as a comodified form of exchange and proof of the worthwhileness of classroom life, and so on. As is often the case in interpretive work, these issues stretch, in Greco-European history, at least back to Plato's *Phaedrus*. Moreover, this history of these issues finds telling counter foils in a wide array of culturally diverse understandings of writing and its place in human life. As well, the issue of the quiet immediacy of lived-experience vis-à-vis the "manipulative abilities of the [inscribing] subject" have long since formed part of many religious traditions as well as many works of contemporary ecological philosophers.

Again, this innocent invocation, "Are we going to have to write about this?", interpretively taken up, becomes a great herald, a great opportunity to understand what is being lived out in the life of reading and writing in elementary schools. Interpretive work does not understanding these phenomena pathologically: Writing and reading are not merely skills that children must learn to command. They are also places of great and troubled history, reflection, controversy, and thought.

Chapter 4

Relentless Writing and the Death of Memory in Elementary Education

David W. Jardine
Pam Rinehart

PRELUDE

I (Pam Rinehart) was excited. The theater performance that my third-grade class had just attended had been excellent. Children and teachers alike had been captivated by visions of dinosaurs in the darkness. As I climbed the stairs to my classroom, children trailing behind, I tossed around ideas for what to do next. It seemed wrong to carry on with daily routines having just experienced such a wonderful play. As I gathered the children at the carpet eager to discuss their impressions, Jessica moaned, "Are we going to have to write about it?"

Her words caught me off guard. My excitement diminished and I felt a little irritated by the guilt her words seemed to conjure up. She had quite accurately "read my mind," for this was one of the possibilities I'd been considering. It was no coincidence that she could have guessed this. Writing in response to an experience, especially a good one, was a common occurrence in our classroom. If an experience left an impact, then it would certainly give us something to write about—provide a way to share our impressions, savor the moment. Record and remember. All the good stuff we're supposed to do as teachers.

But Jessica's words were echoed by all but one of her classmates. They may have been just as inspired as me by the wonderful experience we shared, but they weren't inspired to write. A few days later, our class visited an exhibition at the Glenbow Museum (in Calgary, Alberta) entitled *The*

Face of the Dance, a display of Inuit artifacts. I led the children to a chart entitled "mask maker." Of all the parts of the exhibit, what was written here
struck me the most. To paraphrase, after the dance ceremonies, all the
masks that the participants had worn were burned. A few might escape
burning by rolling from the pile, and these would be gathered up by the vis-
itors who often asked to buy them. Then the striking words of one of the
participants in the dance: "We wondered why they might want to save
them." At first, I'm disturbed by the notion of burning these beautiful
masks. I, too, would probably have been the collector of masks. Save it all,
save everything. Just like I'm afraid to part with any piece of a child's writing. I'm not always sure what to do with it, but I keep it just in case.

Then, again, the words of one of the dancers: "We wondered why they
might want to save them." Such a contrast in thinking. I wonder what it is
like to see life from that vantage point? To experience *endings*. To let go of
something. I thought of education and the desire to save everything. To
make everything savable.

Children have to write about the theater we saw, or it might just end. It
seems so reasonable, but there is a darkness to it.

"THEY HAVEN'T EVEN LEFT A TRACE"

In conversation with Catherine Ingram, poet, folklorist, and ecologist Gary
Snyder hits a nerve about the desire to leave traces and to measure a life by
the traces it leaves. The nerve he hits has telling implications for education
and helps reshape the earlier reflections of a Grade 3 teacher on the taken-
for-granted practices of writing in her classroom:

> *Snyder:*   If you travel over central Alaska, there is virtually no trace of human
> habitation. Yet there have been people living there for 8000 years.
> One way to look at it—the way nineteenth century Europeans would
> have looked at it—was to say that these people had absolutely noth-
> ing going for themselves. They haven't even left a trace. From an-
> other standpoint . . . the fact that they could live there for 8000 years
> and have a very complex and rich intellectual and spiritual culture
> and yet not leave a trace is a considerable monument.
>
> *Ingram:*   Do you know the Chuang Tzu poem called "When Life was Full
> There Was No History"?
>
> *Snyder:*   Exactly, yes. Same kind of thing. We have to re-think what that
> means. (Ingram, 1990, pp. 237–238)

Gary Snyder's words provide a metaphor for re-thinking the desire to get
elementary school children to write incessantly. This re-thinking is espe-

cially urgent when considering its ecological consequences, for the incessancy we sometimes witness links up in convoluted ways to ecologically disastrous images of relentless and ever-increasing consumptiveness and production. We sometimes act as if the Earth, at every turn, needs our articulations and gracious bestowals of meaning in order to be validated. We sometimes act as if the experiences of our children need always to be explicitly articulated and rendered into writing in order to be pedagogically valuable. We sometimes act as if experience must be consumed up into writing and rendered into a product, an artifact in ways analogous to acting as if a forest must be transformable into beard-feet in order to be worthy of our attention. Once inscribed, experience "leaves traces" that can be saved and collected and enumerated like the masks that roll off the fire.

"I'm not always sure what to do with it, but I keep it just in case."

These images are often left unvoiced in current discourse about language arts practices. The power of these unvoiced (and thereby difficult to question) images is undeniable. In a graduate course on the intimacies between ecology and pedagogy, the class explored ways of making schools more ecologically sane. One student suggested that we revert back to individual chalkboards for some writing activities in order to save paper. In response, another suggested that we might simply have children *write less*. It was as if some blasphemy had been uttered. Writing less has become almost unthinkable. As one of the graduate students, a practicing second-grade teacher, said, "Finally I've got my kids writing all the time, and you want me to stop them?"

These phrases are important: "Writing all the time" is mentioned as if it can only be heard as good news, and, now that the children are writing all the time, questioning the incessancy of writing can appear as an oppressive attempt to prevent them from writing. Furthermore, once teachers have gotten children to produce all this writing, they cannot help but save it, even if they no longer know what to do with it. As can often happen in elementary classrooms, teachers can become inundated with "traces" of children's work and find that their ability to attend to it in a pedagogically valuable way is unsustainable, even though it was precisely the issue of pedagogical value that led to having students write so much in the first place. We have something akin to an ecological disaster—an "urban sprawl" of relentlessly proliferating traces that threaten to "crowd out" the very experiences that produced and sustained those traces in the first place.

In some classrooms, children are being encouraged to carry notebooks with them all the time (Calkins, with Harwayne, 1991), to see every experience in light of its note-ability, in light, that is, of the traces it leaves behind in its wake.

"THE SIGHT OF ORANGE SLICES LINED
UP ON A WINDOWSILL"

These issues re-emerge when we consider themes present in the latest work by Lucy Calkins (with Harwanyne, 1991). This book, full as it is of wonderful examples of children's work, contains deep ironies about the relations between our lived-experience, the traces we leave, and our efforts, as teachers, to inculcate children into the undeniable allures of leaving such traces (the allure of "authorship").

Calkins (1991) provided us with compelling considerations of the formative power of writing and the ability of writing to help "young people to cherish the sight of orange slices lined up on a windowsill":

> We can't give children rich lives, but we can give them the lens to appreciate the richness that is already there. (p. 35).

Writing (Calkins is speaking especially of the use of notebooks to record experience) can become a form of mindfulness to the richness of our lived-experience that can be so fleeting and ephemeral. Writing can help us slow down the pace and "take note" of previously unnoticed textures of our experience of the world. It lets us savor our lives more deeply by letting text and the textures of experience play out a dance of mutual articulation. "We let these notebooks help us lead more wide-awake lives" (p. 42).

But there are suggestions in Calkins' work that have an ironic ring to them. Some passages can be read as positive affirmations of the mindfulness that writing can afford us. But these very same passages can "seem so reasonable, but there is a darkness . . ."

"Notebooks validate a child's existence" (Calkins, 1991, p. 35). This statement emerges in the midst of considerations of how children can come to see their own experiences as worthy of note, but it veers so close to Snyder's words: Without such notebooks, "they have absolutely nothing going for themselves. They haven't even left a trace." It must be emphasized that a child's existence is valid without notebooks; notebooks are the noting of moments of a life that is valid already. Therefore, writing does not validate so much as take note of, articulate, and make public something already valid.

The full text of Calkins' work makes it clear that this is not what she intended by these words, but these words (as with any words) have a life that goes beyond intent. These words must be carefully re-thought insofar as they are bound up in North American culture's tendency to see writing as a form of legitimization. That which is written, that which is "in print" carries a great deal more public "weight" if for no other reason than writing is public(ation), unlike the privacies and intimacies of experience itself. And this urge toward "publication-as-validation" must be linked with re-considerations of the ease with which we ascribe the full weight of "authorship" to the youngest of children in school while, at the same time, the adults involved in such ascription would hesitate using the same term to describe themselves. And this ascription itself must be considered in relation to how writing has become so intimately linked to the publishing industry and forces of saleability and marketability. We need only think of how we in academia are not only inundated with texts in ever new and improved editions that we are urged to consume (one suspects that new editions are produced simply to sustain continuous consumption), but how, also, we are encouraged to enter this fray ourselves to gain legitimization as authors.

"Living is, after all, a crucial part of writing" (Calkins, 1991, p. 66). Again, this can be read to say that writing should be full of life and that one must be fully engaged in life in order to write and write well. It also hints that writing can help deepen our living by deepening our mindfulness to the Earth that houses and sustains our lives. But, in fact, writing is (a crucial and irreplaceable) part of life, not the reverse. Notebooks, therefore, are pointedly not "lifebooks" (p. 51) even though one's life may be what the notebook is often about. Put differently, life is more than what is able to be rendered into note-ability. Notebooks are what help writers and readers to attend to something other than the notebooks—"the sight of orange slices lined up in the windowsill."

"In the hurry of our lives and in the rush of the inflated curriculum, we need rituals . . . that invite us to pause and make meaning from the bits of our lives" (p. 57). This again voices the power of Calkins' work to evoke a sense of the deeply spiritual and sacred character that writing can have, causing us to pause over the painful and pleasurable gifts of experience. But it is the pausing over these gifts that is sacred here. Again, the ironies:

> We write. We keep our own notebook beside us as we live. When we and our colleagues keep notebooks of our own, we have wells to draw on when we teach. Then, if we see Rebecca tearing a giant wad of paper from her notebook during social studies because she forgot to bring paper to school, our dismay is deeply felt. "How could you? This is your notebook," we say, and it is not so much what we have said that reaches through to Rebecca but what we have felt. (p. 51)

Embedded here is a sort of unintended emotional tyranny mixed with a dangerous "sacrilizing" of writing itself. For it is being mindful of experience that is the "sacred ground." The violation of this might be so "deeply felt," but not the ripping of pages from the notebook which is, after all is said and done, a thing and nothing more. Sacrilizing the notebook ("How could you?"—as if ripping pages out was some sort of desecration, and as if the child's answer has any options at all, as if this was a real question instead of simply moral outrage hidden in the false guise of a question posed by someone in "authority") once again makes possible the ecologically disastrous turn to replacing the integrity and validity of the Earth's gifts ("the sight of the orange slices") with our articulation of them. "The richness that is already there" does not need our articulation, nor does it gain its integrity from such articulation. Notebooks are nothing but reminders of experience. The experience is not *in* them unless, of course, we sacrilize the written word, sacrilize, not the living, but the traces that living leaves behind.

"Children are great collectors of experience" (p. 44). But to treat one's life as accumulative, to treat one's life experiences like the masks having rolled off the fire (rather than the dance itself, itself uncollected), threatens to betray the darkness of consumerism running rampant over our very existence, an existence now validated by the traces we can collect and accumulate.

"THE PLEASURES OF FORGETTING":
WRITING AND THE DEATH OF MEMORY

> *In this "information age," to forget is seen as a kind of disgrace.*
> —Jackson (1991, A20)

> *It is time to rescue the phenomenon of memory . . . and to see it as an essential element of [our] being. In a way that has long been insufficiently noticed, forgetting is closely related to keeping in mind and remembering; forgetting is not merely an absence and a lack but . . . a condition of the life of mind. Only by forgetting does the mind have the possibility of total renewal, the capacity to see everything with fresh eyes, so that what is long familiar fuses with the new.*
> —Gadamer (1989, p. 16)

Gadamer (1989) suggests that memory is not a faculty with given characteristics that is simply usable instrumentally. "Whoever uses his memory as a mere faculty—and any 'technique' of memory is such a use—does not yet possess it as something that is absolutely his own" (p. 16). Memory, possessed as "one's own," is something that is formed over time and each of us carries—more strongly put, each of us *is*—the unique residues of such formation over the course of our individual lives. Who I understand myself to be is constituted by what I bear forward of my life experiences. The formative processes of remembering and forgetting are thus coincident with the formation of character. Collected and accumulated external traces—for example, notebooks—can remind us of our life experiences, but they can remind us only of what is already somehow borne in memory, however deeply buried. To the extent that these external traces replace the formativeness of memory (like anonymously storing "information" in a computer without digesting it), they can no longer remind us of our lives because they have not entered into the formation of who we are.

Pedagogy, as the formation of character, is essentially the formation of memory, and, Gadamer suggests, forgetting is an essential feature of such formation. There is, in fact, a pleasure involved in letting some experiences "go by," in not saving everything just because we can save it. Graham Jackson's "pleasures of forgetting" (1991) has to do with experience percolating down into the flesh and bones—into a sort of dark, cellular "memory"—rather than this percolating being circumvented through relentlessly saving experience in the arena of the sort of explicitness and brightness that writing allows. Allowing experience to thus "pass away" into "the implicit" allows for the possibility of renewal and regeneration. Experience that is allowed to "root down" in this way (instead of being "pulled up by the roots" at ever turn and rendered into the glare of public writing) can become a sort of fertile "undergrowth" out of which new experience can erupt. Allowing experience to "pass away" allows memory (and thus character) to form through the dialectic of remembering and forgetting.

Writing thus has a paradoxical place vis-à-vis memory and forgetting. Gadamer (1989) cited Hegel's formulation of writing as intimately linked with the "will to hand things down, 'to make memory last' " (p. 391). But we have the paradoxical underside of this formulation as early as Plato's *Phaedrus*:

> You are father of written letters. But the fact is that this invention of yours [writing] will produce forgetfulness in the souls of those who learn it. They will not need to exercise their memories, being able to rely on what is written, calling things to mind no longer from within themselves by their own powers, but under the stimulus of external marks that are alien to themselves. So it's not a recipe for memory, but for reminding that you have discovered. (Plato, 1956 trans., p. 275)

But the forgetfulness that Plato is alluding to here is not the forgetfulness essential to the formation of memory. It is the forgetfulness of never needing to remember in the first place. Writing, Plato fears, avoids or replaces the dialectic of remembering and forgetting that is so intimately "one's own." By forging experience into writing, we force experience into "external marks that are alien" and thus perhaps bypass the formation of character that the dialectic of remembering and forgetting would afford. Writing can circumvent the need to remember (and thereby the formative dangers and pleasures of forgetting). We end up in a paradoxical position: Anything might become memorable, so we take notes and write about everything and this prevents anything from becoming memorable by circumventing the formative effort to remember. An experience is not allowed to stand the test of time, the test of being shuffled and re-shuffled over the course of experience itself (and therefore the risk that over this course, some things will be irretrievably lost). Circumventing this process is circumventing the delicate and contingent interplay we have with the world. Clearly, writing can help slow this interplay and help make us mindful of it. However, as Jessica's moaning, "Are we going to have to write about it?" might attest, it can just as easily interrupt our deep love affair with the world. In the name of ensuring that an experience has been "pedagogically valuable," it can interrupt precisely the formation of memory and character that is at the core of pedagogy itself.

Gadamer (1989) suggested, too, that forgetting allows a certain forgiveness of the past, allowing one to "see with fresh eyes" (p. 15). This may have consequences for our use of portfolios of written work that follow a child throughout his or her schooling (recall Manuel's "file this thick" from chapter 2). This is done in the name of continuity and accountability, but it can be so unforgiving of a child to burden them with a life in which nothing is forgotten. Clearly, an effective teacher will be more concerned with what has "come of" the things "written up" in the file (Gadamer's notion of "formation"), but these "alien marks" often carry a weight of authority that can override such concerns for who the child has become (Field, 1991).

WRITING AND FISSURES IN "THE COMMUNAL ORDER OF MEMORIES AND WAYS"

> *The community is an order of memories preserved consciously in instructions, songs and stories, and both consciously and unconsciously in ways. A healthy culture holds preserving knowledge in place for a long time. That is, the essential wisdom accumulates in the community much as fertility builds in the soil. In both, death becomes potentiality.*
>
> —Berry (1983, p. 73)

An upper elementary teacher of Native children returned from a field trip and told the children to take out their journals and write of the experience they had just had. One child blurted out, "but you were there!", bewildered perhaps at how writing would be necessary for those who had lived through the experience already.

It may be that one of the reasons for the relentlessness of writing in elementary school is that there is no longer a reliable communal order of memory and ways in which shared events can be safely housed without each individual having to inscribe their own individual experiences of it. In educators' efforts to validate each and every child's individual experience by having each and every child write about each and every experience, what is forgone is a deeper sense of communal order, of shared experience (distinguishable from each individual child sharing his or her individual experience), of a roiling, ongoing, constantly re-negotiated "belonging" (Caputo, 1989, p. 201; Gadamer, 1989, p. 462; Snyder, 1980, p. 86). Relentless writing may hint at a sort of individualized democratization gone wild, which belies the growth of essential wisdom in a diverse, sustainable, living community.

With the shifting of teacher populations and student populations, we can no longer reliably say "but you were there!" The relentlessness of writing might belie a fear we all face: Once the communal fabrics are torn, once the threads of the net are cut, things, events, experiences will not be housed unwritten in a common wisdom but will simply disappear altogether. By analogy, once the fertility of the soil is despoiled, new growth will not root but simply disappear altogether. To paraphrase Wendell Berry, in such an instance death becomes, not potentiality and the condition of renewal but simple annihilation.

It may be that saying that "notebooks validate the child's experience" hides the fear that without leaving traces, our individual lives could end without a trace, having never "made our mark." Here is the full turn of the paradox of writing. The desire to save every trace, itself produced by the fear of "disappearing without a trace," consequently produces the lack of "fertile soil" because nothing is allowed to pass away into that soil to sustain its fertility (and to thereby sustain the possibility of "new growth"). And this lack of fertility thereby produces a now completely warrantable fear of "disappearing without a trace," leading again to "save it all. Save everything."

This inability to allow anything to "pass away" means that children's files become often crammed with individual traces and, as Koestler (1959) pointed out, this sort of innundation leads to a paradoxical loss of intelligibility, for there is no longer any formative "remembering and forgetting" done as a feature of the accumulation itself ("save it all. Save everything"). All we have are scattered bits and pieces which we must now try to fit together.

TRACES AS INDIVIDUALLY POSSESSED "CULTURAL CAPITAL" AND THE NEED FOR (AC)COUNTABILITY

The answer to the question, "Are we going to have to write about this?" is so very often "yes." The fear of "disappearing without a trace" is a wonderful–horrible metaphor for the night tremors that teachers experience: the child whose file is empty when her parents arrive for an interview.

Why do teachers have children write about these experiences? It is not simply because they find writing desirable for children to learn to do. Their writing is desirable for teachers to have them do, because it leaves them with collectable, traceable artifacts on the basis of which they can make claims about and stake claim to knowledge of the children they teach. Writing becomes a visible sign of the pedagogical validity of the experiences children have had. It allows teachers to document the life of our classroom by producing precisely this: documents as signs of that life. More crassly put, children's writing validates the teacher's existence vis-à-vis questions of accountability.

There are even more crass consequences that are possible to draw out. Writing renders children's experiences into a marketable form that they can then exchange for marks, for praise, for the allure of public display or publication. We slip easily and unintentionally from lived experience, to mindfulness to such experience, to notability, to documentability, to accountability, to countability, so that the insinuation of children into the allures of writing is at once their (however unintended) insinuation into a view of their experiences as cultural capital which is to be enumerated regarding its current market exchange value, not valued for its depth of mindfulness and attention. Consider the words of Nancy Atwell (1990) who, citing Toby Fulwiler (1987), reminded us that "if learning logs are to be vehicles for learning, they cannot be measured as performances too. Individual entries are never graded or corrected, but they are counted: The student must write something" (pp. xvii–xviii).

Here we have a double turn. In an effort to "democratize" the process of language-arts evaluation, teachers usher children into self-evaluations and then witness how deep is their insinuation into the life view of equating value and enumerability. Consider the extent to which the following excerpts of a child's self-evaluation are full of images "countability" and the subtle equation of numerability with value:

Here's what I'd like to improve: My reading log because I haven't written in it 3 times a week.

My Literature grade should be A because: I read two and 3 quarters Literature books and got an A on my family tree.

My English grade should be A because: I did the amount of pages needed in my writing folder and am finished with my story for publication. (Goodman, Bird, & Goodman, 1991, p. 255)

Consider, too, the teacher's response to this self-evaluation that unwittingly confirms such a life view: "Fine work!" (p. 255). And, finally, consider the fact that Goodman et al. let this go by without further comment.

CONCLUDING REMARKS: THE FEAR OF THE UNUTTERED AND THE PLEASURES OF "WALKING AROUND UNWRITTEN"

> *Notebooks have embodied the idea that we put bits of our lives and our thinking into print not only to produce compositions, but also because we do not want to walk around unwritten. Such writing changes our living.*
>
> —Calkins (1991, p. 38)

Our culture has grown suspicious of that which is held implicitly, of that which is not publically voiced. Withholding is seen as hiding something to the extent that implicit, privately held, embodied knowledge has become pathologized. Everything should be "out" (in journals, in conversations, on television). Explicitness, publicness, publication—what Smith (1999) pointed to as a sort of relentless self-annunciation—becomes a form of healthiness, always and everywhere desirable. Quiet, silence, reserve, become forms of being silenced and suppressed, desiring to write, to speak, but being prevented. Or they mean that someone has something to hide. A telling feature of the relentlessness of writing is that we find it hard to imagine why someone would willingly not pursue it, to the extent that we can say without further ado that "we don't want to walk around unwritten."

So many of the Wisdom traditions speak of the deep pleasure of unarticulated experience, the deep sense of the untterability of the full complexities of our lives. It is precisely "walking around unwritten" that all Wisdom traditions, in varying ways and to varying degrees, hold as most dear and most sacred. It is walking around unwritten that allows the rich integrities of our experience to come forward free of the discursive swirling of human intent. It is the discipline of walking around unwritten that leads to a deep mindfulness of the gifts of the Earth.

It is precisely the near impossibility of walking around unwritten that forms one feature of the ecological disasters we face. Our culture is continuously scribing the Earth and scribing our experience of it. The deep pleasures of finally finding a moment unscribed—a moment of pause, of silence, of the unuttered delight of "this sight of orange slices on the windowsill"— this is the difficult thing.

Certainly, many children find it difficult to write. Many children are estranged from their own experiences and have been rendered mute by the often silencing formalism of schooling. Just as certainly, innovative language arts practices are doing a wonderful job of drawing these children out of their reluctance. The question then becomes, what are they being drawn out *for*? So they can simply "write all the time"? And, to pose the ecological question, is such a drawing out into "writing all the time" sustainable? In conversation with David Smith, the brilliant Indian writer Ashis Nandy suggested that if India pursued the course toward literacy and writing pursued in North America, there wouldn't be a tree left on Earth. Our incessancy is not sustainable without at once requiring a lack of such incessancy from most peoples on Earth. Given this, "writing all the time" might be seen as a type of opulence.

Obviously, writing is not a bad thing. However, its increasing relentlessness might be taken as a sign that warrants careful attention. In the effort to get children to "write all the time," educators may be unwittingly insinuating students into a life view that is no longer sustainable even though it may still be alluring.

Preamble 5

Let's gather together some of the threads so far that define an interpretive understanding of "the basics." We begin with the premise that the living disciplines we have been handed *live* in their openness to being handed along (Gadamer, 1989, p. 284). This is what is "basic" to them, interpretively understood: to understand these disciplines is to participate in their "furtherance" (p. xxiv). Does this at all mean that we simply accept them as fixed and finished givens that are beyond question and simply indoctrinate the young into such acceptance? On the contrary, it means that, say, addition and subtraction cannot be treated as if they are fixed and finish "objects" that are able to be simply indoctrinated through means of control, prediction, and manipulation. Rather, insofar as they form parts of a *living* discipline, that discipline is precisely *not* fixed and finished but is rather, ongoing, still "in play," still "open to question" in our human inheritance. To understand these matters this way is to learn to endure the fact that the seeming fixity of our current knowledge will, *of necessity*, have to experience, to suffer, to endure, or undergo the arrival of an unfixed future and the questions it might hold, questions we might not have even imagined or desired. This open, living endurance, we suggest, is *basic* to the disciplines taught in schools.

Thus, our children and the experiences and questions they bring are not problems we need to fix or stop or remedy. Rather, if such experiences and questions are treated well—treated, that is, as they pertain, not to the psychology of the question-asker, but in regard to how they might open up our

human inheritance—they are basic to the health and well being of these inheritances, because these inheritances *must* remain open to the future if
they are to remain living parts of our world.

Interpretively or hermeneutically speaking, the experiences students engage in our classrooms are not so much something that each "subject" *has*
(as if experience were the subject's *property*). Rather, experience is treated
as something a person *undergoes*. "Any experience worthy of the name"
(Gadamer, 1989) has the character of a journey, a venture into something
that is "more" than my own subjectivity, a place that has character, demands, bloodlines, histories, desires, *of its own*, "beyond my wanting and doing" (Gadamer, 1989, p. xxxviii). Obviously each one of us will bring something different to this place, an angle, a question, a trouble, a discovery that
no one else might have happened upon. But, in the classroom, these differences are not treated as properties of the discoverer, but *properties of the place
itself*, things that this or that individual student has *found*.

This sounds rather arcane, but it simply points to a commonplace experience: those moments when we know that "something is going on," ([*im
Spiele ist*] Gadamer, 1989, p. 104), "something is happening" ([*sich abspielt*],
p. 104), something is "at play," here, in this place and it has something to
ask *of me* beyond what I might imagine asking of it. Rich and memorable experiences ask things of us, and, as such, they are characterizable as "more a
passion than an action. A question *presses itself upon us*" (1989, p. 366; italics
added). Such experiences-as-sojourns-to-a-place take the form of a "momentary loss of self" (Gadamer, 1977, p. 51) and return to oneself, having
learned about that place, say, the territories of Coyote or the hands of time
or the ins and outs of writing and memory. These matters "would not deserve the interest we take in them if they did not have something to teach us
that we could not know by ourselves" (p. xxxv).

Interpretively treated, therefore, "understanding" some topic/topogra-
phy in school means moving into a territory and somehow being "moved"
by *its* movement, (the root of the word *passion*. See chapter 12 on this character of movement as another basic of teaching and learning), being
changed by *its* lessons.

Again, this is why, hermeneutically understood, experience is not
treated as something an individual subject "has," but as something they undergo here, in this place, with others as witnesses to their work. If we go
back to that Grade 2 girl and her questions, they were treated as questions
about the topic/topography of addition and subtraction, not as psychological properties about *her*. Read interpretively, she doesn't precisely *have a
question* as much as she has *happened upon a question* that is indigenous *to this
place*, to *mathematics*. She did need to be "taught" that she had happened
upon something wonderful. She had to learn, from how others treated her
questions, that she had found something. And, of course, as she slowly be-

gan to believe that this might just be true, that there might just be some real venture that could be had, she, this individual child and no one else, slowly seemed to feel and act stronger and more able in this place called mathematics.

A few more turns. As was explored in chapter 4, Gadamer (1989) links these "experiences worthy of the name" with the formation of memory (pp. 15–16) and the formation of memory with the formation of character (pp. 9–19). This last term means simply this: I *become someone* because of what I have experienced, what I have undergone. We have often contended this: that, under "basics-as-breakdown," the work our children do might be memorizable (a version of control, prediction, and manipulation) but it is rarely especially *memorable*. An interpretive version of "the basics" suggests that the disciplines entrusted to teachers and learners need to be made *memorable* if they are to be truly experienced as living disciplines. They need to become things that students *undergo*, not just objects they "have," things that enchant, possess, and capture their imaginations, their passions, and not just things they "possess" and can then exchange, in the market economy of knowledge-as-commodity, for marks (see chaps. 4 and 12). If they do not become things that our children undergo, it is not only students who suffer. The disciplines themselves become characterized *by our students* as little more than commodities to exchange for schoolwork marks (how many pages do you want on this assignment? Is this on the exam? Are we going to have to write about this?).

If we take this interpretive turn, there is a pleasurable sense in which things get *more difficult* for teachers and children alike. The potential memorability of David's tales of Africa, or Sinead's Coyote work, or that Grade 2 girl's "you have to do both" *is not a given*. It is a risk, a venture. But more than this, we find that, at the heart of "the basics" of a living discipline is *difficulty*. This is why Caputo (1987) characterized hermeneutics or interpretation as a "restoring life to its original difficulty" and not betraying those troubles with false assurances regarding controlling, predicting, and manipulating our children's lives. The problem with basics-as-breakdown is that, in schools, we have come to believe too often that *that's all there is* to understanding the world. An interpretive treatment of such matters suggests that mathematics is real work, genuine work, difficult *in its very nature* and to allow our children to get in on the real work makes their school lives more difficult, but also more alive, necessary, challenging.

This is what this next chapter addresses head on: With an interpretive reading of "the basics" things become richer, more questionable, more multivoical and contested, more interrelated and tangled, more ambiguous, more ongoing and unfinished. Classroom topics not only "give way to movement" (Caputo, 1987, p. 2). They reveal that they *are* such movement, and to experience them is to allow ourselves to suffer or undergo this movement.

That is why the offhand characterization of a child in the following chapter is so perfect: This work is pleasurable, but part of the pleasure is the fact that the questions are experienced by all concerned as necessary and long-standing, as parts of ancient conversations and ancestries that have been happened upon in the work of the classroom.

And guess who shows up when you turn your back on those horrid little reader-books that are never about *stories* but always about *assessment*?

The Lady of Shallot.

Chapter 5

Hard Fun: Teaching and Learning for the Twenty-First Century

Patricia Clifford
Sharon Friesen

In a kingdom long ago there was a man who traveled from the farthest city to the nearest town. And as he went he traded things—a pair of shoes for a piece of gold, a parrot for a bolt of silver cloth—until he was more rich than he had ever dreamed possible. The people thought a man who had so many things must be wise, and no matter where he went they followed him, asking questions.

"Our baby cries," said one. "What shall we do?"

"My father went to war. How will we live?" said another.

But though the traveling man could fetch goods from his sack and add up sums, he could not answer their questions.

One day he met an old woman who carried a wooden box. "Inside this box," she said, "are answers to all things."

The traveling man whistled. "I have seen many things," he said, "but I would give all I have to open that box."

"Done," said the old woman.

When the traveling man lifted the lid, he saw to his surprise that the box was filled with coins. Each one was stamped with a curious sentence. "Open the door," said one. "Give him your love," said another. "One hundred and five," said a third.

The traveling man was overjoyed. "I am rich beyond measure," he said. "I have answers to all things.

The old woman smiled. "But what good is an answer," she said, "without the right question?"

—Through the Mickle Woods (Gregory, 1992, n.p.)

We have entered a new millennium. The press teems with articles about what students must learn and what schools must teach in order for society to prosper in the 21st century. Rich and powerful traveling men like the one in *Through the Mickle Woods* (Gregory, 1992) are everywhere, publishing books and magazines, appearing on talk shows, writing newspaper columns. And wherever they go, people press them with questions:

"Our schools are failing. What should we do?"
"Our children are ignorant. How will we compete?"

Equipped with some modern equivalent of the old woman's wooden box, travelers reach in for easy answers:

"Buy more computers."
"Everyone online"
"Return to the basics."
"Charter schools."
"Standardize the curriculum. Give more tests."
"Parent involvement."
"More phonics."
"Make schools run like businesses."
"Cut out all the experimentation and frippery."
"Technology"
"One hundred and five."

Suggestions pile up, each offered hopefully as the coin that will effect real and lasting educational reform. Grasping for certainties in a time of huge social, economic, and political change, people also grasp at these new currencies with genuine hope that this time, in this place, things will be different.

Educators' and critics' faces are oriented, however uncertainly, toward the future. There is a shared, if contradictory sense, that schools need to improve (Barlow & Robertson, 1994)—that the dawning of a new century calls forth changed institutions. No one is content with the status quo. Everyone is looking for answers. In this concern to find solutions that will carry us into the future, however, we are in danger of moving into that future a bit like Marley's ghost, dragging mile upon mile of unresolved chains and incoherent shackles forged, in life, by the accumulation of the curiously stamped coins of countless travelers through the educational landscape.

Concerned educators have long felt the intolerable weight of these chains, and have attacked them, link by link, with well-intentioned but sometimes misdirected efforts at reform. Depending on the dominant concern (cynics might read "fad") of any particular era, teachers have embraced new methodologies, techniques, and programs: phonics, look-and-say, whole language; the "new math," manipulatives, computer-assisted instruction, the spiral curriculum; open areas, cooperative learning, multiaging. The names change from era to era, as do the dominant ideologies that inform whatever program is developed, implemented, tested—and ultimately rejected. Teachers talk about this phenomenon as "the pendulum swing." The particulars of any educational reform are not especially important. Whatever the innovation, it arrives, it becomes the darling of the enlightened, and it goes. As surely as night follows day, what is touted one year will be reviled the next by a new breed of travelers.

It is easy to become discouraged with this cycle of failure. Seeing in this or that new program, idea, or philosophy the grounds for hope that tomorrow *might* be different, many of those in education have committed themselves to one reform or another, only to be left standing at the altar. Jilted two or three times, even the most confident, energetic, and innovative of educators can be shaken by the experience. Sometimes teachers even take our failure to bring long-lasting and significant change to the institution as a personal failure—perhaps of judgment, perhaps of skill and ability, perhaps simply of energy. It is impossible to overestimate the personal devastation that has been suffered by good and caring people who have taken strong and public stands on behalf of a failed innovation to make life in school better for students and their teachers. In this chapter, it is not our intention to add to this accumulated pain or fatigue when we suggest that schools as we know them have to change. Instead, we invite others to take renewed heart, as we have done, from the wisdom of the old woman. Hope lies in learning how to ask new questions.

Without this clear-sighted insistence on a changed focus, all that will happen in the name of educational reform is that the schools of the future will drag longer, more burdensome shackles. If we are to take seriously the idea that schools might enhance rather than impede the development of an innovative society, we must let go of the chain entirely. And in order to do that, we have first to talk frankly about what is wrong with schools today—whether those schools are progressive and innovative, whether they are traditional, whether they are run by principals or parent councils, whether they are site or centrally managed, whether they are filled with computers or completely bereft.

Academics (Egan, 1992; Greene, 1978, 1988; Sarason, 1982, 1990) and practitioners (e.g., Meier, 1992; see chap. 1) have been saying it for a long time. Now even noneducators (Kay, 1995; Negroponte, 1995; Papert, 1993) have jumped into the conversation. Schools are, generally speaking, intellectually boring places, uninteresting both for the students compelled to attend them and for adults hired to work in them. Students and teachers often feel lost and unconnected, "dandelion pods tossed by the wind" (Greene, 1988, p. 3). Despite what Papert (1993) described as a "sort of fifth column . . . of teachers [who] manage to create within the walls of their own classrooms oases of learning," public schools have remained intractable to significant reform:

> Despite the many manifestations of a widespread desire for something different, the education establishment, including most of its research community, remains largely committed to the educational philosophy of the late nineteenth and early twentieth centuries, and so far none of those who challenge these hallowed traditions has been able to loosen the hold of the educational establishment on how children are taught. (p. 3)

It does not seem to matter who is shaping schools, who spearheads this or that reform effort. Students anywhere, any place, in any decade of this century could have said what these students say in *When I Was Young I Loved School: Dropping Out and Hanging In* (cited in Sarason, 1990):

> "I didn't like doing school work. . . . School was boring. And the school work I was learning was boring. Boring, boring, boring."

> "School was boring because you had to [*sic*] many classes to go to. The fun part was skipping or always doing something wrong. You always have to have some kinds of adventure in your life."

> "I don't really mind learning, if I'm talking with somebody and they're telling me something interesting. It's different. But . . . sitting in a classroom with this person teaching you, pointing to the blackboard, and all those people sitting behind their desks. I don't know. If there was a different way to learn . . . I'd do it in a minute." (p. 114)

In a Special Issue of *Scientific American*, Alan C. Kay (1995) recalls a remark of physicist Murray Gell-Man:

> Education in the twentieth century is like being taken to the world's greatest restaurant and being fed the menu. He meant that representations of ideas have replaced the ideas, themselves; students are taught superficially about great discoveries instead of being helped to learn deeply for themselves. (p. 150)

"IF THERE WAS A DIFFERENT WAY TO LEARN . . ."

Children are learners. Everyone acknowledges how much they learn about the world in the years before they come to school: how to talk, how to make and maintain relationships, how to behave appropriately in diverse social situations. They have learned how to pose questions, how to problem solve, how to form and test hypotheses. Even if they cannot yet read print in an adult way, most are literate. They can recognize MacDonald's from a quarter of a mile away, grab exactly the box of cereal they want from the grocery shelf, find the ladies' washroom and Toys R Us. Children age 5 are numerate as well. They have developed razor-sharp acuity of "fair share." Many can count all the candles on their birthday cake, determine who is taller or shorter than they are, and run into the house to get more cookies, marbles, or toys when three kids from down the street come over to play.

Coming from incredibly diverse backgrounds, with a wide range of knowledge and experience in the world, children enter the still-19th-century institution of school and immediately become "students" who are handed the menu, not the feast of real learning. Eager at first to acquire more control of adult ways of knowing the world, far too many of them end up like the dropouts, bored with what adults think they ought to know. Because so little of what they learn outside the school has any place *inside* the classroom, many discount what they learn each day about how to function at work, in shops, and with each other. They can no longer remember a time when they learned things without textbooks, lectures, worksheets, and tests—nor imagine how school might even be otherwise. When asked what they have learned this week, most students will search only their week at school for an answer. Predictably, many will respond, "Nothing." Learning has been reduced to what they do in school. Living is what they do in the real world.

That is what we believe students are getting at when they say that school is boring, boring, boring. Far too little of what most students do in school engages their imagination, fuels their passion to learn, connects them deeply with the world, or wins their hearts and minds. The world of learning shrinks, for far too many, to the size of an 8½ by 11 piece of paper. What understandings they manage to develop are frequently meager and threadbare:

> Students of physics believe in forces that can be mysteriously transmitted from one substance or agent to another; students of biology think of evolution as a planful, teleological process, culminating in the perfect human being; students of algebra plug numbers into an equation with hardly a clue as to what the equation means or when (and when *not*) to invoke it; students of history insist on applying the simplest stereotypical models to the elucidation of events that are complex and multifaceted; students of literature and the

arts prefer works that are simple, realistic, and sentimental over those that deal with philosophical issues or treat subject matter that is not overly beautiful. (Gardner & Boix-Mansilla, 1994, p. 200)

Is it any wonder that students and teachers are bored? And is it any wonder that critics, contemplating the potential of developments in telecommunication and multimedia to put new worlds literally at the fingertips of anyone with access to a computer, are worried? If schools have had little real success in engaging students with knowledge currently available to them—knowledge that is familiar to teachers in both substance and form—what is to ensure that we will do things differently—do things better—as the face of knowledge, itself, changes?

To address this question with any kind of depth, it is important to return to the warning (for so it is) of the wise old woman: What good is an answer without the right question? It is tempting to do what so many have done in the past decades: to rush into answers that look compelling either in their familiarity or in their "techie-whizzy" newness. If we do that yet again as powerful new technologies transform the ways people learn outside schools, the mistakes of the past will be made again. We will likely do what Negroponte (1995) fears: cling to the use of computers in schools advocated in the 1960s:

a crummy drill-and-practice approach, using computers on a one-to-one basis, in a self-paced fashion, to teach those same God-awful facts more effectively. (p. 198)

Only now, he goes on to suggest,

we have closet drill-and-practice believers who think they can colonize the pizzazz of a Sega game to squirt a bit more information into the heads of children, with more so-called productivity. (p. 199)

Schools have a long history of pouring old wine into new bottles. What is called for, this late in the century, are questions that probe beneath the surface of life in schools. We propose that two such questions are these:

1. In what ways are children and young people cast adrift in schools when powerful educational practice instrumentalizes, trivializes, psychologizes—and even ignores—their capacity for imaginative engagement with the world, with ideas and with each other?
2. What can happen in schools when teachers take seriously the power and the right of children to name and to shape their experience of the world? And what does imaginative engagement have to do with that power and right?

The Theoretical Death of the Imagination

Traditional educational practices are in the news these days. Cast as "basics" to which schools must somehow return, cheap coins rattle out of traveling men's bags. It is easy to caricature vocal parents on talk shows: They seem to want every child hooked on phonics. They want schools to buy basal readers instead of novels and picture books, and teachers to arrange classrooms in straight rows of desks instead of clusters of tables and chairs. Frustrated with what they see as ill-considered experiments with child-centered teaching, such parents seem to be demanding a return both to schools that are more recognizable and that are more hard-nosed, more demanding, more rigorous. In one sense, this groundswell represents a new political force in education. In another sense, however, it is very old, with roots that stretch way back to Plato and Descartes.

Distrusting imagination as the most uneducated faculty of the human soul, and fearing its power to seduce and deceive the reasonable mind, Plato banished poets from his Republic. Descartes established a hierarchy of learning, with mathematical reasoning at the top and the fuzzy arts at the bottom. Ever since, Western educational systems have struggled with what to do with children's natural learning, with their intuitions, off-beat questions, and imaginative capacity to see the world as other than it is. Understood as somehow a function of the lower, child-like part of intelligence, imaginative play and representation is given its due in the fingerpaints, water tables, blocks, and house centers of kindergarten. However, the project of schooling is clearly designed to help children banish such childishness as they progress through school. By Grade 3 or 4, children have learned how to work. Cognitive ability becomes cast as their ability to reason in increasingly abstract, formal, and disembodied ways. The generous, expansive and exciting ways children know the world outside the school become cramped and penurious within its walls. The banquet of experiences that feeds all their senses, touches their hearts, and moves their souls shrinks to an anorexic diet of activities, drills, and worksheets.

Thus, for example, the experience of reading changes. Before children come to school, many of them have had the experience of reading with a trusted adult or sibling. Nestled on a lap, hanging over a shoulder or tucked under a friendly arm, such fortunate children experience the delights of reading other times, other places, other worlds. Once at school, however, something happens. The laps are gone—and so are the familiar voices and the loving arms. Sitting alone on their own chairs or in their own spaces during "carpet time" children learn to demonstrate decoding and interpretive competence. The value of the text becomes instrumental: How well is the child sounding out, attending to meaning, learning to recognize familiar words and phrases? That's what teaching and learning becomes for far too many 5-year-olds.

Basal readers, crafted not by strong writers but by committees interested in something quite different from a well-told tale, are not designed to engage the imagination. No one (not even their most fervent advocates) expects a child to be *enchanted* by a reader. That is not what such books are for. They are, instead, designed to develop readers of a particular, rather limited sort. They are designed to teach processes that are assumed to be mental, interior, and private. Moreover, such processes are thought to be sequential and orderly in their development. Missing one crucial step at any juncture is supposed to jeopardize the whole rational, logical, and predictable business of learning to read. From within this traditional paradigm, schools teach a skill—reading.

Bradley, a young child we know, reminded us of how toxic this cramped, disembodied experience can be. Bradley had started kindergarten eager to read and write. By April, his bedtime had turned into tearful pleading: "Please mummy, just read the story to me. Don't make me find any of the letters. Don't make me, mummy." By June, a more bloody-minded Bradley had changed tactics. "Here, mummy," he announced one morning. "Write a note to my teacher. Tell her I broke my arm so I can't write any more." Somehow, for Bradley, reading and writing had become school activities divorced completely from his former delight in stories. And for Bradley's teacher, the point of interest was not Bradley's disappointment with school. It was, instead, his demonstrable lack of readiness to start Grade 1. Before he turned 6, Bradley had become an educational statistic: a child whose problem with the demands of the institution was rewritten as a problem inside his head.

In the orderly world of a traditional classroom, there is generally one best way to do most tasks, one correct answer, one appropriate response. Both our society's longstanding and more recent, born-again commitment to "the basics" as they are understood from within a traditional paradigm make certain key assumptions about the child as learner, about learning competence, about classroom structures and activities, and about the nature of knowledge, itself. The child who comes to school in kindergarten is assumed:

- to be an empty vessel into which knowledge must be poured
- to possess a fixed (perhaps inherited) ability
- to realize her potential through effort and attitude
- to need firm adult guidance and control

Learning competence occurs through an emphasis on:

- memorization
- drill and practice

- direct instruction
- successive mastery of predetermined levels of difficulty

Classroom structures and activities emphasize:

- the same starting points for everyone
- the same materials for everyone. Enrichment is an "extra"
- uniformity of tasks for everyone
- regular examination, often with standardized tests
- acquisition of skills "on schedule"
- the one best way of doing most tasks
- the need to "fix" or "remediate" the child who will not, or cannot, perform according to expectation

And from within this paradigm, knowledge is assumed to be:

- fixed and unchanging
- objective
- discovered rather than created

For many years, teachers, researchers, and scholars have worked hard to address the obvious shortcomings of these assumptions and practices. For schools, these efforts resulted in the progressive classrooms of the 1960s, 1970s, and 1980s—the classrooms that currently bear the brunt of much right-wing scorn. For decades, to be educationally innovative was to be critical of the factory model of schooling outlined earlier. Teachers who sought change aligned themselves with efforts to make classrooms more child-centered; to help children learn by doing; to create a more developmentally appropriate curriculum for the young.

If the roots of traditional schooling reach right back to Plato and Descartes, the roots of this newer philosophy are also older than many teachers recognize. Indebted to the romanticism of Rousseau and the early theorizing of Pestalozzi and Froebel and Dewey, innovative teachers and researchers of the past 40 years eagerly embraced the epistemology of Piaget. Determined to make classrooms more responsive and relevant to the children who inhabited them, such educators introduced innovations that seemed radical at the time—and that critics still brand as "experimental" and radical even today: open area schools, cooperative learning, multiaging, field trips, learning by discovery, math manipulatives.

Like the traditional paradigm it attacks, the more progressivist, child-centered paradigm also centers on certain key assumptions. The child:

- is a "growing flower" or "innocent savage" in need of nurturing, care, and protection
- re-creates knowledge through the process of developing and unfolding his or her inner potential
- is an individual whose needs, rights, and self-esteem are paramount
- has inherently different thought processes from adults

Learning competence develops through an emphasis on:

- the interior, private, individualistic, and natural growth of mental processes
- the acquisition of "personal knowledge" through experience
- discovery
- activity
- self-realization
- expanding horizons of meaning from concrete experience of the immediate world to abstract thinking

Innovative classrooms designed from within this framework emphasize:

- the teacher as facilitator of personal exploration. Intervention by an adult is seen as interfering with "natural" development
- positive reinforcement and reward
- success without struggle or correction
- self-esteem
- immediately accessible and appealing, child-like resources
- process rather than product

Whether by accident or by design, the ages and stages through which children progress in their psychological development correspond to the three major periods of schooling:

The first epoch, called the *sensorimotor stage*, is roughly the same as the preschool period. This is a period of prelogic in which children respond to their immediate situation. The second epoch, which Piaget calls the stage of *concrete operations*, is roughly coextensive with the elementary school years. This is a period of concrete logic in which thought goes far beyond the immediate situation but still does not work through the operation of universal principles. Instead, its methods are still tied to specific situations, like those of an expert at kitchen mathematics who is incapable of handling a paper-and-pencil test on fractions. And finally there is the *formal stage*, which covers high school—and the rest of life. Now at last thought is driven, and disciplined, by deduction, by induction, and by the principle of developing theories by the test of empirical verification and refutation (Papert, 1993, p. 152). This neat and tidy view of the stages of child development is pervasive in education today. Seen as *natural, developmental,* and entirely inevitable, these Piagetian stages form the basis of curriculum design and innovative teaching practice in every Canadian province.

For far too long, debate about innovation in education has cast one "ism" against another: the shortfalls of traditionalism against the promise of progressivism. The battle has been waging for long enough that it is now becoming clear how seriously flawed *both* arguments are. Thus, it is not our intention to align ourselves with either side. Practices that derive from both paradigms have proven useful. Ideas from each have led to important discoveries about how people learn. What is important, at this juncture in the reform debate, is to recognize that educational questions for this new century lie quite outside the traditional/progressivist dichotomy that teachers, parents, and researchers have framed.

STILL EATING THE MENU

When we speak in public about the need for educational reform, sympathetic educators find our criticisms of traditional practices easy to accept. They say to us, "But we haven't supported *those* ideas for a long time." What these educators find more difficult to understand and to accept is that the two of us are no less enamored of the progressivist camp than we are of the one it supposedly supplanted. Although we recognize (and use) some of the practices most closely identified with progressivism, like hands-on learning through discovery, group work, and broadly based assessment, we draw firm lines in places that often surprise people who feel we should be singing from the same hymnal.

If a brief examination of what often happens to children's reading and writing experiences in the traditional classroom helps to shed light on some of its flaws, a discussion of what has gone so badly wrong with mathematics innovation over the past three decades might elucidate some of the pitfalls of newer, supposedly progressive, practices.

In 1997, we taught Grade 7. Students arrived in our classroom with at least 6 years of formal mathematics teaching and learning under their belts. Our school is very large, and draws from many elementary schools. Some of these schools are very traditional in their approach to teaching mathematics. Students use worksheets and textbooks. They are taught to memorize algorithms and procedures. The only problems they solve using mathematics are the word problems that most of us recognize from our own school days: "If Johnny has two apples and Mary has one apple, how many more apples does Johnny have than Mary?"

Others, however, have had very different experiences. They have used blocks and counters, geoboards, cuisinaire rods, and calculators. Some have learned how to use a simplified form of Logo, the computer programming language developed by Papert.

Given the huge differences in beliefs and practices that derive from these radically different approaches to teaching math, it would be reasonable to have assumed that we would be able to spot which students had received which kind of mathematical training. The claims, particularly of teachers who use manipulatives in their programs, would lead reasonable people to assume that children who had a hands-on, direct experience of carefully chosen resources would also have developed much deeper mathematical understandings. If the claims of progressive mathematics educators were correct, these students should have been confident problem posers and problem solvers. They should have liked math and been intrigued by its relevance to their everyday experience.

Well, they didn't, and they weren't, and they couldn't. There was no way to tell (except by asking) who had had what kind of teaching in math. Children who had received a consistent diet of drills and work sheets were no different from the ones who had played with blocks and counters. In a traditional classroom, children learn very early to manipulate mathematical symbols. As the children say, they get good at plusing and minusing and timesing. But they do not learn how to forge strong links between the procedures they are memorizing and the mathematical understandings from which those procedures derive. That is not news. What *seems* to be news is that children can learn to manipulate blocks with as little mindfulness as they manipulate symbols.

Progressive educators have long recognized that shoving symbols at young children can produce superficial learning—and that, in fact, such practices can mask deep and pervasive misunderstandings of basic mathematical concepts. We have no problem with this criticism. Like many teachers, we live with the consequences of such practices every day. What progressivist theorists and teachers did, however, was to make a leap that denies children's everyday mathematical competence and insists that children cannot actually be *taught* mathematics until they are developmentally, cognitively ready for instruction. Until this supposed readiness has set in, children are given blocks and activities that pander to their supposedly "concrete" stage of development. Without assistance from a teacher, they make patterns, pictures, and constructions from which, on their own, they are to derive mathematical insight. Somehow, without what is cast as the interference and imposition of a teacher, each child's mind is supposed to traverse the space between concrete operational and abstract reasoning. Each child's mind is also assumed to recapitulate the development of human, mathematical understanding. Left to their own devices with artfully chosen materials, such children, it is assumed, will re-invent arithmetic. Moreover, they will find that learning easy, pleasurable, and natural. And when they do not—or when they are required to do less palatable things like "math facts," the questions are glued and laminated, say, to teddy bears' tummies to make them cute, attractive, and easier to digest.

Written this boldly, the theory sounds a bit silly—but the romantic practices with blocks and counters that derive from it are pervasive in primary education. In Grade 4, however, many children find that the blocks disappear and the real work of manipulating symbols begins, resting, it is supposed, on a firm foundation of concrete operations. Abruptly, traditional practices take over. The time for playing is past—and mathematics becomes much more recognizably traditional for teachers and for students. It becomes work.

There are more problems with this approach than we intend to discuss here. For now, it is enough to draw attention to two fundamental ironies of progressivist thinking. First of all, it denies categorically the ability of young children to think abstractly. Yet, as researchers and teachers and parents all know, children have already formulated very strong mathematical hypotheses before they enter school. Some of these theories and sets of beliefs about how the world works—what Gardner and Boix-Manilla (1994) call "theories of mind, theories of matter, theories of life" (p. 200)—provide real promise as the groundwork for future understanding of mathematics. Progressivists, like their traditional counterparts, tend to discount the sophistication of such thinking. What progressivists who argue the virtues of unfettered, easy play also seem to disregard, however, is that left to their own devices, children often develop very flawed understandings based on their personal experiences of the world. A romantic would argue for the mental growth of a child uncorrupted by adults' efforts to rush them to premature levels of abstraction and thought. We stand much closer to Gardner and Boix-Manilla in saying that these powerful, informal habits of learning established before school begins often lead children to trouble as well as to insight. Unproductive habits of mind (Gardner & Boix-Manilla, 1994, p. 200) can be remarkably robust. Such habits are just as likely to lead children to construct powerful stereotypes about people and events and to overlook the meaning or implications of activities in which they are engaged. The result, say Gardner and Boix-Manilla (p. 201) is "ritualistic memorization of meaningless facts and disembodied procedures"—the very evil against which progressivists had pitted themselves in the first place. That is, perhaps, one of the reasons that we saw no difference, ultimately, in the children we taught. Both groups had learned how to "do" the activities their teachers had provided. It mattered little whether the activities were pencil and paper or hands-on: they were just activities, after all.

This observation leads to our second major criticism of progressivist practices in mathematics. It would be easy to misunderstand our concern, and to assume that we fault the blocks, the rods, the resources, themselves. We do not. We use them every day. What we note, however, is that when the concrete materials are not used to *model* more abstract concepts and processes, they become just another thing, just another fad, just another coin in the traveling man's purse.

What is so clearly missing from children's experience of mathematics is mathematics, itself. Seen mostly as developmental stops along the way, work with blocks and counters remains largely untied to the very context from which such work should spring. Children are not often taught how to derive equations from the patterns they construct; how to link the activities that engage them both with their mathematical experience in the world and also with the fundamental mathematical issues that underlie these activities and experiences. Just "doing" can be as mindless as not doing at all. The *doing* of activity-based, hands-on learning by discovery can remain as divorced from the contexts that give them meaning as any other kind of rote activity. Innovative teaching in mathematics or any other subject involves making visible that which has largely remained invisible:

> To make contexts visible, make them objects of discourse, and make them explicitly reshapable and inventable are strong aspirations very much in harmony with the pressing needs and on-rushing changes of our own time. It is therefore the duty of a well-conceived environment for learning to be contentious and even disturbing, seek contrasts rather than absolutes, aim for quality over quantity and acknowledge the need for will and effort. I do not think it goes too far to say that these requirements are at odds with the prevailing values in American life today. (Kay, 1995, p. 150)

Learning, ultimately, should help students see that things can be other than as they seem, other than as they are. Learning entails a commitment to human freedom, to "the capacity to surpass the given and look at things as if they could be otherwise . . . the capacity to choose [and] the power to act to attain one's purposes" Greene (1988, p. 3). This is hard work, and not easily accomplished—which, in itself, poses problems for North Americans hooked on quick fixes and instant gratification. As Kay (1995) insists,

> difficulty should be sought out as a spur to delving more deeply into an interesting area. An educational system that tries to make everything easy and pleasurable will prevent much important learning from happening. (p. 150)

When we insist on recognizing how pervasive the boredom of schools is, we are not saying that curriculum should be more "relevant," in that easy talk of the 1960s. We are not calling for entertainment, "warm fuzzies," or Disneyfied diversions of the work at hand. Such thin gruel fails to nourish the intellect. It starves the imagination and withers the soul.

Children like to work hard—if that work is meaningful, engaging, and powerful. Negroponte (1995, p. 196) cited an 8-year-old, pressed during a televised premiere of Media Lab's LEGO/Logo work at the Hennigan school. A zealous anchor, looking for a cute sound bite, kept asking the child if he was having fun playing with LEGO/Logo. Clearly exasperated, but not wishing to offend, the child tried first to put her off. After her third attempt to get him to talk about fun, the child, sweating under television lights, plaintively looked into the camera and answered, "Yes, it is fun, but it's hard fun."

Hard fun. We cannot think of a better way to describe the kind of learning that life in our rapidly changing world calls for. Life has become harder both within and beyond the classroom.

Change has accelerated so rapidly that what one generation learns in childhood no longer necessarily applies later in adulthood. In other words, each generation must be able to quickly learn new paradigms, or ways of viewing the world; the old ways do not remain usable for long (Kay, 1995, p. 150).

We contend that despite lip-service acknowledging the importance of "learning to learn," there is little in institutional schooling that could be called "hard fun." There is too little that nourishes the romance, the adventure, the enchantment of learning. There is too little that links children, young people and their teachers with the voices of the past, with the world we inhabit together, or with the possibilities of the future.

Schools are, so to speak, "from the neck up" sorts of places that divorce children and teachers from their bodies, from their feelings and intuitions, from their experiences and from each other. Lately, new traveling men have appeared on the horizon suggesting that things will be different in the information age. Schools will have to become different, they tell us, because knowledge is now so different. And that may be true. But at this crucial juncture, while right-wing fundamentalists are calling for a return to the past and high-tech gurus are calling for expensive ventures into computers and telecommunication, we have some important questions to ask. How will teachers and students do any better with computers in schools than we have done with anything else? Instant access to the information of the world is likely to be as mind-numbing as anything else we have done unless we look squarely at issues of imagination, engagement, and power.

Educators, as Seymour Papert insists, are at an early stage in understanding the power of computers to change schools. Our fundamental educational structures remain almost untouched by any of the major revolutions of the last century. Technology may be another of those revolutions that passes us by. Or educators might, as Papert says, simply try to strap the jet engine of powerful computers to the old, worn-out frame of our horse and buggy schools. If that is done, the end result will be unfortunate. All that will happen is that the force will shake the buggy to bits and scare all the horses. Wise men and women need to ask different questions as the coins rattle out of diverse and powerful purses. On the surface, those questions have little to do with technology or the prevailing political winds. They have everything to do with deeper issues of the human spirit. We have already asked—and attempted to answer—the first of the questions with which we began: In what ways are children and young people cast adrift in schools when powerful educational practice instrumentalizes, trivializes, psychologizes—and even ignores—their capacity for imaginative engagement with the world, with ideas, and with each other?

In the next part of this chapter, we return to the second question: What can happen in schools when teachers take seriously the power and the right of children to name and to shape their experience of the world? And what does imaginative engagement have to do with that power and right?

THAT'S NICE, CHARLOTTE . . .

The power of classroom activities in traditional practices lies in their instrumental capacity to achieve measurable, objective ends. In traditional classrooms, no one worries much about the development of imaginative capacities. There is other, supposedly more important work afoot in teaching children how to decode, how to spell correctly, how to "attack" text, how to add, subtract, multiply, and divide. Learning is what children do in order to demonstrate their ability to read and calculate. Imagination has little, if anything, to do with these developing abilities.

Imagination is also a problem in more "progressive" practice. Thought to inhabit a separate sphere of innocence, children (as they are understood from within the progressive paradigm) share few of—indeed, must be protected from—the concerns of adults. Moreover, each child makes up his or her own fantasies. And because these fantasies are private, mental, and individual, they cannot really be discussed, challenged, or built upon except to say things like, "Oh, that's nice." Or "Thank you for sharing that with me." Or "How interesting." We believe that there is a real danger, in progressive teaching practices, of killing imagination not by starving it completely, but by rendering it so trivial, so "made" up, so bizarre, or so private that no one really cares about it at all.

We think, for example, of what sometimes happens when teachers work with *Charolotte's Web* from this sort of progressive perspective. Often encountering the novel as part of a Pig or a Spider unit, children are encouraged to write about topics like this: "Send a letter to Charlotte telling her how you felt when you finished the book." On bad days when we hear teachers talk about such assignments, we are tempted to say, "Excuse me, Charlotte is a spider. She's dead. She won't write back." Why, we wonder to ourselves, would a robust, intelligent child with an enquiring mind finish a powerful book and want to do something silly like writing to a dead spider, except perhaps to please her teacher? There are far more engaging, thoughtful, and—may Plato and Rousseau both rest in peace—philosophical ways—to talk, and write, and draw about the ideas E. B. White raises (and does not raise) in this interesting book. The least important thing about *Charlotte's Web* is that it deals with pigs and spiders—but in the name of imagination, that is *precisely* the part some teachers fasten on to most relentlessly. Children, they think, adore talking animals. And Disneyfied, talking animals may be about all that children have left to talk about.

That debased understanding of imagination worries us a great deal. What we work with in our own practice is an entirely different understanding of imagination. By way of example, and of a simple beginning of a conversation that could go on far beyond the bounds of this chapter, we want to speak about Jason and David, two boys we taught when they were in Grade 2.

BEYOND A WINDOW-FULL OF LIFE

One day we were reading aloud to the children the version of *The Lady of Shalott* illustrated by Charles Keeping. This in itself is unusual in progressive Canadian schools, first because the classics are generally considered too tough for young children to grasp, and second because many teachers have long since abandoned the supposed oppression of studying a single text with an entire class in favor of programs with names like "community of readers."

We had chosen the poem because of a question one of the girls had asked in response to an investigation of some King Arthur stories earlier in the month. "Where," she wanted to know, "were all the ladies in that King Arthur time?" The question is an important one, and as we picked it up, we followed Andrea's insistent lead in finding stories about medieval women in both history and fiction to discuss. We wanted to talk about what women actually did, what the stories said they did—and in so doing, to raise questions that would help students read both with the grain of a lovely poem, and against the grain of the romance plot that still figures so prominently in the lives of contemporary girls and women. Thus, we took the Lady of Shalott seriously as a person, asking questions about how she might have got in the tower; how she might have got cursed; how the presence of the villagers changed her life and she, theirs; why she insisted on writing her name on the prow of the boat.

But we also asked questions about the crafting of the story: Why was it always ladies who seem to get shut up in towers? Why do knights get to be the ones to go riding two on two? And we talked about the text of our own lives: How come boys get to play rough and girls have to be nice and do indoor stuff? If you had a choice, we asked, who would you be: the Lady of Shalott or Sir Lancelot? No one, as we recall, wanted to be the lady. And what did we make of her decision to leave the harp, to leave the loom, to take three paces through the room? Was she, this woman no one wanted to be, was she strong and brave, or foolish and silly?

For a couple of days we talked and argued and wrote about the poem. It was a public, noisy conversation that engaged 55 children and their teachers. Together, we created and debated and inhabited a world inspired by a modern telling of a Victorian account of a medieval story. The melancholy lady and her cramped, unwelcome destiny resonated for all of us. And the resonance went far beyond ferreting out what each individual thought of the poem. It existed most strongly, most vibrantly, in the questions, challenges, and answers we built together. From across the span of more than a century, the words of an old dead White guy lit up the classroom of Canadian 6- and 7-year-olds who felt, somehow, the tragedy of those final, dismissive words of Lancelot's: "She has a lovely face. God in His mercy grant her grace."

Now, children are not supposed to be able to talk and think about such things. The progressive view of curriculum tells us this. At 6 and 7, children are supposed to be studying the details of their immediate, concrete, real world. Only much, much later are they supposed to be able to take on history, narrative poetry, and philosophizing about life, death, irony, and fairness. Indeed, even the current Junior High School Program of Studies in Language Arts in use in Alberta specifically advised teachers to abandon "the classics" in favor of young adult novels thought to be more appropriate and relevant to students' stage of development.

And yet here we were, sitting on the floor and on little chairs, doing the impossible. On one of those days, Jason, a rough and tumble boy's boy looked up from his place on the outer edge of the circle, and he said, "You know, it would be so awful to be the Lady of Shalott. All she ever gets is a reflection of a window full of life."

Years later, we still remember how the children swivelled around to look at Jason. Somehow, in one image, he had gathered up all the threads of our conversation. Excited by this new way of seeing the poem, we all looked at the illustrations again and again to see how Keeping had drawn her mirror-world. We wondered what such a life would feel like. Some children drew and wrote their own insights. No one wanted to write a letter to the Lady, or find other pictures of boats or knights to draw. That wasn't it at all. They cared about the Lady's dilemma, and they cared about the questions she raised about their own lives because those questions *were* real. It was a glorious time.

If our experience with *The Lady of Shalott* had ended there, it would still be an instructive story about how literature of substance engages even the youngest children in robust, fascinating talk and debate. Read alone, it would still challenge the debased understanding of imagination that permeates school curricula and activities. But something else happened almost 2 years later. Unexpectedly, in the middle of a lesson on statistics, the Lady of Shalott floated, singing, into our midst once again.

It is important to note that our school was organized in such a way that we kept the same group of children together for up to 4 years. We pick up the story again when David was in fourth grade, 2 years after his first encounter with Tennyson's poem. Our classroom now comprised children in Grades 1, 2, 3, and 4. The two of us now had our own Internet accounts, and we had jumped at the opportunity to participate in an international study of the television watching habits of upper elementary students. An Ottawa teacher had invited classrooms in Canada, the United States, and Europe to participate, through SchoolNet, in a survey called "Taming the Tube." We had already learned, years earlier, that children can display a remarkably sophisticated ability to describe and interpret statistics in meaningful ways when they generate "data that are not merely numbers, but numbers with a context" (Moore, 1990, p. 96). Even our youngest students worked diligently with school-wide data derived from monthly "pizza days," describing patterns of consumption from class to class, grade to grade. Older students began to look for trends that allowed them to predict the next month's patterns. The father of two of our students, a professor who routinely taught first-year statistics at the local university, insisted that his daughters had a firmer grasp of statistics than did students three times their age. Good data, we had learned, are not merely numbers; "they engage our knowledge of their context so that we can understand and interpret, rather than simply carry out arithmetical operations" (Moore, 1990, p. 96).

Confident that our students would yet again be able to engage imaginatively, emotionally, and mathematically with this new opportunity, we enrolled them in the project—even though most of them were considerably younger than the target audience. We set out together on the Information Highway, learning together a little bit more about how to navigate the Net because we really, really wanted to know how we stacked up against TV fans across the globe.

As part of the study, the children collected, organized, and graphed data from our classroom. We compared our findings, noting remarkable similarities from group to group, and also laughing at and debating anomalies: the two boys who decided to quit watching TV cold turkey that week so they could bring in 0 hours on their logs; the girl whose family was in the middle of moving and who watched more than 50 hours because there was nothing else to do in the house; nutty Gaston, the proud addict who turned on the set 2 hours before he came to school each morning and left it running until late, late at night.

We also learned how to do important calculations to determine range, mean, median, and mode. Terms like *average* came alive for children who came to realize that their own, individual data were subsumed by the larger group. They learned that they could make some statements about the group's habits, generalizing from the data. But they also saw, especially in their anomalies, that they could not make the reverse move: use the average figure to determine what any individual had, in fact, watched that week. We shared stories with them about debates that were raging in the school district about test scores on provincial examinations—and the demand by some concerned but ill-informed citizens that students in Calgary score above average on the next set of exams. "Above average?" raged David. "Above average? How can everybody be above average? Don't those guys know anything about statistics?" We just grinned. If half the adults in Calgary (speaking of statistics) had the insights and dispositions of these children, the level of public debate around student achievement would be bound to rise!

Once again, we note that if the children had gone only that far, had achieved only these mathematical insights, their accomplishment would have been considerable. But they did far more—and in what happened next, they showed us as clearly as we have ever seen how imaginative engagement with mathematics lends power and meaning to life.

Discussing patterns that emerged through all the idiosyncrasies of individual circumstances, the children noticed that as girls got older, the amount of television they watched increased substantially. At the time, we had just fed our own data into the larger study, but did not yet have results from other places. We had identified a trend in our own class, and were wondering together whether that trend would hold in other parts of Canada and in other parts of the world. And if it did, we wondered, what would that say about girls' experience of the world? The survey had been conducted in the spring, and the boys thought that their own TV habits were influenced by the time of year. Soccer season was underway, and they did not want to sit around indoors. So what, we asked them, do you make of the fact that while the boys are out playing soccer, the girls are inside in front of the tube?

The question caused a ripple of argument through the whole group— not about the data, which was clear (at least for our class)—but about girls' relative lack of activity and engagement as they grew older. In the middle of the debate, David spoke up again. "Remember," he said, "what Jason said about the Lady of Shalott? Remember about seeing only a reflection of a window full of life? That's what's happening. If boys are outside playing and doing things and the girls are just watching television, they are just like the Lady of Shalott. All they are getting is somebody's reflection of life."

Because so many of us had been part of that conversation 2 years earlier, David's comment was very powerful. He took all of us back in an instant to the whole wealth of the earlier discussion: the story, the pictures, the questions, the feelings and arguments that had inspirited our classroom. Sitting on the floor in the present moment of a mathematics lesson, he took us back to an earlier image that we had built together and drove us forward to a new understanding of the import of the numbers on the chart paper in front of us.

The question about girls' experience of the world and the half-life so many of them inhabit is tremendously important. We had asked and answered Andrea's question—"where are the ladies?" in many different ways over the intervening years, reading and discussing *Alice in Wonderland*, the story of Lady Ragnall and Sir Gawain, venturing into ancient China and Greece, opening forbidden doors in fairy tales. All of this talk and reading came together in David's analysis. As members of a classroom community, we had developed a community of memory grounded in the stories and knowledge we shared together. We had developed habits of thought and discussion that respected the power of stories, mathematics, science, and art to inform our lives. We took learning seriously. We took the children's questions seriously. Reading both out of and back into our community, we became who we were to each other through the stories, the talk, and the work. And our becoming situated us in time and place, connected not only to each other but also to our ancestors and to the disciplines to which our studies had committed us all.

This sense of connection was made possible *only* by imaginative engagement. David's comparison helped us see that what was happening in the present moment of girls' experience had happened many, many times before. It wasn't a fluke; it wasn't an accident. What we saw on the chart paper in front of us was systemic, deeply rooted, and seductively appealing. And moreover, David helped us frame new questions: "So, what did it take for the Lady of Shalott to break out of her prison? What did it cost? Does it cost girls today the same kinds of things when they refuse a shadow life? What does it cost them if they do not? And what kind of courage might it take to live life differently?"

And those, we propose as we conclude this chapter, are precisely the questions that press educators today. What will it take us to break out of the 19th-century institutions that imprison us, teacher and student alike? What will it cost to refuse a shadow life—to demand a seat at the banquet, not just a menu in the waiting room? What will it cost us as a society if we do *not* break free of the chains that we drag behind us into the millennium? What if we do nothing? What if policymakers, administrators, parents, teachers, and students continue to stare steadfastly into the mirror, weaving and singing to no purpose as life passes us all by?

What kind of courage, we ask, will it take to live life differently—to change our schools, to change ourselves so that children have a chance to emerge from public education as passionate, robust, committed learners?

Preamble 6

The City of Tomorrow Has Fewer Children
Cheryl Chow, acting principal of Garfield High School said, "To me that would be one of the scariest things to imagine, to live in a city without all the generations."

—*The Seattle Times*, Sunday, April 2, 2001, A8.

This is quite an image: a human place without all the generations present. Except, of course, that is very often what schools premised on "basics-as-breakdown" seem to be. In fact, many of the materials presented to our children in schools are geared *precisely* to *not* be something all the generations might gather around and work on—all the generations, for example, of those interested in mathematics. An interpretive treatment of the basics treats this phenomenon as one of the most pernicious manifestations of basics-as-breakdown–the breakdown, so to speak, of the full family of learners and knowers. Interpretive work proposes that basic to any living tradition of work is the necessary co-presence of all the generations. As we suggest in the following chapter, mathematical truth is an intergenerational phenomenon, such that our children's learning of mathematics is part of *its* well-being and life.

Let's try an analogy here. When I go out into the garden with my 7-year-old son, I don't send him off to a "developmentally appropriate garden." I take him to the same garden where I am going to work. Now, once we get there and get down to the work, of course, each of us will work as each of us

111

is able. We are not identical in ability, experience, strength, patience, and so on. But *both of us* will be working *in the same place* doing some part of the real work that the garden requires, part of the "continuity of attention and devotion" this place needs to remain whole.

In an interpretive understanding of "the basics," each person's work in the classroom is not treated as a subjective or interior possession, but is treated as something that happens out in the world, with others, in the presence of others and their work in this place. Each person's work is therefore taken up as adding itself to the richness of the place that we *all* find ourselves living in. This is why Gadamer (1989, p. 140) suggested that the inheritances we've been handed undergo an "increase in being" when they are furthered. All these conversations add themselves to what we had heretofore understood these matters to be. When we have explored the phenomenon of the "belonging together" of addition and subtraction with our student–teachers, this exploration also adds itself to this furtherance. And we demand, in such explorations, that these student–teachers realize that they are deepening their understandings of this feature of this wondrous place of mathematics because a child had gone there before us, tripped over something and asked her fellow traveler in that place, the person, so to speak, who went *with* her, "I'm not sure, did I add or subtract?"

Student–teachers (and teachers, and university researchers and mathematicians) are embarking on *precisely the same enterprise* as that Grade 2 girl. Where each starts, how much each gets done, how much any one of us knows of this place ahead of time, and how surprised any of us can be when we attempt to teach something we think we know well—all these things will vary, sometimes greatly, but all concerned are doing (part of) the real work of mathematics as a living discipline. As a living discipline, it not only has room for them both. It needs this full range of exploration and cultivation and questioning to remain hale.

Here is the real rub of interpretive work, one of its most thrilling and most difficult ideas. As we demonstrate in chapter 6, when a large group of first- through fourth-grade students and their teachers and university colleagues start to explore a particular mathematical phenomena together over several days (and eventually weeks, once the great implications of this experience were unfolded; and, of course, here, still, years later, in a book), what occurs over time is not merely an aggregate of subjective conceptions. What occurs over time, collectively, is that the place we have been exploring starts to open up and we begin to see, *because of our different explorations*, that *the place* is full of possibilities. It has room for us all.

Thus, as Gadamer (1989) put it, such an interpretive exploration of "number" and its composition in a mathematics classroom is "not at all a question of a mere subjective variety of conceptions, but of [this phenomenon's] own possibilities of being that emerge as it explicates itself, as it were, in a variety of *its* aspects" (p. 118). This phenomena of "number" and its composition, as a living inheritance, *is* all the ways that it has "gathered and collected itself" (p. 97) over time. And now we, too, in our explorations, step into to this already-ongoing conversation and add our voices, our objections, our discoveries to it.

So if we are going to be exploring mathematics interpretively, it becomes necessary that we find materials and experiences for children that are rich and fulsome and real enough to sustain a broad, intergenerational array of care and attention. So guess what we picked?

A worksheet.

The problem with that second-grade girl's worksheet is not that it was a worksheet, but that it *wasn't*. There wasn't any real work to be done that hadn't already been fully figured out by someone else. That girl's worksheet was telling her that her work wasn't really necessary. So math worksheets are fine providing they require some *mathematical* work.

What if we re-imagined Jean Piaget's notion of developmental stages. Instead of picturing them as strung along a line, where each new stage subsumes and overcomes the previous ones, what if we were to imagine them as, so to speak, a *field of relations*? As a field of relations, each of our explorations of the mathematics worksheet described below is co-present to all the other explorations. Because of this, each seemingly individual exploration makes all the other explorations surrounding it stronger, more interesting, more complex, more rich and alluring than any one would have been alone. Each adds to the other, puts it in perspective, fills it out, deepens it, questions it, and so on. This is why we have so often had mathematicians or poets or chemists along for the ride in the classroom, because their work, too, is one of our relations. Just as with the youngest of children counting out steps with his mother on the stairs, the mathematician in the classroom is *one of us*, that one, who does that job for a living.

This intergenerational co-presence places each person's efforts, not inside their head, but *in* the whole field of work into which not only this whole class (teachers and students) venture, but into a field that has been worked already, beforehand. The traces of other hands are found there, ancestors, earlier travelers. Interpretation always reads the part any one of us plays in such explorations, not pathologically, but as part of the whole field of human endeavor we have taken on.

and all the consequent memory loss that ensues in the collapse into clear, memorizable (but not especially memorable) equations and operations. The young child's presence, if carefully and generously read, helps keep mathematics open to the arrival of renewal, of difference. If educators forget how our children might be raised up into this logico-mathematical knowledge and how their work is thereby a real, irreplaceable part of mathematics as a *living* tradition, our knowledge becomes worse than dangerous. Under such conditions, education becomes crazy-making, because it begins to work against the real conditions under which it might go on. We can, it seems, too easily forget that the traditions and disciplines of mathematics live, not in fixed, self-enclosed rules and equations, but in the living conditions that constitute its being *passed on*. This is how we might understand Piaget's (1970a, p. 731) invocation: "How, *in reality*, is science [e.g., the science of mathematics] possible?"

In this odd sense, then, pedagogy, as an openness to the arrival of the young, becomes inscribed into the heart of mathematics. Pedagogy is not simply a conduit or vehicle for the inculcation of a knowledge that is already finished and complete. It is, rather, part of the very renewal of mathematical memory that makes mathematics, *in reality*, possible.

This sort of reading of developmentalism therefore suggests something similar to the premise of genetic epistemology: that mature adult thought requires genetic grounding (Piaget, 1968, pp. 116–117; 1971b, p. 143, Piaget & Inhelder, 1969, p. viii), or, as Piaget playfully put it, "the child explains the man as well and often better than the man explains the child" (Piaget & Inhelder, 1969, p. ix).

One way of reading this notion of genetic grounding is that the discipline of mathematics cannot remain simply self-enclosed and self-referential. Even though such enclosure might describe "an ideal, perhaps a hope" (Piaget, 1970b, p. 7) of a structuralist *theory* regarding the ways in which this community of principles and operations gain their sense in reference only to each other (such that the messy ins and outs of mathematics as a living tradition can be formulated as simply "extraneous elements" [p. 7]), in reality, as the life of the classroom attests, mathematics also requires something else. It requires the arrival of the young into that community of relations and the inevitable difference that such an arrival of new relations (and therefore new ways of seeing old relations) makes. It requires attesting to the fact that, if it is to continue making sense as a living, human enterprise, the "others" to which mathematics refers must include all its *real* relations. Or, to use Piagetian terminology, "the concepts and categories of established science" (Inhelder, 1969, p. 23) require genetic grounding.

This different reading has profound pedagogical consequences. It suggests that the child's understanding of a certain mathematical nuance must be read for the ways in which it is true of mathematics, for the ways in

Meditations on Classroom Community and the Intergenerational Character of Mathematical Truth

Sharon Friesen
Patricia Clifford
David W. Jardine

I

Sometimes my teachers try to make things so simple that they don't make sense any more. I need to know where I am going to know where I am.

These words of a 13-year-old boy, full as they are of wonderful geographical/topographical images, hint at an unintended pedagogical consequence of developmentalism: the overcompensation for children's "developmental levels" to the extent that any particular activity or event or understanding starts to become incomprehensible because it no longer occurs within a large, patterned, disciplined space of relations and possibilities. Developmentalism has, in some quarters, unintentionally become an excuse to fragment children's learning in the name of developmental appropriateness or in the name of the child's individuality and difference. Often, teachers narrowly target children's needs and activities, and in the process can, however unwittingly, damage or undo the deep communities of relations that make various bodies of knowledge whole, comprehensible, and sane and that make the child's learning coherent and true.

Many student–teachers often lament this situation, rightly claiming to be overwhelmed by the fact that there are so many individual developmental needs in their classroom, and that each child's needs must be individually met. This image of the pedagogic requirements of the classroom quickly becomes monstrous: 25 individual students, each with their own life and history and abilities and troubles, suddenly becomes multiplied times the number of desired learning outcomes, times (e.g., in Alberta), 107 mandated curricular-developmental strands in language learning alone, times multiple curriculum guides for each developmental area.

Teaching with any sense of coherence or continuity or community begins to appear to be virtually impossible in the midst of such developmental proliferation.

In response, the ability and willingness of teachers, student–teachers, and university education faculty alike to learn about the discipline of, say, elementary mathematics, becomes fragmented. Talk of mathematics as being constituted by a deep community of relations becomes vaguely incomprehensible, too theoretical and not really, as one student–teacher said, "hands-on practical, like what I can actually *do* with the kids." A sense of mathematics as a community of relations becomes replaced with a flurry of unconnected, hyperactive "activities" frantically pursued in the name of meeting students' individual needs and keeping students' interest. And, as the child cited earlier hinted, in any particular activity, students and teachers alike very often no longer know where they are because all of the topographical relations that provide a sense of direction and place have been severed or dispersed.

As a consequence, everyone involved in classroom life (students, school teachers, student–teachers, and university teachers) becomes extremely *busy* and extremely *active*, and no one feels they have time (or energy) to do any real work. Worse yet, sometimes it seems as if "the surface is all there is" (Smith, 1999, p. 177) and that there is no real, abiding community of work even possible, let alone required. The community of mathematics, like the community of the classroom, becomes dispersed into the odd and unintended isolationism of developmental difference.

When we were in the process of having conversations about writing this chapter, Sharon gave a compelling picture of how, especially in mathematics education, something like memory loss figures in this dispersion:

> The problem with math in particular is that all the work you do, all the ins and outs of conversations, little details—it can easily collapse and condense. As the next generation enters, it has to try to pick up all the conversation all over again that has since collapsed into one clear equation. Math collapses like that all the time and all the work that gets you there, all the community memory you've built up in the class, gets lost and the next generation try to simply memorize the equations. What the memorized equation loses is all the memories, all the sense of membership. It loses all its relations and acts like its got none. In many classrooms, you can't get in on the conversations about all the relations of math because *there aren't any such conversations.* Instead each child gets shoved into all these separate, "appropriate" activities. There is no place to *meet.*

It's not just that teachers don't like math; they don't know what's happening because they can't remember what the real work really is. All they remember of math is the equations and the rules and the facts they've memorized—the surface activities with all the relations forgotten. Teachers always talk about children "showing their work," but unless you base serious mathematical conversations on that work, children end up believing that the answer, the clear equation or just following the rule, is all that counts, and the activities just become stupid distractions, entertainment. Just for "show." For *all of us.*

As a consequence of such a loss of memory and depth, not only does the community of the classroom become frayed into what Dressman (1993) described as a place not unlike a shopping mall, where everyone comes together only to mind their own business. The community of relations that constitute mathematics itself never comes forward as a generous and alluring "place" in which children and adults might meet and might do real work together. Mathematics becomes simply a place where everyone can come together to mind their own "developmentally appropriate" business.

II

We wish to directly confront this (however much unintended) legacy of developmentalism. We have been involved in reading the work of Jean Piaget differently from the schooled, "curricularized" version of developmentalism (and the consequent version of mathematics pedagogy) might allow. We suggest that Piaget's work, if read interpretively rather than literally (Jardine, in press), does not so much lay out a developmental line along which children's abilities might be strung, as much as it opens up a large, generative space full of rich, interdependent, co-present relations. For example, Piaget shows how bodily and concrete manipulations of objects in the world, like the footfalls of the young child on a staircase counted out with each descent, bear a "family resemblance" (Wittgenstein, 1968) to the operations of logico-mathematical knowledge. *Each of these* seemingly particular, discrete phenomena, helps open a space around the other, making the other more comprehensible than it would have been without the co-presence of all its "generations," all its multiple "relations." Each is thus potentially "fecund" (Jardine, 1992b). Therefore, the halting steps of the young child do not need to be conceived simply as in need of maturation, refinement, and eventual replacement, or as some sort of protomathematics. Rather, these steps are steps paced out by one of us, one of our kin, and they articulate mathematical kinships and relations in ways that are irreplaceable in a full understanding of the whole of mathematics. This young child's steps thus have the power to keep logico-mathematical knowledge in place, in relation. They have the power to prevent logico-mathematical operations from becoming simply self-referential and self-enclosed

which it has a real, abiding place in the community of relations that constitutes mathematics. It must not be abandoned or trivialized or, as Piaget suggested in an early work, understood as an "exceedingly suggestive deformation of true conceptions" (Piaget, 1974, p. 50), conceptions that are developmentally "destined" (Piaget 1952, p. 363) to be replaced through maturing.

Through an interpretive turn in Piaget's idea of genetic grounding, children's work must be ushered in to the real world and real conversations about real mathematics and that it must be understood as such if teachers are to act in a pedagogically responsible way and students are to be allowed to participate in pedagogically viable work. This does not mean simply affirming "the child" and their efforts. It means carefully reading the child's *work* out into all its mathematical relations, finding ways to help make it strong, stable, and *true of mathematics.* It means reading the stubborn particularity of child's work in relation to the sense of the community of relations that constitutes mathematics that is building in the classroom—*these* children, re-membering in *these* ways what *this* thread of mathematics is about (Jardine, 1995b). It means, for us as teachers, taking on for ourselves the task of deeply understanding the geographies and topographies of mathematics, so that we can hear the child's comment, not just as indicating something about her or him, but as indicating something about her or his presence, place, and orientation in the world of mathematics itself (and therefore, indicating something about mathematics which would have been lost without that presence).

Interpretive work contests Piaget's (1965) suggestion that "a single truth alone is acceptable when we are dealing with knowledge in the strictest sense" (pp. 216–217). Rather, interpretively understood, the truth of mathematics is found *within* the conversations that ensue *between* its multiple relations, *within* the conversations *between* multiple generations of understanding (both in the sense of mathematics' traditions and histories and in the sense of the co-presence in the classroom and in the discipline of mathematics of the old and the young, the experienced and the less experienced).

We are suggesting, therefore, that the truth of mathematics is *intergenerational.*

But we are suggesting something more than this. We are suggesting that the truth of mathematics is also inherently *generative.* That is to say, the arrival of *this* child in the classroom, and the odd and wonderful way that he or she has formulated some mathematical theme, does not signal the arrival of simply one more formulation of some mathematical concept that can be simply added to all the rest or that can be shelved because we have heard this before. Rather, as we have often witnessed as teachers, (and as we show by example next), such arrivals can sometimes precipitate the transformation and regeneration of what all members of the class have heretofore understood this theme in the field of mathematics to mean. *This* child's work can cause our understanding of the whole of mathematics to "waver and tremble" (Caputo, 1987, p. 7); it can open what was previously closed, make questionable and provocative what was previously a given, cause us to re-read and re-think what was previously obvious. It can make the brutal clarity of an equation or a previously merely memorized rule something about which we might now have a real *mathematical* conversation. Each new arrival has the potential to rattle through the whole of our previously established relations and can make our understanding of the whole (however slightly) different than it would have been without this arrival. As with the arrival of a new child in the class, this arrival is not just "one more." And, as our following example attests, even though the clarities of the mathematical principle of cardinality might suggest that such arrivals can be counted as simply "one more," the actual taking up of cardinality in its full meaning as a topic in the classroom requires treating children's responses as more generative and difficult than this merely additive notion allows. For cardinality to become comprehensible, we must break below its clean, clear surface definition and remember all the difficult ins and outs that make it possible to understand, possible to pass on. This is the messy work of teaching the young and the equally messy work of making mathematics teachable.

In terms of classroom practice, this process of taking the truth of children's work seriously requires something different than the ever-narrowing targeting of developmentally appropriate activities (and the consequence hyperactivity that often ensues in the effort to "keep up" [Jardine, 1995b, 1996]). It requires pursuing deeply disciplined classroom work ("*real* work" [Snyder, 1980]). This work must be open and generous enough to embrace the full multiplicity of understanding in the classroom and create a sense of a real, mathematically devout community. And it must be strong enough to hold together as well the deep communities of relations that constitute the disciplines of mathematics.

This pedagogical commitment to intergenerational community includes a deeply ethical and ecological act (Jardine, 1994a). It requires of all concerned simply saying "no," refusing those classroom activities or philosophies that trivialize, flatten, or fragment the real work we do as teachers.

We now begin an exploration of this notion of the classroom as a community of relations in which children's work is taken seriously in its claims to truth (Jardine, 1995a) through an example. This classroom experience hints at a sense of generous, intergenerational, conversational space in a concrete way. This experience began in a large Grades 1 to 4 classroom of 70 children. It has since spilled over into our work with student–teachers and with a large group of seventh and eighth graders in an inner-city setting. It thus involves the deliberate, difficult work of building both individual and collective memory and the deliberate attempt to open a *mathematical* space that can bear such memory, that invites exploration at many levels and in many ways. Rather than developmentally delaying some of the questions and patterns of mathematics, we looked for ways to inscribe into each classroom venture the possibility of moving back and forth between the simple and the profound.

We had been working with the origins of counting. We had imagined ourselves as shepherds tending our master's flock at the time when numbers had not been thought of. We wove together a story that involved all of us as characters. Only through a story was it possible to put aside what we knew, or assumed, or had memorized about the number system to think of a time when there was none. Only stories have the imaginal power to place us elsewhere (Bogdan, 1992; Bruner, 1990; Clifford & Friesen, 1994; Egan, 1986; Hillman, 1983).

Children added to this tale as we kept the plot line moving along. Even for first graders, it was almost impossible to put aside what we knew about the number system to think of a time when there was none, to put ourselves into that other space. The fourth graders, too, found this tale compelling. They faced the real question of what one would do without the mathematical knowledge that they had come to learn so well (which, implicitly, is similar to the pedagogical question of what one does with the young child who does not yet know how to count, or who is just beginning the work that we ourselves thought we had finished—see Daniel's story in the Concluding Remarks section of this chapter).

We, as adults, were ourselves taken: What is it, in what we have assumed about these seemingly simple events, that we actually know? When the habits are stripped away, and when the memorized surface clarities of mathematical definitions and equations no longer suffice, what, after all, *is* counting? What is it about the world to which counting might have provided a sensible response? And how can a real conversation about counting ensue *for us all*, children and teachers alike?

We needed to devise a way for keeping track of the sheep we were to care for each day. Each sheep needed to be accounted for at the end of the day. Eventually, we decided that we would use pebbles to represent each of the sheep we took from the master's house and into the field. At the end of the day we would return and the sheep and the pebbles would be counted and if they matched, we would be allowed to continue to live and tend sheep for another day.

We employed the principles of cardinality in these conversations. The children understood that the two sets of sheep and pebbles could be considered equal in number if they could be put into one-to-one correspondence with each other. (Some student–teachers later balked, at first, at the suggestion that musical chairs might itself be *real* mathematics.) Our counting went like this: we have one, and another one, and another one, and. . . . And for each one, there was a matching pebble until all the sheep were accounted for. We saw how easily we could make the leap to a tally but we still had no way of describing an ascending set of quantities. We had no way, yet, of denoting any sequential relationship.

We continued to work, over several days, with various counting systems. We moved from our system of ones to a system employing two numbers (one and two). With two numbers, we could count: one, two, two and one, two and two, two and two and one, two and two and two, and so on. Our sequence did not need to include "one and one," because, of course, one and one is two. But now, this "of course" which everyone in the class knew before we began our tale is no longer so simple, now that we have seen it *arrive* up out of real work and real questions. Or, differently put, its simplicity becomes suddenly *brilliant.* We didn't only have a counting system with two numbers. We also had emerging the understanding that there is a *relation between these two numbers* and that two stands in for one *and* one.

At this point in the class, Alex rose onto his knees on his table and started to rub his hands together: "but you can make five by two and one and one and one. And you can make five by one and two and two."

The rest of the children in the class caught Alex's excitement. A space had opened and questions rushed in. Just how many ways were there to make five? What if you were not limited to ones and twos? We were *in,* and the glances between us told the tale. As Daniel (Grade 4) once said about a similar moment in the classroom, "I can always tell we've hit something because you two [Sharon and Pat] look at each other in that way."

Witness, too, was given when this activity was shown to student–teachers at the university. They, like us (children and teachers alike), gasped with delight when they, too, "got" it. It was clear that what they *got* was not simply "here's a bunch of hands-on activities for the children in my practicum class." What they got was the feeling of a generative rush of insight, the rush of opening. Their gasp (and ours) was caused by a sense of vertigo caught in Alex's excitement. The space he opened for us all was larger than just his particular questions. It was as if we had come with him over a rise and that just these few particular steps, taken seriously and followed, had opened up a huge horizon of possibilities around *all of us.* And it was not simply that we now had new territories to traverse. We also now came to understand territories already traversed in a new way.

Clearly, *no one* present could experience or understand every possibility. But even the youngest or least able of us (sometimes this was, of course, the adults involved) knew that what had arrived had to do, somehow, with the work that we ourselves were somehow already in on. Even if we did not fully understand all of the implications, we knew that we were *there,* with these others, doing part of the real work. Even the child (or adult) who did not initially "get it" at all could now be *understood* better and more generously treated, and could experience the classroom as having such generosity, such openness and sense of possibilities, even if the work is not yet especially understood.

It was our obligation as teachers to take this opening seriously. We gave each of the children a 10 × 10, 2 centimeter grid and asked them to color in all the different possible patterns of adjacent squares they could in order to make five.

What occurred here was important: Even the youngest or least able of children, if they could count and color, could find a way in to the real work that was now going on in the class. And our work with the youngest or least able child was still the same: to help each of them with the work that was now necessary in this common place. If necessary, we or their classmates helped them to count out five or to make a pattern on the paper. Some children were given small blocks to use at first. Some children simply needed initial encouragements or the detailed one-on-one talk of counting and patterns and coloring and "how many do you have now?" Some needed only the example of the questions and wonderings of a neighboring child whose work they might imitate or whose questions might propel new lines of work and wondering. But these individual "needs" were not allowed to fragment or disperse, because each of them was taken up as necessary for the full range of the work of this place to be done, for the full range of the community of mathematical relations to be seen and understood.

Some of the children colored in five squares in a row. They decided they could represent these by 1 + 1 + 1 + 1 + 1. When they grouped the five squares like this (see Fig. 6.1). Those who knew the mathematical designations wrote 3 + 2 = 5. Those who didn't were able to write 3 beside one column and two beside the other, so that when talk of "+" occurred, they were able to experience their work as *already in that space*—that this "+" referred to what they somehow already knew, familiar territories and terrains.

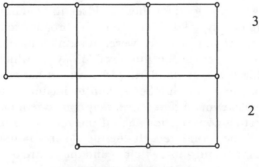

FIG. 6.1.   3 + 2 = 5

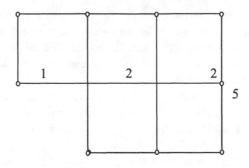

FIG. 6.2.   1 + 2 + 2 = 5.

And, of course, some children, using the very same figure, wrote 2 + 2 + 1, as such (see Fig. 6.2). With a lot of good talk, it was clear and obvious that both of these were correct. And—this is vital—not only were both of these each individually "correct." Each of them makes the correctness of the other more comprehensible than it would have been without the presence of that other. With each other, each becomes not simply an isolated "actual" answer, but a possible answer which could have been answered otherwise. Paradoxically, then, one piece of work makes the individuality and difference of another piece of work appear, each giving the other dimensionality and depth. Without the other solution, each solution loses its sense of topography and place and relation. Without this sense of place, each becomes less fully *mathematical.* The nest of relations continued: Some children, from this figure, decided that five can be understood as two times two plus one only if you do the two times two first and *then* add the one, thus opening up the whole issue of the order of operations and how $2 \times (2 + 1)$ is not equal to $(2 \times 2) + 1$. Other children struggle to make these five shaded squares into a rectangle and raised questions about the workings of prime and composite numbers.

Some of the children found the challenge of counting out five squares and coloring them in and recording their way, quite sufficient for now, and opportunities were provided for these children to remain in this place and explore it more deeply, all with an eye to the broader relations inscribed, but not yet visible, in this place. However, it wasn't long before some of the children seemed to exhaust all the possible ways in which to make five.

Several children began wondering what would happen if we included zero, thus expanding our number system to include whole numbers. It didn't seem to make much difference, they concluded, but it certainly led to some interesting conversations about the role of zero. "What kind of number is zero?" they wondered. "It doesn't add anything. What's it *for?*"

"Zero is a number and a place holder and the centre on the number line between positive and negative numbers" answer Alex.

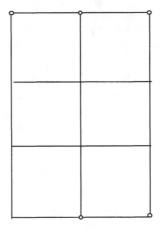

FIG. 6.3.   3 × 2 = 6

Some children pictured six as follows (see Fig. 6.3).

In the conversations that followed, they glanced up against how it is that six is two threes, or three two times, and how three times two is two times three, and both of these are two and two and two (and, of course, three and three).

By this time, small groups of children began to form around different places of work. Onlookers from different tables joined in with these groups—with the groups that offered a mathematical place they could inhabit themselves, with the groups that were asking the questions they understood and that compelled them. Because this activity was not targeted to meet individual needs, it allowed precisely those wonderful, alluring differences to come forward, often in specific, meticulous ways that we could not have anticipated, however careful or well-informed our targeting and developmental planning might have been. Moreover, because of the space created, these differences came out also *in relation to each other* and to the whole community of the classroom. "Individual difference" came forward, now, as *mathematically instructive* for us all, rather than as pathological conditions of isolated individuals. Differently put, we were able to experience the individual differences, not just of these children, but *of mathematics itself.*

"What if we don't limit ourselves to whole numbers? What happens then?"

For some children, out came the rulers and a small group of students started to divide the squares into halves. Justin (Grade 2), who understood what was happening, ran into his own inability to handle a ruler and pencil well enough to draw from corner to corner and ended up, for a few moments, standing full height on his table, pointing down at the paper, crying in frustration. Sharon helped him back in to the work, and helped the student–teachers who were present at that point to understand that it wasn't helpful to see what occurred with Justin as a "management problem." It was better, more pedagogically sound, to take it up as a *mathematical* problem, and to deal with the child's frustration by going back, carefully, with love and attention, to the mathematical work that caused the trouble in the first place. What was so clear with Justin was the absolute physical intensity that occurred. He did not want to be rescued from his dilemma. He deeply wanted to learn how to do this because he knew that was the work that needed to be done.

The group (which Justin soon rejoined, now standing on his chair, beaming, full of "I told you I could do this!") became determined to find all the ways in which halves (and, eventually, quarters and smaller) could be used and their equations were getting longer and longer (meanwhile, concretely, less able children were easily able to see how you need two halves to make a whole and how, if one colors only one half, you have one out of a total of two, how, then, you have something that could be represented as 1/2).

Some children spun off into issues of how many different patterns "5" could make, and children were encouraged to cut out the different patterns, fitting them together, turning them around. Talk of tessellations ensued with some as did talk of how "two squared is just two in a square."

With the following work, one child made it so obvious to us how the equation for the area of a right-angled triangle works (see Fig. 6.4). The child colored in "four" as follows (to his shape we have added our letters):
He then cut out the triangle ABC, cut it along the line AD and placed the new triangle ABD so that the line AB became adjacent to AC (see Fig. 6.5). clearly showing us all something that had become a too clear equation: that the area of this right-angled triangle is half of the base (DC) times the height (AD): $2 \times 2 = 4$.

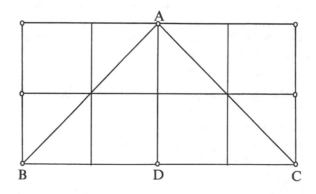

FIG. 6.4. $1 + 1 + \frac{1}{2} + \frac{1}{2} + \frac{1}{2} + \frac{1}{2} = 4$

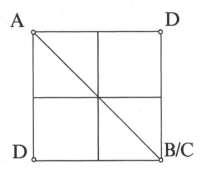

FIG. 6.5. $2 \times 2 = 4$.

Then came the work of Cartesian planes which laced together this 10×10 grid with earlier, meticulous work on the number line and lovely questions about the existence of negative integers. This, of course, is not exactly another story, but it will have to wait for now.

CONCLUDING REMARKS ON DANIEL'S RETURN

Long after traveling the Cartesian planes, Daniel, Grade 4, went over to look at a Grade 1 child's work and remarked that he could have never done that stuff when he was in first grade, and that they were so smart, doing such hard work.

This is a wonderful image of an older student returning to work that he had, in fact, done, now with a broad and generous knowledge that allowed him to see the depth and hidden detail in the simplest of events, allowed him, a fourth-grade child, to see something that Piaget couldn't quite see: that the world of "other generations" is more than simply exceedingly suggestive deformations of the truth. This is a wonderful image, too, of the experienced older boy treating the young so graciously, letting them and us know that they are doing real work.

Daniel was correct. The Grade 1 children were doing hard work. And, as we talked, he also came to understand this work differently than he did when he himself undertook it. Because of the continuing presence of the younger children in the classroom, he was able to remember this work he thought he never did because now, he could see where it belonged and where it was going.

This, again, bears witness to the intergenerational character of mathematical truth because, of course, the younger children engaged in such hard work because of Daniel's presence to them. They knew—each as they were able—that the work they engaged in was real work.

Preamble 7

If we provide enough room for restlessness so that it might function within the space, then the energy ceases to be restless because it can trust itself fundamentally. Meditation is giving a huge, luscious meadow to a restless cow. The cow might be restless for a while in its huge meadow, but at some stage, because there is so much space, the restlessness becomes irrelevant.

—Trungpa (1988, pp. 48–49)

Conversation is a process of coming to an understanding. Thus it belongs to every true conversation that each person opens himself to the other, truly accepts his point of view as valid and transposes himself into the other to such an extent that he understand not the particular individual but what he says. If one transposes onself into the position of another with the intent of understanding not the truth of what he is saying, but him, the questions asked in such a conversation are marked by . . . inauthenticity.

—Gadamer (1989, p. 385)

This might seem like an odd juxtaposition of texts, but what follows is a rather odd chapter.

We were attracted to the citation on meditation by Trungpa because it provides a helpful analogy to our thinking on "the basics." What very often happens in schools when students become restless and encounter difficulties with the work they face is that teachers (and sometimes assessors, testers, and remediators) zoom in on that trouble, narrowing attention, making the "meadow," the "field of relations" available to that student (see

129

Preamble 6) less huge, luscious, rich and spacious. In the face of restless-ness, lesson plans "lessen" (see chap. 1) as we more narrowly target school work to the individual child's needs. This sort of pedagogical intervention is commonplace under the auspices of basics-as-breakdown. The more trou-ble a student has, the smaller and simpler and less interesting the "bit" doled out to them.

In the process of such narrowing, the restlessness does not become irrel-evant. It becomes paramount. But, under the auspices of basics-as-break-down, this restlessness now no longer has places that are patient and forgiv-ing and rich and rigorous enough so that our troubled relations might be able to work themselves *out*.

In an interpretive understanding of the basics, the restlessness brought to the classroom by an individual child's question or concern or trouble or confusion is dealt with differently. The interpretive task is to open a space around the troubles so that those troubles can be worked out, not just worked *on*. As the passage cited from Gadamer suggests, in classroom con-versations, any one of us can have read back to us our own restless experi-ences and questions in ways that no one of us could have accomplished alone. In the presence of other fellow travelers in these terrains, "experi-ences" can be "de-pathologized." They can be taken seriously as perhaps re-vealing *of this place* and not simply revealing about the one having the expe-rience.

This process of "reading back" opens a space around individual troubles so that they might be able to open up into more than what I have myself un-derstood. In our introductory example, the reading-back to that Grade 2 girl made it possible for her to take up her own experiences in light of, so to speak, a "space of possible relations" different from those she might have intended. As we have seen so often as teachers, students are more than will-ing to step up into what they feel is a stronger and more insightful, less pathological version of their ventures that they could have imagined by themselves. This is what Gadamer (1989) called "the art of strengthening" in a true conversation:

> [It] consists not in trying to discover the weakness of what is said, but in bring-ing out its real strength. It is not the art of arguing (which can make a strong case out of a weak one), but the art of thinking (which can strengthen . . . by referring to the subject matter). (p. 367)

Once such an art becomes part of the classroom climate, students them-selves become increasingly willing to read the ventures of others in strong ways, ways that open up rich and luscious spaces for others. This might be an opening for re-thinking the idea of "classroom community."

This sense of "opening up" is precisely what is meant by the notion of "truth" in hermeneutics (Jardine, 2000). For something to be true is for something to be opened up to a living array of potentialities and possibilities and prospects. The "reality" of something like mathematics is thus defined as "standing in a horizon of . . . still undecided future possibilities" (Gadamer, 1989, p. 112). This "standing" is another way of understanding the character of mathematics as a living discipline. Mathematics is real only to the extent that it is vulnerable to such undecidedness. Thus, our children's questions are not only indicators *about them* but are also indicators of the openness of mathematics to question, *its* basic undecidedness.

As mentioned in Preamble 5, for something to be true in this interpretive sense is for it to be open to the future, because, by being open to the future, it is a *living* inheritance that those who follow us will, of necessity, understand otherwise. And, of course, "those who follow" are our children.

Thus again, in an interpretive treatment of the basics, children have a place, not as individuals into whom a fixed and finished set of "basics" must be downloaded, but as inheritors of shared and contested traditions in relation to which their own work will, if allowed, if properly cultivated and cared for, have a say as to how, whether or when these things get handed on.

So, the chapter at hand is another example of how an off-hand comment by a child—if treated as true of something other than his own pathology—can provide the possibility of opening up questions that seemed to be closed, bringing forward matters that seemed to be given. Here we have an individual child with his own mathematical question, but his question is not handed back to him as if it were a question about him. His question is, in a small way, worked *out* into the field of relations about which it is *true* (i.e., recall, this means "opening").

A chapter, now, on the "fecundity of the individual case" of "x."

Chapter 7

A Play on the Wickedness of Undone Sums, Including a Brief Mytho-Phenomenology of "X" and Some Speculations on the Effects of Its Peculiar Absence in Elementary Mathematics Education

David W. Jardine
Sharon Friesen

Car ride to school. And I'm (David Jardine) quizzing my 14-year-old son, Eric, about how mathematics is going lately, what they have been doing, whether he understands. The class has just entered in to the nebulous beginnings of algebra, and Eric offhandedly says, "I don't really get this stuff about 'x'."

Suddenly I am drawn away. I have been working since 1992 with Sharon Friesen and her teaching partner, Patricia Clifford, who have been working both in elementary and middle-school classrooms. Sharon is a brilliant mathematics teacher, and part of her brilliance is how she is able, even with the youngest of children, to maintain the integrity of the discipline of mathematics and help children find ways in to its real work, underneath the burgeoning and often seductive trivialities that pass for some elementary school mathematics "activities."

Our conversation, now so oddly coincidental with Eric's quandary: no mathematician would ever write "5 + 3 = __." They would always write "5 + 3 = x." If you do not write in the "x," you turn what is, mathematically speaking, an equation into an unanswered question, as if you are saying "five plus three *equals?*" with a rising pitch of voice at the end.

More disturbing still, without the "x," equality is turned into an *operation*, something you have to now *do*.

We talked through all those long lists of so-called "math facts" that children are given in school, each one missing an "x."

And how each one becomes filled with an odd and inappropriate form of anticipation and suspense, as if, with "5 + 3 = _," a pendulum were pulled over to the left-hand side, tensed, unable yet to let go, needing our concerted intervention in order to achieve its blessed release.

Once the "x" is returned to its proper place, this suspense is not fulfilled but lifted. Equivalence becomes, not a question but a state, a point of rest.

It loses some of its compulsiveness.

With "5 + 3 = x," we can finally admit that *there already is* equivalence (even though *what it is* may be undetermined). Equivalence is now no longer an operation. It no longer longs or waits or demands to be *done*. It no longer needs us to *do it*. We need no longer be actors or manipulators or constructors drawn into the frays of action and manipulation and construction.

As this once-taunt pendulum now rests in equivalence, we, too, can now rest *in it*.

Without the "x," vision becomes narrowed and singular: answer it, *make* this equivalence (in school talk, "five plus three *makes?*" is commonplace). With the reappearance of "x," a wide field of movement and choice and decision and consequence flowers open. What was once made narrow and singular by the absence of "x" is now an open topography of relations, a "space," a "place" with relatives and kith and kin.

So now, a new pleasure arises to replace the tensed pendulum jitters. Now that we know *that* there is an "x," we ourselves can rest with some existential assurance in a given field of equivalence, with all of the multiple possibilities involved. Against such a background of possibilities, manipulation becomes careful, measured. We can (carefully!) manipulate the equation "5 + 3 = x," into "5 + 3 − x = 0" or even "−x = − (5 + 3)," and so on.

Without the "x," the very idea that you can do anything to one side of an equation as long as you do the same to the other side is not simply meaningless.

It is impossible.

Without the "x," children can come to believe that subtraction is one more damn thing to be done (and teachers can come to believe that subtraction is one more damn thing to be taught).

With the "x," it is possible to see that *subtraction is already co-present in the givenness of "5 + 3 = x"* as an implicate relation living at the very heart of addition.

With such existential assurance *that*, we can now safely ask "What is 'x'?" We are safe, now, because our actions and manipulations and constructions are no longer necessary to the very being of things: *that* is given, it is already assured, even though *what* it might turn out to be still suffers the indeterminacy of "x."

Constructivism, we might say, has found its limit.

A "that there is" of implicate family resemblances flowers opens without us.

Alethia: the word hermeneutics invokes for truth as uncovering, opening up.

"5 = 3 = _," we might say, is lethal, deadening. Nothing can open up.

Truth in this hermeneutic sense is not possible with out an "x" which throws open a field of relations and revelations that we can now *come upon* and cannot simply "construct." With such a field of relations, we must be careful, considerate, quiet sometimes, sometimes full of vigor and ebullience. Our actions are held in place.

We are no longer little gods, and the stories of mathematics are no longer stories only about us and our heroic deeds of construction. We are *in a place*, and our deeds become heroic only if we do what is needed, what is proper to this place.

What is regained with the re-placement of "x," then, is a hint of the deep pleasures that mathematicians experience in entering into open play-fields of possibilities, feeling the exhilarating rush as relations rattle open like the furls of wings, the heartpump sense of potency and option and quandary and challenge and difficulty and adventure and arrival *within* a still place.

Without an "x," the walls close in and smother movement and breath.

Trapped.

Spotted in sights.

The Teacher's Question: "5 + 3 *equals*? David? *Well*?! You weren't listening, were you?"

("No, actually, I wasn't.")

Clearly, some young children (and many adults I know) would not be able to or interested in doing the work of opening up this mathematical field and exploring it, taking its paths, seeking its ways, its patterns, its semblances, its seasons, its quandaries and comforts and thrilling perfections.

However, with the systematic early absence of "x" in mathematics education, *there is no such field*. The systematic early absence of "x" is thus akin to an ecological disaster, and the image of the Child-as-Constructor-Without-Limit is ecologically ruinous. Without an "x," mathematics loses its openness. It loses its truth. It becomes distorted into monstrous little "equivalence as operation" math-fact-question-lists in the early years.

Deadly.

And our children become distorted into little manipulative monsters roaming the landscape without regard.

So, back in the car, I asked Eric to recall all those addition and subtraction questions that, in his earlier grades, were written "5 + 3 = _".

"It should have been '5 + 3 = x'. The 'x' should have never been left out."

A moment's silence.

"Okay, so, algebra. Right. I get it. Why didn't they tell us this in the first place?"

Speculation: that the systematic and deliberate absence of "x" in early mathematics education turns the learning of mathematics into something more desperate than it needs to be. Perhaps worse yet, it turns mathematics itself into something that cannot fully make sense, that is distorted, misrepresented, flattened out, often lifeless, robbed of the truths of family resemblance and topography. It becomes "the solving of problems," and loses its character as an open world of relations. It becomes "unworldly"—nothing more than mental operations in the omnipotent, manipulative charge of a thinking subject whose competence is bewilderingly beyond me and, let me admit it, frightens me to no end in its confidence and blindness.

More than once, I have written the word "mathematics" on the chalk board in my Early Childhood Education teaching methods classes, and have turned around to tears, looks of panic, like deer caught in headlights, transfixed, unable to move or speak.

Horror, if you will, at the spittlefear smell of something awful impending.

Lifelessness: *lethia*.

This is the lifelessness these students experienced in their own mathematics education and the lifelessness that they are now dreading to pass on to their own children, as part of their professional responsibility.

So much of this because of an odd absence of "x."

Preamble 8

It's a name they give you; it's nothing to tell you about the kids, you know, or what they're like, or how to deal with them, really. I want to look at the child and see what they can do, and see how I can get them to the next stage, instead of expecting something, because everyone is different.

—Beck (1993, p. 62)

These words of "Kay, a third-year education student doing her second practicum" were captured by Dahlia Beck in her brilliant book *Visiting Generations* (1993). In the present context, two things are especially revealing about these words.

First of all, Kay is invoking what so many teachers and student–teachers invoke: a concern for children and the practical matters of teaching them well. All that other stuff "they [University personnel] give you" is just "theory," "just talk," "just names." This is one of the great, perennial inheritances of the profession of teaching: the great and heated love–hate relationship between "theory and practice." The image of basics-as-breakdown has a profound effect on our images of what this relationship is about.

One form of breakdown that basics-as-breakdown induces is precisely a breakdown in this relationship between theory and practice, between academics and "the field." Practice, in this view, is pictured thus: It is all the concrete things, all the know-how, tricks of the trade, get-in-there-and-do-it stuff, file cabinets full of generously offered (see chaps. 9 and 12), tried and true "activities for the kids." It is, as many student–teachers have ventured,

137

all the "real" stuff about what actually happens. And theory, in this view, is the abstract, arcane, not-really-necessary, overintellectualized, mostly irrelevant, not helpful with the day-to-day, philosophical stuff. It is, as many student–teachers have ventured, all the stuff you say when "you haven't really been there" and you "don't really know what it's like" and "you aren't giving us what we really need to survive out there."

And let's be clear about this. Under the auspices of this very same breakdown, there are university teachers and researchers who believe a version of the very same thing: that there is not much of scholarly, intellectual, or academic interest in the day-to-day, everyday events of the classroom. One might be able to set up a "research project" where "data" could be collected and later analyzed. But coming into an elementary school classroom and doing the work of thinking, for example, about addition and subtraction with a Grade 2 child, and thinking about what might be showing itself in such intimate relations between adult, child, and world—for the most part, this is not part of the job description.

Such Grade 2 conversations and the thinking that follows certainly is not considered "real research" in this view. It is not considered research because such day-to-day work does not issue from a methodology aimed at controlling, predicting, and manipulating isolated (broken-down) variables. Because that Grade 2 conversation with that child is not produced of breakdown and therefore is not really "data" for research purposes.

For the most part, educational researchers do not consider this day-to-dayness as something that calls for thinking (Heidegger, 1968). "It's just the practice stuff," a colleague admitted; "driving from school to school and waving the flag" another suggested. Another called colleagues interested in such practical busywork "the worker bees."

Apparently this was meant to be funny.

An interpretive treatment of the basics makes quite a mess of this familiar situation. It is not precisely that it provides a solution to the ongoing debate between theory and practice as much as it simply steps away from this debate and begins elsewhere, with a second enticing feature in Kay's words cited before.

This is basic to interpretation and its image of "the basics": The living, day-to-day world of the classroom is *always* and *already* full of roiling faces, ghosts, ancestries, names, ideas, and images. We are "always already affected" (Gadamer, 1989, p. 300). Such faces, ghosts, ancestries, names, ideas, and images do not need to be imported or read into those everyday, "practical" events in order to "theorize" about them. Rather, interpretively understood, we *find* such things *working themselves out*, often "beyond our wanting and doing" (Gadamer, 1989, p. xxviii), in such events. This is the ontological claim of hermeneutics: Everyday events *are* their ancestries and renewals.

When we say along with Kay, with all genuineness and heartfeltness, that "I want to look at the child and see what they can do, and see how I can get them to the next stage, instead of expecting something, because everyone is different," our words, whether we meant it or not, are *already full* of the echoes of long songlines that criss-cross the terrain of teaching. Listening to Kay's words as issuing some "truth" about our profession and following the leads that it suggests is a matter, not of methodological control, prediction, and manipulation, but a matter of "entrusting ourselves to what we are investigating to guide us safely in the quest" (Gadamer, 1989, p. 378), entrusting ourselves to the fact that we *already belong* to the world of teaching, for good or ill.

Bluntly put, listening to Kay's words for the bloodlines they invoke *is* interpretive research. And, to mess things up even further, listening to that Grade 2 girl's words for the mathematical bloodlines they invoke *is* interpretive research. And further, provoking that Grade 2 girl to hear in her own experience the possibility of a genuine, living mathematical adventure is teaching that child to treat the world of mathematics as a living inheritance. That is to say, it is teaching her to treat mathematics *interpretively*. So, as is becoming clearer as these chapters proceed, we do not treat interpretive work simply as our "research methodology" for understanding classroom events. The sorts of classroom events we are trying to describe *are already themselves interpretive* for teachers, students, and researchers alike. They are the sorts of events that, if well-treated, if treated "strongly" (see Preamble 7), open our collective attention (students, student–teachers, teachers, researchers) to the interpretive character of the world.

To return to Kay's invocation, one of the "name[s] that they give you" is, of course, Jean Piaget. And it was Piaget's work that introduced into the bloodlines of education the idea that children "go through stages" and therefore that "get[ting] them to the next stage" might be a sensible thing for a prospective teacher to say about the children in her care. It is through Piaget's legacy that we believe that, because children go through stages, we can, within certain limits, "expect something." It may be, as Kay suggests, that "everyone is different." But Piaget is telling us that, in the movement from childhood to adulthood, everyone is not *just* different. There is, according to Piaget, an identifiable pattern to this movement. So, all at once, Kay has invoked Piaget and the idea of stages in order to rescue a sense of the uniqueness of each child. And she has invoked Piaget—"I want to . . . see how I can get [the child] to the next stage"—as a way of turning her back on the fact that, for her, he is "just a name they give you."

This is not to say *at all* that Kay was being "unreflective" or disingenuous. Rather, it simply says that an interpretive interest in everyday classroom events—including an interpretive interest in the musings of student–teachers on their practicum experiences—is not a matter of imposing arcane theories on to practice, but of attempting to listen, to hear, to heed, to take seriously, all the "multifariousness of voices" (Gadamer, 1989, p. 295) hidden there. This means taking seriously the scholarly, academic, and intellectual invocation of such events and doing the work of opening them up into the myriad shared and contested possibilities and potentialities they might portend. Rather than pathologizing Kay's words into simply "her opinion," we can take them up as laying claim to us. If I am the one in the education faculty who knows his way around Piaget's work, I can hear in Kay's words that all we had heretofore thought we knew about this Piagetian inheritance has been *called to account.* Why? Because, interpretively speaking, right in the everyday words of a student–teacher, here is how this inheritance is being handed along.

Interpretively speaking, then, the question becomes this: How can we, now as Kay's teachers, help her hear *in her own words—right there,* in that nearness and taken-for-grantedness and obviousness—that she has kin, she has relations that can help her strengthen, open up, celebrate, and challenge who she is becoming as a teacher. Right in the midst of her own words there is a transformative, educative potentiality. She is, right in the midst of her own words, already living out living relations to others who have also ventured into such places. So reading Jean Piaget becomes a matter of searching out the traces of the work he has left behind because, at least in part, it is precisely these traces that educators, along with Kay, are living out in their profession, more often than not "over and above our wanting and doing" (Gadamer, 1989, p. xxviii).

This means, of course, that we have to start reading Jean Piaget interpretively as well, for the witness he can give us to the troubles being lived out in education. Interpretively understood, Piaget is not a *theory,* he is not just "a name they give you." He is a *relation* that inhabits the world of teaching in many, often contradictory, ways, that very world of teaching that Kay is entering, that very world of teaching that Grade 2 girl and faculty of education university folks and classroom teachers inhabit.

As such an "old man" (Jardine, in press), Piaget has stories to tell—with all his foibles and excesses as much as with all the insights and care that has come down to us. Along with Piaget we have family relations: all the debates about stages, about their gendered character (see, e.g., Gilligan's [1993] responses to the work of Kohlberg, a student of Piaget's), about the tense relations between Kay's "everyone is different" and Vygotsky's musings on the social constitution of one's self in the acquisition of language, and so on, and so on. Kay (along with the rest of us concerned with education, *including* that Grade 2 girl and her math worksheet) is *right in the middle of something*: the fact that these matters are neither "theory" nor "practice" nor both added together. They are, interpretively put, living threads, live debates, blood relations that constitute the living profession of education.

Piaget has handed teachers and students and researchers a way to treat this difficult task of understanding our children and raising them well. Unfortunately, he has handed us what sometimes becomes a form of blindness rather than insight: There are those who would invoke developmental theory to suggest that that Grade 2 girl could not possibly understand this idea of the belonging together of addition and subtraction because, as it is often put in the everyday parlance of schools, "kids think concretely." As with any blood relation, it is not necessarily the case that how matters have been handed down to us is all good news. And, of course, those who follow us, including the students and the student–teachers (and, in our graduate classes, the practicing teachers and administrators) we teach, will have something to say about what all this might mean in the future.

It is very hard to get a glimpse of these blood relations, because, very often, our view of things is constituted and formed *by means of* these blood relations and not necessarily *about* these blood relations. They are, for the most part, simply taken-for-granted as obvious and as going-without-saying:

> It is impossible to make ourselves aware of [these things we take for granted, these] . . . prejudice[s] while [they] are constantly operating unnoticed, but only when [they] are, so to speak, provoked. (Gadamer, 1989, p. 299).

As was mentioned in the Introduction, chapter 3, and Preamble 7, interpretively speaking, "understanding begins . . . when something addresses us" (Gadamer, 1989, p. 299). That is, understanding in the interpretive sense begins in the face of something happening to us such that things no longer go without saying, things are no longer simply "obvious." Kay's words, so to speak, *struck us* when we read them, they "hit home." This seemingly "individual case" of Kay expressing what some call her "teacher beliefs" suddenly becomes, not simply and only what "Kay believes" but what Gadamer (1989) called "participating in an event of tradition" (p. 309). That is to say, right in the midst of what some would treat as an isolated, only personal, "individual case" something "opens up" about the *world* of teaching: a "portal," an "opportunity." The ordinariness of that world begins to "waver and tremble" (Caputo, 1987, p. 7). What was dull and obvious starts to become suggestive, starts to show itself as rich, complex, difficult, full of hidden relations, stories to tell, whispers and hints, obligations, and implications.

The following chapter is a mixture of these considerations. What if we considered the ordinary things in our world, like the sun and the moon, not as singular self-same objects to be controlled, predicted, and manipulated? What if, instead, we understood them as multifarious ciphers that hide all of the myriad and often contradictory ways in which such things have been handed to us? Interpretively understood, the sun and the moon are not just objects of scientific discourse. They are figures in the tales our ancestors have told each other, they are lunacy and sun-dogs and the bodily immediacies of day and night, all of these presences in our lives.

Jean Piaget, as we see in chapter 8, had lovely things to say about understanding the sun and the moon *animistically*. Unfortunately, as was often his wont, Piaget tends to mean by this "understanding the sun and moon *as if* they were alive" and *they aren't really alive.* For this old man, animism is just a developmental feature of how children think. It is true *of children's thinking* but it is not true *in the world*. Interpretively speaking, however, it is also a truth, an "opening," in the world. One of the threads in the following chapter is an exploration of how interpretive work might liven up Piagetian theory and therefore, how interpretive work might be deeply pedagogical at its heart, seeking out how the new voice, like some young child in a first-grade science class, might be calling the world to account.

It is becoming obvious by now that an interpretive treatment of the basics as involving the living disciplines educators have inherited has something animistic about it and that in school classrooms where the basics are treated interpretively, there is a certain sense of "life" involved beyond the deadliness of basics-as-breakdown. Liveliness, in the basics-as-breakdown classroom, is a *management issue,* having to do with the wildness and woolliness of children. And, of course, if you are a university researcher, there is no intellectual venture to be had in engaging children in their liveliness, because, after all, in this set-up, *you* are the inquirer, the researcher, and they are not. Best leave the wildness and the woolliness to those "in the know": the worker bees, full of an accelerated (see Preamble 1) buzz.

More of this in Preamble 9.

Chapter 8

"Because It Shows Us the Way at Night": On Animism, Writing, and the Re-Animation of Piagetian Theory

David W. Jardine

> *Let us imagine the* anima mundi *neither above the world encircling it as a divine and remote emanation of spirit, a world of powers, archetypes and principles transcendent to things, nor within the material world as its unifying panpsychic life-principle. Rather, let us imagine the* anima mundi *as that particular soul-spark, that seminal image, which offers itself through each thing in its visible form. Then* anima mundi *indicates the animated possibilities presented by each event as it is, its sensuous presentation as a face bespeaking an image, in short, its availability to imagination.*
>
> —Hillman (1982, p. 174)

PART ONE

Does the sun know anything?
Yes, it heats.
Does the moon know it shines?
Yes.
Why?
Because it shows us the way at night.

—Jean Piaget (1974, pp. 205–206),
in conversation with "Vog," age 8;6 months

Jean Piaget explored the ways in which such animistic thought was true of a certain stage of the development of objective, scientific (mid-20th century) conceptions of physical, mechanical causation.

143

There is a fascinating, mysterious sense in which "Vog"'s words can also be treated as somehow true of the sun and the moon.

What if we entered the imaginal realm and allowed "the sun" and "the moon" to no longer be literal designations of univocal objects? What if we took "the sun" and "the moon" to be multivocal ciphers, holding in their hearts all of the ways that they have arrived here, in our fleshy, human lives, through the pores, as the gods, in the tales, on the tongue, in the leafy-chlorophyllic gobbles of sugar production, and in the tumbles of burning gases and their reflected light that shows the way at night?

So that sun and moon "bear witness to [themselves] in the images [they] offer, and [their] depth lies in the complexities of [these] image[s]" (Hillman, 1982, p. 128), and not just in the tales that the sciences have to tell about literal, objective states of affairs:

> I am not anthropomorphizing. It's more like a thing is a phenomenological presentation, with a depth, a complexity, a purpose, in a world of relations, with a memory, a history. And if we look at it this way we might begin to hear it. It's an aesthetic appreciation of how things present themselves and that therefore they are in some way formed, ensouled, and are speaking to the imagination. This way of looking is a combination of the Neoplatonic *anima mundi* and pop art: that even a beer can or a freight car or a street sign has an image and speaks of itself beyond being a dead throwaway object. (Hillman, 1982, pp. 132–133)

But we must delve deeper here: Even "dead throwaway objects" now *bespeak themselves, show* themselves as what they are. Thus, science and its tales of the world becomes *a living part* of these imaginal complexities, not an exception to them, a thread among others, needing to find its proper place and needing, as we all witness, to learn how to conduct itself with more grace and care and generosity in relation to all its kin.

Thus, interpretively taken up, "Vog"'s words must be understood in their address (Jardine, 1995c) to the full range of these phenomena of sun and moon in our lives, as evoking true, real relations uttered by one of our kin, and not simply as immature developmental precursors to the texts of the sciences. "Only in the multifariousness of such voices do [the sun and moon] exist" (Gadamer, 1989, p. 295).

What happens in bypassing the monotheistic (Hillman, 1983) canons of noncontradiction and giving up the hope that Piaget expressed, that "a single truth alone is acceptable when we are dealing with knowledge in the strictest sense" (Piaget, 1965, pp. 216–217)? What if we gave up Piaget's suggestions that children's tales are odd "deformations" of the truth (Piaget, 1974, p. 50), that children often become "duped" (Piaget, 1972, p. 141), "victims of illusion" (p. 141), where the tales they tell become "traps into which [they] consistently fall" (Piaget, 1974, p. 73) to the extent that "the whole perspective of childhood is falsified" (Piaget, 1972, p. 197)? What if, instead, the truth were to be had in the spaces "in-between" (Gadamer, 1989, p. 295) all our kin—ourselves, our children, our shared and contested ancestors, and the Earth that holds us all here in relations of kind?

What if we were to look at the life of these words, their animating spirit, allowing ourselves to be drawn in to the wondrous cosmologies they bespeak, drawn out of our selves—a "momentary loss of self" (Gadamer, 1977, p. 51), a type of self-dispersal out in to the ways of things, out into the voices beyond my own, out into "all my relations" (King, 1992)?

PART TWO

> Of course, the most fruitful, most obvious field of study would be reconstituting human history—the history of human thinking in prehistoric man. Unfortunately, we are not very well informed about the psychology of Neanderthal man or about the psychology of *Homo siniensis* of Teilhard de Chardin. Since this field of biogenesis is not available to us, we shall do as biologists do and turn to ontogenesis. Nothing could be more accessible to study than the ontogenesis of these notions. There are children all around us. (Piaget, 1971a, p. 13)

Thus, for Piaget, the child is the real primitive among us, the missing link between prehistorical men and contemporary adults (Vonèche & Bovet, 1982, p. 88).

When Piaget (1971, pp. 12–14) speculated that ontogeny (the stages of growth of the individual) might recapitulate phylogeny (the stages of growth of the species), he was not deliberately contending that our ancestors were like children, or that those of cultures other than Europe might be full of the naivetys and simplicities and immaturities and petulance of childhood.

He was not deliberately demeaning the great tales of sun and moon and stars and gods and demons that still hold us spellbound in the tales we still tell our children (and this despite the fact that we and they are "destined to master science" [Piaget, 1952, p. 369] somehow instead). The alert ears that come in the moonlight when vision fails, the deep, darkening woods and the messages housed and hinted in Coyote's moony giggle—these things still trickle thick in our blood and in the blood of our children, despite our seeming destinies.

Let us give him this much, even though speculations such as these were rife in the spirit of the times (Eliade, 1968, 1975). Such tales were understood as:

belonging to a different mentality [than scientific discourse]: savage, primitive, underdeveloped, backwards, alienated, composed of opinions, customs, authority, prejudice, ignorance, ideology. Narratives are fables, myths, legends, fit only for women and children. At best, attempts are made to throw some rays of light into this obscurantism, to civilize, educate, develop. (Usher & Edwards, 1994, p. 158)

Much has been made of such parallels as those very "un[der]developed others" read our Eurocentrism and its colonial presumptions back to us (LeGuin, 1987, 1989; Minh-Ha, 1994; Nandy, 1987).

Let us give him this much, reading him perhaps more generously that he could have read himself (Jardine, in press); let us give up talk of what readings his legacy might angrily deserve and take up the task of making his work speak whatever truths it might hold—its openings, its portals, its wounds, its ways.

Let us grant him what we wish that he might have granted "Vog" and his tales of the moon and the sun.

PART THREE

In that land of beginnings spirits mingled with the unborn. We could assume numerous forms. Many of us were birds. We knew no boundaries. There was much feasting, playing, and sorrowing. We feasted much because of the beautiful terrors of eternity. We played much because we were free. And we sorrowed much because there were always those amongst us who had just returned from the world of the Living. They had returned unconsolable for all the love they had left behind, all the suffering they hadn't redeemed, all that they hadn't understood, and for all that they had barely begun to learn before they were drawn back to the land of origins. (Okri, 1991, p. 3)

When Piaget speculated that ontogeny (the stages of growth of the individual) might recapitulate phylogeny (the stages of growth of the species), he was certainly not deliberately contending that our children might somehow be our ancestors, potential clarions of what our prized 19th-century hallucinations of "development" may have somehow forgotten. Children as reminders of past lives, as holders of memory, living nearer-by old springs that have lasted, that still nourish, nearer to remembering old tales that objectivism has dispersed, dispelled, or demeaned as not really telling of the ways of the Earth.

What if we were to give up picturing "development" as a line in which one stage is replaced by another, in which one is more precious than the other, where we must somehow make a moral choice between youth and age and the tales each might tell? What if we were to imagine "development" as an open field of relations, in which each voice, each tale, each breath requires all the others, all its relations, to be full and rich and whole and healthy and sane? What if we were to understand development thus ecologically, full of Earthy relations of the flesh? So that, in fact, the old never replace the young but live *with* them, so that one does not fulfill any destiny in aging, but simply becomes who one becomes, generous or not, able to live well with all the voices of the Earth, or unable, disabled, desperate.

The articulations of adults and children might thus each protect and cradle the other from the mortalities that entwine us (see chap. 6 on the idea of "intergenerationalness").

This is *almost* what Piaget contends, that the "concepts and categories of established science" (Inhelder, 1969, p. 23) require genetic grounding, and that science—what Piaget took to be an unquestionable sign of "maturity"—is not comprehensible without delving in to its genesis, into its arrival. The ways of age are not properly understandable in isolation from the generations that have brought them to be what they are. And again, whether this means that ancestors, and our current attraction, in curriculum, to the old tales, the "old ways" (Snyder, 1977), are child-like or our children are ancestral becomes alluring again, far more interesting than Piaget might have been able to imagine.

If we pursue a study of the child and her "course" (curriculum), we cannot presume the presence of logico-mathematical knowledge and turn children and the coursing of their lives into our object. *It is that very presence of logico-mathematical knowledge, that very presumption, which is drawn into question by genetic epistemology,* but it is, *at the very same time,* left in place as the method genetic epistemology uses to give answer to that question. Piaget was unwilling to risk this much, not because of cowardice or malice, but because he believed that to produce a science of children was to raise children up into their truth and, at the very same time, to ground that very scientific truth in its fragile, intimate genesis.

However, he need not have feared quite so much. If we are to engage our children—meet them as our kin and not just as our object—we must allow our ways of proceeding to come into conversation with them in such a way that their ways and ours "converse"—turn around each other, each becoming different in the movement, each held in place, held in check, by the other.

Dead ordinary, this. We live in a world *with* children, and we live in it as adults who are defined in concert with our kin. When we read these books full of spooks and spirits, we ourselves are drawn down into deep entrails of belief that work in the guts, that perk the sensuousness and sonorities that ring and hum through our throats (Abram, 1996), and that haunt in the "sedimented layers of emotionally resonate metaphors" (Fischer, 1986, p. 198) housed in our language. Resisting the ascendancies of "development"

(Piaget's stages are always pictured as ascending, like a spirit rising up in the flesh, finally becoming free and pure in the fleshlessness of the pure operations of logic and mathematics [Jardine, in press]), we plunge down into worlds that are alive beyond the mechanisms allowed by logico-mathematical reasoning, beyond what is allowed by our feigned "maturities."

In such an interpretive descent, logico-mathematical reasoning *itself* becomes full of life as well, haunted, as Piaget *almost* suggests, by old family ties that bind it to our living: "part of the history of the human spirit" (Gadamer, 1989, p. 283), and not some abstract, other-worldly exceptionality cut loose from the ways of the flesh.

Youth or age and the tales they have to tell—each without the other loses its sense of place and proportion and relation. Each without the other becomes monstrous (Jardine, 1994a; Jardine & Field, 1992). And, as hinted with the sun and the moon, perhaps these too, "youth" and "age," are themselves ciphers that ought not to be pinned squarely and solely on certain chronologically specifiable objects.

PART FOUR

> The whole leap depends on the slow pace at the beginning, like a long flat run before a broad jump. Anything that you want to move has to start where it is, in its stuckness. That involves erudition—probably too much erudition. One wants to get stuck in the history, the material, the knowledge, even relish it. Deliberately spending time in the old place. Then suddenly seeing through the old place. (Hillman, 1991, p. 154)

If one pursues a hermeneutic study (say, into Piagetian theory and his work on the animistic child [1974]), it is not enough to write about different things than are common in curricular discourse. I must also *write differently*, in a way that acknowledges, attends, and waits upon the agency of the world. Hermeneutics is therefore akin to the opening up of "animating possibilities presented by each event" (Hillman, 1979a, p. 155).

Hermeneutic writing is premised on the eventful ("Understanding proves to be an event" [Gadamer, 1989, p. 309]) arrival of animating spirit. This is why its name is the name of a god of arrival, of youth, of fecundity and fertility and agency. It is premised on the belief in a resonant, animate world, full of voices and spooks and spirits which require a form of attention that extends beyond one's self, out into the living ways of things.

It is premised on the arrival of the young boy Hermes, flitting and flirting. Little wonder that Piaget identified animism with the young child, for the young child, in fact, is one of its gods. It is premised on "the [animated/animating] leap" beyond the old and established; in a sense, an enlivening leap *into* the old and established. Hermeneutics represents a conversation with the old borne on the breath and in the face of "the new, the different, the true" (Gadamer, 1977, p. 9). This is not precisely a leap that I *do*, even though I must prepare myself through immersing myself in the voices of the ancestors, spend time in the old place, the "resting place" (Ly, 1996, p. 1). I must, for example, carefully read Piaget's work down into all its meticulous details; it must become familiar, cellular, memorable, at the tip of the tongue in immediate ways. And then, "the leap"—some insight arrives, it seems, from elsewhere, a "provocation" (Gadamer, 1989, p. 299) carrying its own agencies and consequences and desires.

"To understand . . . hermeneutically is to trace back what is said to what wishes to be said" (Grondin, 1995, p. 32)—just imagine, things *wishing* to be said.

Thus, when the issue of animism is posed to Piaget's work as a hermeneutic task, a question is posed to what is left unsaid and unheard in this work and, in such posing, "the whole" of it wakes up by being called to account from elsewhere than it has come to rest. "The whole" of it seems somehow new and different and true. Piaget's work suddenly becomes visible as in the sway of age-old tales already told. Piaget's decision to focus on scientific knowledge and its genesis is suddenly recast, suddenly visible as a profoundly spiritual, even cosmological decision to cast the gods and ancestors as children.

A way therefore opens to carry on a conversation with this elder, but it is a way that is beyond his intent in his work, beyond his wanting and doing (Gadamer, 1989, p. xxviii), and, insofar as I pay careful attention as well to the lessons he leaves, beyond mine as well. Something, so to speak, happens (Weinsheimer, 1987) and this happenstance of meaning—a "breaking forth" as Gadamer (1989, p. 458) described it—is revivifying, re-generative, "fecund" (Gadamer, 1989, p. 32). "It has to be epiphantic. [It has] to come forth and surprise us" (Hillman, 1991, p. 50). "This is the first condition of hermeneutics," that "something addresses us" (Gadamer, 1989, p. 299).

PART FIVE

The Idea is an organism, is born, grows, and dies like organisms, renews itself ceaselessly. "In the beginning was the Idea," say the mysterious words of the Christian cosmogeny. (Piaget, 1977, p. 27)

The calm of the Idea . . . brings [us] closer to God. (Piaget, 1977, p. 28)

The good is life. Life is a force which penetrates matter, organizes it, introduces harmony, love. Everywhere life brings harmony, solidarity in the new and vaster units that it creates. (Piaget, 1977, p. 31)

Life is good, but the individual pursuing his self-interest renders it bad. Every individual instinctively, unconsciously serves its species, serves life. But self-interest may lead the individual to keep for himself some of the vital energy which he might bring to others. One day intelligence appeared, illuminated life, opened new domains to mankind, and through him God thought to attain his ends. But here again self-interest appeared, now armed with reason. Life is threatened, instinct evolves and is transformed into a sacred feeling which sets man on the right path again, and brings him back to God. But man, having tasted of the fruits of the tree of life, remains caught in this conflict between self-interest and renunciation. (Piaget, 1977, pp. 29–30)

The individual can only attain true life . . . by sacrifice, by force of the Idea, harmony with life. (Piaget, 1977, p. 30)

It is the Idea which is the engine of life, it is the Idea which will animate our corpse. Let us restore the Idea! (Piaget, 1977, pp. 32–33)

Piaget's work originated in a mystical, near-ecstatic image of "life itself," an identification of "life" with Christ as the *eidos* of the Cosmos. In his later claims regarding the "self-organizing principle inherent in life itself" (Piaget, 1952, p. 19) are hidden evocations of a biogenetic vision of the Living Word and a vision of humanity and human development as a progressive, developmentally sequenced shedding or renouncing of one's selfishness (egocentrism and the individual, psychological subject), and the progressive participation in the pure functioning of life itself. The functioning of "life itself" in earlier stages of development is encumbered by the body, by the flesh, by the animate corpse, and the progressive of development is a shedding of such encumbrances.

Underwriting development and all the multifarious changes one undergoes in becoming an adult, is the "absolute continuity" (Piaget, 1971b, p. 140) of the functioning of "life itself." Development, therefore, is a matter of the slow, sequential achievement of a state in which such functioning is expressed purely (even though it is present from the beginning of life). It becomes clear from this why a single truth alone is acceptable: Under the monotheistic rubric of Christianity, the pristine principle of identity in mathematics ($A = A$, which, for Piaget, underwrites the concepts and categories of established science as a pure expression of their functioning, their operations, their "methods") becomes entwined with God's self-affirmation of the "I am that I am"—and, in Piaget's genetic epistemology, such pure (self-)identity is properly called an *operation*, that is, a *function* which represents in a pure form the self-regulating or "autoregulatory" (Piaget, 1971b, p. 26) character of life. Development is a process of life "coming to" so that the highest stages represent perfect self-identity, where the operations of logico-mathematical knowledge, and the objects of such knowledge are the same.

In such knowledge, one has an experience akin to a re-union with God.

And again, this work frees the animate spirit, the fiery *logoi*, of the disciplines of logic and mathematics. The purity and self-enclosure and pristineness and anonymity of logic and mathematics to which Piaget's work attests becomes visible as full of old, familiar, oft-told tales of ascendancy beyond our fleshy, human countenance, images of purity, of purification beyond the putridities of the bowels and the blood.

But here is an odd twist. Piaget's earlier works are concerned with the animistic realm in which "life itself" is still deeply embodied—bodily reflexes, bodily functions, language, cosmology, imagination, play, dreams, images, clouds, and sun and moon. As his work progressed, it became more and more fixated on issues of logic and mathematics. His earlier work, then, is more childish in its concerns. His work as a whole, then, betrays the very movement of development that his work is about at its core: the struggle of the animate sprit, the breath of the world, to escape its mortality and free itself.

PART SIX

> The sole work of *La Loba* is the collecting of bones. She is known to collect and preserve especially that which is in danger of being lost to the world. . . . [H]er speciality is said to be wolves.
>
> She creeps and crawls and sifts through the *montanas* . . . and *arroyos* . . . looking for wolf bones, and when she has assembled an entire skeleton, when the last bone is in place and the beautiful white sculpture of the creature is laid out before her, she sits by the fire and thinks about what song she will sing.
>
> And when she is sure, she stands over the *critura*, raises her arms and sings out. That is when the rib bones and leg bones of the wolf begin to flesh out and the creature becomes furred. *La Loba* sings some more, and more of the creature comes into being; its tail curls upward, shaggy and strong.
>
> And *La Loba* sings more and the wolf creature begins to breathe.
>
> And *La Loba* sings so deeply that the floor of the desert shakes, and as she sings, the wolf opens its eyes, leaps up, and runs away down the canyon. (Estes, 1992, pp. 27–28)

Clarissa Pinkola-Estes' re-citing of the tale of La Loba can be read as an expression of the deep experience that hermeneutic writing entails. It is a mytho-poetic evocation of the life of those who, in some sense, gather together the dry bones of a particular topic (snippets, passages, citations, references, suggestions, turns of phrase, hints, clues, and page numbers, all the bones of the old place, the resting place) and who must carefully and patiently sing over them, hoping that they will come to life, hoping that the song sung, this enchantment, will result in a re-enchantment (Berman, 1983) and a reanimation of the world—a wonderful twinning of the formative power of the living Word and its profound helplessness (Gadamer, 1989, p. 390; see chap. 4) before the ways of things.

Helpless, of course, because we must wait upon the things to arrive (in hermeneutics, truth is epiphantic, it *arrives*). Fearful, too, provoking "all these deeper fears of the spontaneous and eruptive. The *invenio*: the coming-in of something" (Hillman, 1991, p. 68). A hermeneutic reading of Piaget is a deliberately creative act of reanimation. Like *La Loba*, breathing, sitting firm on the ground, resting in the old place, abiding, waiting upon the Earth for the leap of life beyond the singer.

And look where we have ended up—in a giddy, fearsome place. Who would have imagined that underwriting our dull and dusty images of curriculum development was such a whirlwind of ancestral voices, such a living world, such mystical hallucinations and hope.

PART SEVEN

> All things show faces, the world not only a coded signature to be read for
> meaning, but a physiognomy to be faced. As expressive forms, things speak;
> they show the shape they are in. They announce themselves, bear witness to
> their presence. They regard us beyond how we may regard them, our perspec-
> tives, what we intend with them, and how we dispose of them. This imagina-
> tive claim on attention bespeaks a world ensouled. More our imaginative rec-
> ognition, the childlike act of imagining the world, animates the world and
> returns it to soul. (Hillman, 1982, pp. 177–178)

What breaks here is the closed seal of constructivism which places the making of all things in our hands, in which Piaget envisaged the development of the young child as a progressive move from the chaos of early experience to the construction of a cosmos (Piaget, 1971c, p. xvi). Things regard us beyond how we regard them, and however active our knowing might be, it must rest in the grace of things—"entrusting ourselves" to the ways of things (Gadamer, 1989, p. 378)—if our knowing is to not be ecologically and spiritually insane. A fearsome insight. A world re-enlivened, where all the old alignments shift and flutter.

PART EIGHT

Recently in a first-grade class, the children were learning the science curriculum requirement of living and non-living as part of "science." As the University supervisor, I arrived and the student–teachers handed me an 8½ ×

11 sheet of paper, divided in half with a black line, with the words "living" and "non-living" at the top of each column. This large double classroom of children were then divided up between eight adults, myself included, and, after a brief discussion, we were sent out on to the playground to search for objects and decided where they might be placed on the chart we were given.

Our group quickly checked out cars and dogs walking by. One child then picked up a popsicle stick.

"Non-living," one child insisted.

Another said, "That's not non-living. It's dead. That's different."

"Write that down," I insisted. "Here, I'll help." The children had been encouraged as well to simply make drawings on the paper if they had trouble with the writing, whatever might help remind them when we gathered to talk later in the classroom.

Later, all of us gathered together and the student–teachers, on a large version of our worksheets, started taking down children's discoveries, probing for why they chose to put things where they did. I nudged a child in my group.

"We couldn't decide where to put a popsicle stick. She said it's 'non-living' and I think it's dead."

"They were in *your* group, right?" the student–teacher said, smiling at me, and we had a good laugh with the kids about "university teachers" and the odd questions they can bring.

Then, one child said, "I don't know where to put the sun." A *huge* debate broke out, with questions and counterquestions, examples and counterexamples.

"It keeps us alive so it *has* to be alive."

"It's just a big fire." And on and on. So, for now at least, "the sun" was printed on the line between.

There is little room to move in many schools, and we do not want to confuse our children. But a door opened here that is at the heart of education: a moment of age-old indecisiveness, an indecisiveness that holds some truth about "all our relations" (King 1992; see chap. 2) and how we have come to be who we are. What about this sun on the line in between? What does it do? What are the Helios tales of its arcing across the sky? How do these green leaves feed on its gifts? Where does it fit in this precious Earthly life we live? What have the old ones said of it? How are our lives placed and positioned by its heat? The Tropic of Capricorn, and the Sun's turning in the heavens, Old Sol static for a moment, turning (*tropos*) in the sign of the Goat.

And, too, it heats. St. Francis called it brother, and such calling was not simply foolishness. Such calling called up some truth.

Why do this? Because, interpretively treated, the issue of the life of the sun is not new, not trivial, not easy, and not yet decided once and for all times. The line between living and non-living is an age-old *decision* that was made, that it could have been made otherwise, and that we sweet humans divide purposefully. And this dividing in the Grade 1 curriculum guide is a profound cosmological choice that hides great wisdoms that are left unaddressed if we simply place objects where they unthinkingly and obviously belong.

Our children, in such dull-minded placing, are robbed of their relations if we do this.

Piaget's decision to trim the narrows of contemporary scientific discourse is a profound spiritual and mythopoetic decision to take up the world in a certain way, and, as the late 19th century warranted, he splayed all other beliefs in developmental sequences of great progress toward our own age.

And that the decision to drain the agency, drain the daimons from the Earth and take it up as mere mechanism, not as our home, our brother, our lover, our guide, our fearsome teacher—these are tales far too archaic to map out here in full. But, oddly, as Piaget discovered in his searching of the child's animism, the spirits and faces of long-forgotten ancestors remain. Children still place the sun "between" in an odd imaginative space full of many more "animated possibilities," much more "sensuous presence" than the lesson-as-planned allowed.

There is something beautiful here. Something *shows*.

PART NINE

> One need only think of the great effort that structuralist poetics has put into shedding some light on myth—and yet without even coming close to realizing the aim of letting myth speak more clearly than before. (Gadamer, 1995, p. x)

> But what is animism? It's *esse in anima*. It's living in the world via the soul and sensing the soul in the world ... feeling the world as personified, as emotional, as saying something. [We] live in the *anima mundi*, in a world full of figures, omens, signatures. (Hillman, 1983, p. 91)

> Things have skins and faces and smells. Now that would be a revolution. It would give the world back to its soul, and let the soul out of our private personal subjective idea of it. We might then love the world and not be in terror of it. (Hillman, 1982, p. 175)

It is not enough to simply replace a literal take on science and its voices with a literal reading of animism. This opens up nothing at all, and engulfs interpretive work in paradigm wars premised on the very literalism that is killing us. What a serious, playful fugue on animism does is attempt to breath life into our work, even the often brutal works of an old crank like Piaget. His work is full of spooks, full of spirit, full of animated possibilities beyond the hard edged readings of curriculum development.

As I hope my own child will know, the world is full of wonder, full of agency beyond our own, and we need not be in terror of it, although its fearsomeness can sometimes cause the breath to halt. We need not simply learn about animism. This is not what the mythologies of curriculum hold.

We need to learn from it.

Let us end by dedicating a little word to "Vog" and the moon and sun he knew.

Preamble 9

We came as infants, "trailing clouds of glory," arriving from the farthest reaches of the universe, bringing with us appetites well preserved from our mammal in heritances, spontaneities wonderfully preserved from our 150,000 years of tree life, angers well preserved from our 5,000 years of tribal life—in short, with our 360-degree radiance—and we offered this gift to our parents. They didn't want it. They wanted a nice girl or a nice boy.

—Bly (1988, p. 24)

One of the vile products of a misguided philanthropy is the idea that, in order to obey gladly, the child has to understand the reasons why an order is given and that blind obedience offends human dignity. I do not know how we can continue to speak of obedience once reasons are given. These [reasons] are meant to convince the child, and, once convinced, he is not obeying us but merely the reasons we have given him. Respect . . . is then replaced by a self-satisfied allegiance to his own cleverness.

(Kellner, 1852, as cited in Miller, 1989, p. 40)

It would be wrong to give the impression that everything one might come upon in interpretive work is cause for celebration. Some inheritances are horrible and many of the hidden corners we turn in seeking out ancestries and bloodlines in interpretive work are as often painful, humiliating, and unpleasant as they are the opposite. Usually, in fact, there ends up being a bit of both in interpretive work.

It would be equally wrong, therefore, to give the impression that what is come upon in interpretive work is always an inheritance one would wish to hand on to our children untransformed and uninterrupted. Interpretive work always places in front of us, not just the epistemological task of understanding the often contradictory, often ambiguous meanings of these inheritances, but the ethical task of deciding now, here, in the face of these matters, what shall we do, what shall we say, how can we properly go on, given what we've found? This is why Smith (1999) so simply and clearly stated that hermeneutics has to do with human freedom. Once we allow that, interpretively treated, the inheritances handed to us become opened up to question by the arrival of the new, we can no longer pretend that they are just a given or that we are helpless in the face of them and their traditionary weight.

> *It goes without saying that pedagogues not infrequently awaken and help to swell a child's conceit by foolishly emphasizing his merits. Only humiliation can help here.* (From *The Encyclopedia of Pedagogy*, 1851, as cited in Miller, 1989, p. 22)

The italicized passage just cited and the following ones from Alice Miller's terrifying and important book, *For Their Own Good* (1989), are from mid- to late-19th-century European childrearing manuals. They therefore sketch out, for the three of us, the atmosphere in which our grandparents were raised. They sketch out as well a discourse that was commonplace at the advent of contemporary schooling.

> *The child does not yet understand enough, cannot yet read our feelings clearly enough to perceive that we are compelled to administer the pain of punishment only because we want what is best for him, only because of our good will.* (From A. Matthais, 1902, as cited in Miller, 1989, p. 38)

But, as school and university teachers, it sketches out something nearer than this. The desire for control, prediction, and manipulation inherent in basics-as-breakdown are full of similar motives, and the image of the wild and wilful child is no stranger here. Neither is the image of women as equally willful and wild and therefore the horrifying potential implications of basics-as-breakdown for (especially elementary) education.

Interpretively understood, every text can be read as an answer to a question that could have been answered differently. To "understand" a text—a child's statement or question, a curriculum mandate, a taken-for-granted image of "the child" or "the teacher"—is to understand how it is not *necessary* to the way things are but always only an eventuality that could have turned out differently. Inheritances are thus full of *possibilities* the furtherance of which must, of necessity, be somehow decided upon, whether by thoughtfulness, acceptance, reflection, default, inclusion, exclusion, prejudice, transformation, cooperation, coercion, or otherwise.

Pedagogy correctly points out that even a baby in diapers has a will of his own and is to be treated accordingly. (From *The Encyclopedia of Pedagogy*, 1851, as cited in Miller, 1989, p. 42)

Interpretively understood, inheritances don't remain true—recall, remain an "opening"—forever. Our knowledge is not immortal and our insight is not omniscient and we do not have in our control all of the circumstances that the future will bring, circumstances that will make what we heretofore took to be "given" seem simply unseemly to still hand down:

> . . . we are always educating for a world that is or is becoming out of joint, for this is the basic human situation, in which the world is created by mortal hands to serve mortals for a limited time as home. Because the world is made by mortals it wears out; and because it continuously changes its inhabitants it runs the risk of becoming as mortal as they. To preserve the world against the mortality of its creators and inhabitants it must be constantly set right anew. The problem is simply to educate in such a way that a setting-right remains actually possible, even though it can, of course, never be assured. Our hope always hangs on the new which every generation brings; but precisely because we can base our hope only on this, we destroy everything if we so try to control the new that we, the old, can dictate how it will look. Exactly for the sake of what is new and revolutionary in every child, education must be conservative; it must preserve this newness and introduce it as a new thing into an old world. . . . (Arendt, 1969, pp. 192–193)

Some tales we tell each other are no longer telling, or have become telling of things we no longer can tolerate. Sometimes the furtherance required of interpretive work involves saying "no more." But even in these cases, the interpretive task remains of showing how worn-out bloodlines remain at work in our world, even if we no longer might explicitly subscribe to them.

In this next chapter (and in chap. 10 as well) is a great confluence of difficult news. Part of it has to do with old images of women and children and wild(er)ness. Part of it has to do with the angers often experienced by whose who desire to be able to reduce human life to those overarching patterns (those—excuse the etymological mess—patri/arches) that can be controlled, predicted, and manipulated. And, as Miller (1989) has so frighteningly pointed out, we attempt to control the wild "for their own good" for we believe, under this deeply buried version of basics-as-breakdown, that their wildness is a problem to be fixed (recall Manuel, e.g., in chap. 2, where the "wild" of Coyote comes forward). If we believe that the basics of the world of teaching are those things that can be properly controlled, predicted, and manipulated, "the wild" becomes only that which has violated, transgressed, or not obeyed the orders we have given. The wild (and we must add here "the immature," "the uncivilized," "the underdeveloped" [see chap. 8]) are the disobedient: the ones who "just wouldn't listen" (*ab audire*, to heed, to mind, to listen) and therefore we *must* "teach them a lesson they'll never forget."

At the roots of basics-as-breakdown is the necessity, not only of management but of violence. Once living, sustaining, in-their-own-way disciplined relations are severed, the resulting fragments must be re-ordered under the rule of law. And, as the vigilance of the monitoring and management increases, the restlessness of those so "ordered" increases, unwittingly caused by the very act meant to fix things. If we recall Trungpa's "restless cow" (see Preamble 7), such increases in restlessness are then blamed on those who refuse to "mind."

In some of our other work (Abram & Jardine, 2000; Jardine, 2000; Jardine, Clifford, & Friesen, 1999), we have explored the tremendous *ecological* bloodlines at work here—the fear of the wild and the desire to control it, a parallel fear of the liveliness and lividness of children, the fearsome insight of ecology that the earth may have a life beyond our control, monitoring and ordering and desire, the old ecological tales of the Earth's blood relations and the place women have had in these ways.

Here, in this chapter, some familiar figures show up: Eve, Pandora, and Lilith. What shows up, too, is a great lament for the wilful child and the women who, having denied their own wilfulness, are commissioned to break the wills—the wildness—of the children they teach.

Re-read the passages from Alice Miller and think about how that Grade 2 girl's question was treated by some of our colleagues: "She was just trying to get your attention." "She was just trying to get out of doing her work." "You should have ignored her or re-directed her back to her own work." And, in the invoking of The Sirens that drew great heroes from the straight and narrow (see chap. 12), "You let her suck you in."

And imagine, along with that, that the worksheet she had in front of her was designed, "beyond our wanting and doing" (Gadamer, 1989, p. xxviii)—after all, we didn't *intend* this—to break her will.

> *As far as willfulness is concerned, this expresses itself as a natural recourse in tenderest childhood. If willfulness and wickedness are not driven out, it is impossible to give a child a good education. It is impossible to reason with young children. Therefore there is no other recourse than to show children one is serious. If parents and teachers are fortunate enough to drive out willfulness from the very beginning by means of scolding and the rod, they will have obedient, docile and good children. If their wills can be broken at this time, they will never remember afterwards that they had a will.* (J. Sulzer, 1748, as cited in Miller, 1989, pp. 11–13)

Interpretively speaking, "all the children are wild" (LeGuin, 1989, p. 47) and this is not bad news, even though it might be difficult to face. If treated out from under the basics-as-breakdown, it is a glimpse of the generative energy that necessarily surrounds living disciplines and the difficult task of listening for the truth (the openings) in the heralds our children bring to the world. To use Arendt's phrase, with such energetic arrivals, generously heeded, things can be "set right anew." Without such arrivals, things become leaden, more calcified, more angry and more paranoid.

This is why, in other contexts, we have suggested that interpretive work, the work of opening up how these ideas have been handed to us, where they have come from, where they belong, and what strings are attached, can sometimes be a form of *healing*:

> [These] wounds need to be expanded into air, lifted up on ideas our ancestors knew, so that the wound ascends through the roof of our parents' house, and we suddenly see how our wound (seemingly so private) *fits.* (Bly, n.d., p. 11)

One more thread before we proceed.

As was mentioned in chapters 3 and 8, there is a fascinating linkage between an interpretive treatment of the basics and a recovery of what could be called the "body" of knowledge (Abram & Jardine, 2000). The energies that children bring to school are deeply embodied, and if we treat the basics as constituted by breakdown, education becomes something that only occurs "from the neck up." Therefore, through breakdown, the body itself becomes a problem to be fixed. The body becomes, as Jim Paul, one of our colleagues, has put it, simply the thing that carries your head to school. We'll end this Preamble, then, with two more passages about body-knowledge from Alice Miller (1989, pp. 46–47):

> *And yet, a boy should know how the female body is fashioned, and a girl should know how the male body is fashioned: otherwise, their curiosity will know no bounds [curiosity, like wilfulness, is a "body function."] All these worries disappear if one makes use of a . . . corpse. The image imprinted on his soul will not have the seductive attractiveness of images freely engendered by the imagination.*
>
> *I would suggest that children be cleansed from head to toe, every two to four weeks by an old, dirty, and ugly woman. This task should be depicted to the children as disgusting.*

Chapter 9

The Transgressive Energy of Mythic Wives and Wilful Children: Old Stories for New Times

Patricia Clifford
Sharon Friesen

The Wilful Child

Once upon a time there was a child who was wilful, and would not do what her mother wished. For this reason God had no pleasure in her, and let her become ill, and no doctor could do her any good, and in a short time she lay on her deathbed. When she had been lowered into her grave, and the earth was spread over her, all at once her arm came out again, and stretched upwards, and when they had put it in and spread fresh earth over it, it was all to no purpose, for the arm always came out again. Then the mother herself was obliged to go to the grave, and strike the arm down with a rod, and when she had done that, it was drawn in, and then at last the child had rest beneath the ground.

This is an old and terrible fairy story, that, if interpreted literally, should never be told (Evetts-Secker, 1994). As a cautionary tale warning children about the perils of disobedience, it is a brutal and terrifying narrative that is best left hidden within the pages of ancient books. Read symbolically in other ways, however, the tale invites us, as teachers, to think about much that is wrong with schools today—and to consider the potential within each of us to offer, through wilful transgressions, genuine hope for change.

Speaking as women, we are immediately on shaky ground when we mention transgression. Our mythic fore mothers Lilith, Eve, and Pandora tried transgression already. Read as cautionary tales, *their* stories have come to us through the ages as warnings: Don't presume equality; Don't pursue knowledge; Don't disobey the master or displease God. Women who do not do as

163

they are told, we have been instructed, are the source of all evil in the universe. And their stories, told from generation to generation, re-inflict the primal punishment of the initial sin upon each one of us, generation after generation. What we propose today is a new reading of those ancient tales of wilful women. Read literally, their cautionary purpose is oppressive, and read only literally, they deserve the same fate earned by so many forgotten, grisly Victorian stories. Opened to new readings of possibility woven within their folds, however, such stories (while still uncomfortable to contemplate) become disturbing in a completely different way. The energy of their single acts of rebellion transformed utterly the worlds in which these women lived, making those worlds, and not just the women's acts, readable in new and exciting ways.

ECCENTRIC CHILDREN AND TEACHERS

Let us situate that awful story about the wilful child in North American classrooms. Sent to school as very young children, both boys and girls learn very early that the Procrustean standards of "normalcy," "being good," and "doing school" create a very narrow band of acceptable thought, speech, and action. Children are forced to learn very quickly how to discipline their bodies, how to color between the lines, how to print neatly, how to please their teachers by doing "their work" in a neat, orderly, and timely fashion. Those who will not, or cannot comply with what schools and teachers demand are rapidly and effectively marginalized under the claim that early intervention is in the best interest of the child. They are scrutinized for symptoms of learning disabilities, behavioral disorders, developmental delays, experience deficits. The institution of the school, geared up and waiting for the first signs of abnormality, like not being able to read by Christmas of Grade 1, not talking properly in the first month of kindergarten, or not forming letters correctly right from the start, begins its work of culling the abnormal into "learning resource rooms" and burying their difference under a dead weight of pathology.

Children learn early on in school that they have to "be good" in order to survive. School robs far too many of them of the ability to feel, touch, and embrace the world with energy, imagination, and ferocious appetite. Instead, school reduces children's experience to a round of activities, exercises, and programs that exist nowhere except in school. Being good in school means being quiet, obedient, orderly, passive. It means staying "on task" no matter how dull, meaningless, or demeaning the task may be. Despite the rhetoric of education that claims an interest in the development of creativity, critical thinking, and independent judgment, the daily experience of far too many children is that the genuine exercise of these faculties generally lands them in hot water.

It may well be that getting "good at school," especially for girls, is potentially toxic. When the obedience training takes, children in school are often indistinguishable from one another. They do the same worksheets in the same way in the same time frame as everyone else. They modulate their voices, discipline their bodies, perform their tasks carefully within the cramped boundary of "normal" that admits of very little deviance. It is as if, ushering students into a banquet hall of potential learning, educators hand them workbook and activity sheet menus and say, "Here, eat this instead" (Kay, 1995). As an ironic aside, in a technological age, Internet surfers plunge headlong into the same dilemma. Told that the age of communication is upon us, that the Internet opens up the world of information at the click of a mouse, the intrepid adventurer on the Web is fed screen after screen after screen, not of text, not of real *stuff*, but of factoids and tables of contents. Devouring the hype that has grown up around electronic communication, people are in danger of starving on the *promise* of substance that so seldom actually materializes.

Unresisted, the story of the wilful child is a terrible one. Read as a metaphor of educational confinement, it begins to make a different kind of sense—particularly when we examine the mytho-poetic portrayal of the mother as the ultimate agent of subjugation and conformity. It is pedagogically worrisome that so much of children's experience in school is reduced to rote, meaningless activity. It is politically untenable to us that teachers, in the name of nurturing and caring, are cast into the role of mother. Primary teaching is almost universally regarded as the mastery of mothering: of zippers and caring and wiping noses and drying little tears. Rarely does someone champion the intellectual, spiritual, and physical rigor that the job, thought of differently, demands. Early childhood teachers thus appear as institutional mothers—with all the attendant problems that accompany society's view of that calling.

Read within the context of "The Wilful Child," institutional mothering takes on a horrifying dimension that goes far beyond hugs and warmth and cookies at snack time. It is we, the mothers, who are called upon to smack little, resistant arms back into the grave. We, the mothers, are the vigilant ones, calling in psychologists, resource teachers, social workers, specialists of all stripes and hues the minute things go awry. It is we who pronounce judgment, who feed back to parents the first public assessment of their child: "is learning to cooperate"; "shares nicely at the Home Center"; "is starting to take her turn properly"; "is beginning to sit still during group time"; "is learning to direct his energy in a more positive way." These assessments are often written in the careful code of "learning to," "beginning to," "starting to," recognizable in an instant to other teachers as a sign of struggle and trouble within the classroom; struggle and trouble that is often disguised from parents until it rears itself as irremediable, calling for a signature for special placement in a special class. Early childhood teachers are carefully trained both to spot and remediate troublesome abnormalities in a child's adjustment to school—and also how to cocoon those judgments in soft, modulated phrases that sound so *positive*, so attentive to the child's self-esteem and development.

However softened and euphemized, however, the blows to the eccentricities of the wilful child are sure and swift. The relentless, institutional job of normalizing falls to the mother-teacher whose professional competence is judged largely on the success of these efforts. Eccentric herself, refusing to normalize or subjugate little children in cheerfully repressive ways; refusing to hand out 30 pairs of scissors and 30 bottles of glue so that 60 little hands can glue identical woolly beards on 30 identical paper Santas by snack time, such a teacher can run into huge problems (Jardine, Graham, & LaGrange, 2000). For the institution has then to normalize *her*; bring *her* into line; cool her down; call in the professionals to adjudicate her failures of practice, her failures to conform; document her institutional failings and her peculiarity; transfer her out.

What the institution has done to wilful, eccentric children it must do first to its wilful, eccentric teachers. What we are taught to revile in children's inability to be institutionally normal we first learn to revile in ourselves. What we strive to modulate, dampen, tame, and obliterate in children's energy, we first modulate, dampen, tame, and obliterate in ourselves. And in that sense, our very success becomes our spiritual, emotional, and intellectual undoing. It is the story of Lilith and the story of Eve, the story of Pandora. To win at the game of "ordinary," of subservience, obedience, and silence is to lose the very best of ourselves—to lose passion, conviction, bloody-mindedness, curiosity, humor, intensity, and joy. It is, as the old tales tell us, to become the spawn of demons and the mother of evil.

For the two of us, the story of the wilful child is partly a story of horror and repression—a story we lived in painful ways in the years we taught young children in eccentric and unusual ways. But it is more than that. It is also a story that contains the seeds of resistance, a story that points to the courageous possibility that any one of us—even the smallest and most nameless—can stick our arms out of the institutional grave over and over again, steeling our minds and bodies against the blows that inevitably follow yet another deliberate transgression. There are always ways to resist. We believe that one of the ways we can learn to resist is to read again, and differently, the stories of Lilith, Eve, and Pandora—our foremothers in crime.

THE WILFUL WIVES OF ADAM

In rabbinic literature, Lilith is sometimes depicted as the mother of Adam's demonic offspring following his separation from Eve and sometimes as his first wife, a wilful woman who assumed her equality with him, who "stood her ground, amazed/By the idea of differences" (Fainlight, 1991). Undaunted like the traditional Eve whose eyes were downcast in the presence of her difference from Adam, Lilith had the audacity to presume, on her own behalf, that it meant something to be formed in the reflection of God.

As it turns out, Adam had some thoughts on the matter as well. To know the will of God did not mean, for him, taking joy in the dappled multiplicity of life; it did not mean celebrating difference and reveling in chaotic wonder and possibility. For Adam, to know God and to act in accordance with the will of God meant assuming the right of domination over a creature "as constrained and resentful/As he was" (Fainlight, 1991). And God encouraged him to think this way, this version of story goes. God *gave* him Eve to rule: a subservient woman whose existence on the planet became, in this story, a source of nagging irritation—a right royal pain in the ass.

And as for Lilith—her fate was to be cast out in disgrace. Her "disgrace thus defined/Good and evil" (Fainlight, 1991) for all time, and she, herself, was condemned to roam, hungry, enraged, and dangerous, on the margins of others' lives. Warnings were issued, signs posted, amulets crafted: Beware this wilful, angry woman. She will ruin your children, destroy the good order of your constrained and resentful lives.

So what is to be made of this mythic oddity—this woman whose story is hardly known? What is to be made of our first mother, enchanted by difference and charmed by the power of inhabiting the spaces that difference opens? What is to be made of the Lilith by those whose simple, primal sin is delight? Well, we're not quite sure—for we, ourselves, have only recently stumbled on Lilith's story. We have learned that there was a cult of Lilith that existed until the 7th century A.D., and we puzzle over the way her story, her presumption of equality, and her courage to stand ground have disappeared from the world. We grew up knowing about Eve and how *she* screwed up. We cut our mythic teeth on Pandora and her ditzy inability to follow even the simplest command, "Don't open the box, dummy." But Lilith was a stranger, and we have only begun to explore the contours of her expectations and her courage.

So what we offer here is just a beginning, just a feathery teasing out of some of the connections we sense between Lilith and the story of the wilful child with which we began. As teachers, the two of us are enchanted by the differences we see in children. We are intrigued by the pedagogical possibilities of creating spaces in which children will take up ideas, projects, issues, and enthusiasms in ways we could never have imagined. We are committed to finding ways to organize our classroom so that the unexpected is the most welcome guest of all. We teach and write out of a conviction that the concept of childhood as it is currently constructed in both traditional and progressive theorizing and practice is repressive, driven by images of deficit and insufficiency that render much of the experience and the possibility of children institutionally invisible. We work the space of difference. And we stand our ground over and over again in the face of power politics that demand that we constrain, restrain, confine, and pathologize difference.

Maxine Greene (1978) speaks of the malefic generosity of education: the "killing" that is done "for the child's own good." For too long, teachers have been like Adam, knowing the power of God through our own power to subdue creatures given to us to control. And for too long, we have been like Eve, "eyes downcast," embarrassed by the generative power of our difference, waiting to be shown and told what to do next.

But Lilith was right, and her delight and simple insistence on the generative power of difference inspires us and give us hope. Not that her story guarantees that life lived as Lilith will be safe or easy. It is not. Lilith teachers, thrusting unwelcome arms out of graves of conformity over and over and over again, find themselves often "on the outs" with the institution. Superiors may well try to beat them back into submission; colleagues may well fashion amulets to ward off the power of their presence. We know from hard experience that the Lilith in us is often enraged, ravenous, and dangerous. We speak out, demand change, stir the pot, and keep on keeping on—calling from the margins when we must, but refusing, ever, to abandon the center. For the power of Lilith is simple: It is the power of delight, passion, engagement, enthusiasm, wonder, and tenacity. It is the power of equality, of voice, of standing firm and true in a world in which you claim the symmetry of your own creation. Lilith knows that the reflection of God is incomplete without her—however much Adam conspires with his creator to deny that simple fact. Somehow, and in ways that we have only begun to apprehend, we are inspired by the sheer audacity of her reminding the two of them that she, Lilith, is a force to be reckoned with.

EVE

But what of Eve in all of this? In the version of Eve's story we just told, and in versions that have come to all of us through the generations, Eve is a pathetic creature. Unable to resist the obvious temptation of Satan, Eve turns her back on God and implicates Adam—history's first unindicted co-conspirator—in a horrendous fall from grace that has condemned all human beings to suffering. Women are told the cautionary story of Eve in a particular, careful way: Look what happens to you if you can discipline neither desire nor thought. And look what happens to you and all your children when you displease God. Disobedience, the primal sin, is the sin of woman.

Is it possible to understand Eve differently, to see something else in her simple act of transgression? We think so—and, once again, we find ourselves energized by new understandings of Eve's deal with the devil. What happens, we wonder, when women claim that first bite as a deliberate, mindful act of rebellion? What happens when we understand that Eve, ushered into the presence of knowledge—the banquet hall of learning—refuses to remain content to nibble politely at the corner of the menu and insists, instead, in taking a huge bite of the real thing? And what happens when Eve dares Adam to cut loose, too?

We think that such a reading changes everything. Adam cast Lilith aside for insisting on her own equality and difference. He married again, hoping the second time to find a creature who would not only start out, but who would also remain, with downcast eyes, obedient, maybe even playful in her ignorance and helplessness. Adam expected, in his second wife, a meek and compliant girl—one who knew and would stay within the confines of her place. He certainly did not expect a full-grown woman who would insist on knowing *everything*, and who would willingly share her desire to know with him.

What happens when we understand, as teachers, that in the Garden of Eden the compliant never eat? (Evetts-Secker, 1994).

Here is what happens, we think. First of all, as women and as teachers we are released from the mythic shackles that a repressive reading of the story of Eve impose. We come to understand the power of seeing, in Eve's transgression, a strong and deliberate choice. Life does not have to come to us as given, as inevitable, as predestined. Choices are possible. Simple, deliberate choices that change everything in an instant. For teachers sickened by the marginalization and pathologizing of children who do not or cannot conform, choices to live differently *are* within our grasp. Listening to voices other than the ones that control access to the garden, we *can* find new ways of seeing, new ways of being. However strong the institutional pulls to make us into malefic mothers, we can find within ourselves the courage and the means to resist.

And our resistance is crucial. First of all, it makes meaningful action possible for those of us who, like Eve, cannot accept the status quo. However comfortable it might be to inhabit orderly, idyllic classrooms in which we do things the way everyone else does them; in which we make no waves or ask no rude questions; in which all the lovely pictures line up nicely on all the lovely walls and all the lovely children line up nicely in all the polished hallways, we can resist. We can say no. We can also say Yes! Yes, there are other ways to think about our work. Yes, there are more generous ways of understanding why some children do not fit in easily. Yes, we can learn about ourselves and about our profession by attending carefully, thoughtfully, imaginatively to the lessons offered by children who do not color between the lines. Eve shows us how we can free ourselves. As we thrust our hands out of the graves of conformity, there is something out there beside the rod that would strike us down. There is also the fruit of knowledge. The knowledge of what the next right step into the unknown might be. The knowledge of pedagogical possibility. The knowledge of what is morally right to do for ourselves and for others.

For Eve did not act alone, however much partaking of the apple was *her* act, claimed by her. As the story goes, Eve took Adam and the rest of us down with her. She, herself, was conned by the serpent and she turned around and seduced Adam to follow her, against his better judgment. That, as we say, is one way the story goes. But that is not the only possible reading of Eve's transgression. Consider this possibility. In her defiance, Eve did not condemn anybody. Even though she and her daughters had to pay dearly for the freedom she bought, we think she rescued Adam and all of her children from the lives of conformity and order to which Adam might otherwise have condemned us all (Evetts-Secker, 1994). What she took upon herself in both act and consequence she offered to others. "Follow me," she said. "I cannot promise that I will make your life easier, but I can certainly promise that it will be adventurous, dangerous, thrilling, and wild. Your life is in your hands."

Before Eve, there was no choice in any meaningful sense of the word. She and Adam could play with anything else in the Garden—anything except the one thing that really mattered. Like children, they could color predrawn pictures, paste beards on fabricated Santas, chant the words to songs already measured out by someone else. They would have remained such children—sexless, docile, obedient, normal, never overstepping bounds laid out it advance; never shoving or pushing or calling out in big voices; never laughing too loud or too long; never questioning or wondering or imagining how the world might be otherwise than they found it.

In the Garden, as we say, the compliant never eat. Eve broke that anorexic chain, not only for herself but also for the generations of unknown children who followed her. Without Eve, the Garden would have remained a prison. Comfortable, yes. Pleasant, yes. Available to us all without toil or effort, certainly. But a prison, nonetheless. The Garden of Eden was like a perpetual kindergarten in which humankind could play and play all day long. Had we remained in Paradise we might have suffered the same fate as Peter Pan: We would never have had to grow up. Eve would have remained, perhaps, our perpetual Wendy-mother: sweet, warm, kind, and nurturing. A good, Wendy kindergarten teacher. And the rest of us would have been her cheery, Lost Boys.

Instead, Eve's transgression allowed all of us to grow up. And in consequence, we have had to pay for that growth, generation after generation. So—is that the worst that could have happened to us, we wonder? However painful the consequences, Eve opened up possibilities. She teaches us that we can create both ourselves and the world quite differently. And she shows us what real power means. Born into a universe of givens, Eve found the one true act that would crack everything open and allow us to conceive and generate anything we could imagine.

PANDORA'S TRICKS

In traditional readings of the stories of Eve and Pandora, all evil and suffering in the world derive from these two impulsive women. God, the story goes, gave us Paradise for our use, and we lost it. Prometheus, the kind benefactor, parceled up all the spites that might plague humankind into one jar to keep us safe. Pandora lifted the lid and turned it all loose in the world. Tempted beyond their strength to endure, we are told, these beautiful, mischievous, foolish, and idle women condemned our race to the vicissitudes of old age, disease, pain, labor, war, insanity, vice, and (Hesiod tells us) passion.

That is how our mothers come to us: as evil, foolish wantons who robbed us all of immortality. How not, then, to feel only scorn and anger for their daughters through whom successive generations of pestilence are born into the world? Why not, indeed, beat the arm of the wilful, disobedient daughter into the ground before she causes even more damage and destruction?

As we said when we began, if that is the way these stories continue to be told, we wish that they would simply disappear from the landscape. They are hopeless stories that justify the scorn and violence wrecked upon women generation after generation. They justify a blueprint for pedagogical repression and conformity that kills the spirit of eccentric children and teachers in the name of comfort, stability, and order. They are vengeful and nasty, and we would wish such stories dead.

Read differently, however, the stories of Eve and Pandora offer exciting hope. They offer a chance both to heal old and horrid wounds and also the opportunity to look forward to new ways of thinking about what so many lament as the problems of educational practice: the learning disabled, the poor, the unruly, the severely gifted—all those eccentric children whose arms and legs stick out from the confines of the Procrustean bed of schooling. All those whose difference we pathologize and then attempt to "normalize" in the name of learning.

We see in the transgressions of Eve and Pandora a wonderful audacity that charms and energizes us. Led by their boldness, we propose to open up what Greene (1988) called "places for speculative audacity" that draw the mind to what lies beyond the accustomed boundaries and often to what is not yet. They do so as persons become more and more aware of the unanswered questions, the unexplored corners, the nameless faces behind the forgotten windows. These are the obstacles to be transcended if understanding is to be gained. And it is in the transcending, as we have seen, that freedom is often achieved. (p. 128)

Understood as audacious rather than foolish, Pandora has lessons to teach. In what, one might well ask, does this audaciousness consist? How is it possible to see Pandora (or Eve) as the people who secured our freedom?

Consider this. Pandora, conceived in Zeus' spiteful imagination as revenge for Prometheus' theft of fire, is intimately tied first and foremost to issues of knowledge. Zeus cared about the theft of fire because it was the theft, for humankind, of the most god-like power of all: knowledge. Having had the best of him stolen away, Zeus musters the other, lesser attributes of the immortals. "Give this creature your greatest glories," he orders the lesser gods. And so Pandora is given it all: beauty, music, everything. And from Hermes, she got a most curious and interesting gift. Hermes, the tricky messenger of the gods and inspiration of hermeneutics, gave Pandora voice: the power to speak her mind and heart. History is silent about Athena's gift to Pandora. But if each of the gods gave the gift most closely associated to them, then, we wonder, did Athena give Pandora a mind? If she did, whatever would be the use of giving someone a faculty if they could never exercise it?

In our schools do we perform the Zeus trick, the god trick (Haraway, as cited in Bogden, 1992, p. 218)? Do teachers do to children what the gods did to Pandora? Do children with bright active minds enter the institution only to find themselves, given both voice and mind, forbidden to use either? When asked to name the sides of various geometric figures, children are encouraged to chant: "Triangles have three sides, squares have four sides" and so on. When asked, "How many sides does a circle have" children who answer "millions and millions" are too often silenced. "Wrong," their zealous if uninformed teachers respond. "We all know that a circle has only one side, don't we?"

Whether we are stomping the life out of children with authoritarian rigidity or smothering it in gooey praise, we chill the life from the spirit and kill the soul of all but the most bloody minded.

Schools co-opt terms like critical thinking, creative thinking, and independence without offering many genuine opportunities for students to exercise any of those faculties. It is the promise of the banquet and the reality of the menu. It is pedagogical bad faith. It is the god trick. After often it works.

Given faculties of judgment, Pandora exercised them. Opening the jar was a mindful deliberate act of rebellion. Told to ask no questions, seek no answers, behave herself, be a good girl, color softly within the bold lines that others had photocopied for her, Pandora refused. She knew where the action was. It was shut inside that jar and she would not be denied. Life as she was living it was deadly boring. What did she have to look forward to: doing her nails, playing with Epimetheus, combing her hair, looking pretty for that foolish young man who could not see beyond the end of his own nose? What good is a mind if you can never use it? This is the question that the Pandora story insists we ask.

But what of the suffering? What can be made of the fact that Pandora's choice cost so much? Part of the answer lies in Prometheus' attempt to cushion human beings from the fullness of life. However how well motivated Prometheus' attempts to bottle up all suffering, pain, and sorrow, he was wrong. For life to fashion itself, it needs everything: gladness, joy, beauty, pain, suffering, war, and sorrow.

Prometheus attempted to fashion his gift to humankind from all the beauty of the world: the clouds as round as pearls, light shimmering across an expanse of water, dewdrops on grass blades (Gregory, 1992). Having given knowledge with one hand, he tried to deny it with the other. Knowing what he himself would suffer for his transgression, he tried to protect humankind from the same fate. Prometheus was a kind and generous benefactor. He did what he could to protect us—but especially Prometheus would have known that the fabric would not hold. Prometheus if no other would have known with clear and absolute certainty that Pandora would open the jar. The hope that is there is the hope of our transgression and the courage to live out the consequences.

If teachers erect boundaries around learning that are rigid and unyielding they attempt another god trick. If we curtail children's curiosity, questions, and freedom of inquiry in the authoritarian belief that such freedom will lead to disaster, we are like Zeus jealous and stingy with our knowledge. Or if we wrap knowledge up in soft cocoons in the mistaken belief that children cannot handle big questions, abstract thought, passionate engagement, we are like Prometheus.

Either way, it makes little genuine difference. Both god tricks deny the power of children's minds and the power of their difference. Whether the motive is punitive or protective, freedom is denied. Genuine engagement with the world becomes impossible.

The pedagogical act that addresses the god trick is the transgression of Pandora. It is the act that creates spaces in which freedom, imagination, creativity, and possibility are created. It is our hope. Again we quote from Maxine Greene (1988). Transgressive acts, like art,

> have the capacity, when authentically attended to, to enable persons to hear and to see what they would not ordinarily hear and see, to offer visions of con-

sonance and dissonance that are unfamiliar and indeed abnormal, to disclose the incomplete profiles of the world. As importantly, in this context, they have the power to defamiliarize experience: to begin with the overly familiar and transfigure it into something different enough to make those who are awakened hear and see. (p. 129)

Should we be surprised that this is so? Not when we consider that Pandora, whose name means "all giving," was delivered to the world by Hermes. And therein lies another story.

Preamble 10

In a hermeneutic conception of understanding, identity and difference are not the alternatives. In dialogue with another person, I do not become identical to my interlocutor, but neither can I remain simply different. In dialogue, mutual understanding is sought, but it is sought in such a way that our real differences are preserved while, at the same time, kinships, resemblances, or analogies of understanding emerge. In the area of education, this phenomenon of analogical interrelatedness is especially important. We find ourselves constantly in the presence of those who think differently than we do and, at the same time, finding these others as persons whom we wish to engage, to understand, to educate, to learn from them, not just about them. As teachers, we find that "the full meaning of a child . . . resides in the paradox of being part of us but also apart from us" (Smith, 1988, p. 176). We find ourselves in kinship with children, belonging together with children, while neither being quite the same or simply different. We find, as teachers, that we must live in the dialogue between same and different in which mutual understanding is sought. Effective teachers cannot begin with a refusal: namely, a retreat into their own constructions and the limits of their own strategic action. In the pedagogical act, then, children cannot become the passive object of mastery and control, but neither is this act simply handed over to children as an inglorious compromise with their difference. The analogical character of dialogue lives in a tension between same and different, and understanding is not produced by dispelling this tension, but by sustaining ourselves in it. We find, in such an orientation, that "genuine life together is made possible only in the context of an ongoing conversation which is never over yet which also must be sustained for life together to go on at all" (Smith, 1988, p. 174). The other voice thereby becomes a moment in my own understanding and self-understanding. It is only in being open to another voice that I can hear my own voice as authentically my own (Jardine, 2000).

The commonplace educational adage "Lifelong Learning" can mean several things, depending on how the basic matters of education are treated. Understood under the auspices of basics-as-breakdown, this adage can become very weak and debilitating. It can mean that the teacher "learns along with the children" in the sense of learning what the children are learning. And this can mean that (especially the work of elementary) school teachers can easily become infantilized. As addressed in chapter 9, educators cannot do to our children what they have not already done to themselves. When their work becomes thin and weak and fragmented and unworthy of "a continuity of attention and devotion" (Berry, 1987, p. 33), learning along with the children becomes the same. There is an even worse potential consequence here, that the child becomes an empowered learner and the teacher becomes only a facilitator who themselves never grow up (see chap. 9 and Preamble 11).

Under the auspices of basics-as-breakdown, imagine how Lifelong Learning sounds to a student:

- Just learn what the teacher tells you to learn.
- Remember only the stuff you need to for the tests.
- Treat your questions as pathological problems that *you* have, submit (and it better be gladly) to regimes of monitoring and management about which you have no say.
- Realize that your contributions are irrelevant except insofar as they allow others to more easily control, predict, and assess the knowledge you have accumulated and can now properly dispense.
- *It is going to be like this for the rest of your life.*

Of course, no one ever intended for Lifelong Learning to mean this, but, as we have seen, interpretive work is not necessarily or even primarily about the *mens auctoris*, the "author's meaning," as if good intentions alone can save us from thinking through and deciding anew what is at work in the logics we are living out in schools.

So, what would Lifelong Learning entail if we treated the basics interpretively? It cannot mean that we are only identical to our students, ready for and in need of precisely the same learning that they are undergoing, as if, over the course of our careers, we have taught but never learned our way around. And it does not mean the opposite of this either, that we already know everything we need to know *without* our students, such that they become simply a problem of how to downloading what we already know:

> The truth of [an interpretive treatment of] experience always implies an orientation to new experience. "Being experienced" does not consist in the fact that someone already knows everything and knows better than anyone else. Rather, the experienced person proves to be, on the contrary, someone who . . . because of the many experiences he has had and the knowledge he has drawn from them, is particularly well-equipped to have new experiences and to learn from them. Experience has its proper fulfillment not in definitive knowledge but in the openness to experience that is made possible by experience itself. (Gadamer, 1989, p. 355)

Lifelong Learning, interpretively understood, means having become experienced and, as a consequence having become better able to engage the truth (opening, eventfulness) of what our students bring to the topographies we mutually explore. Unlike the image of the cynical, know-it-all "expert," "being experienced" means becoming more sensitive to the subtle differences and openings and opportunities that new experiences can bring.

The following chapter describes the experience of reading and rereading a novel with a group of 55 troublesome eighth-grade students. But it describes more than that. It also shows how the teachers involved came to face *their own* learning in the face of this work, learning that was neither simply different or simply identical to the tasks their students face. But, more than this, the understandings that students brought to the tasks at hand transformed what the teachers understood *their own* tasks to be. As is the case in an interpretive understanding of a true conversation, we do not listen to what others have to say in order to understand *their* understandings better. We listen to what others have to say in such a way that we can understand *our own* understandings differently than we could have understood them alone.

In the following chapter, weaving, waiting, and loss became visible, not only as generous and alluring themes in the book being read. They became, as well, visible features of the students' experiences of reading and, most tellingly, features of the very task of teaching itself. Mark's experiences in *I Heard the Owl Call My Name* (Craven, 1973) became great analogues in which students and teacher alike came to share, each in their own ways. These teachers, having entered a school community unaccustomed to treating students' experiences seriously, found a situation where the students themselves had learned this lesson well, not unlike Mark's experience in the wilds of Kingcome, up the coast of British Columbia. Thus, as part of the experience of reading this novel with this group of children in "one of *those* schools" (as a local school administrator called it) the teachers had to learn their own lessons of waiting, weaving, and loss. Such lived mutuality makes Lifelong Learning sound less trite, like less of a platitude, because it means, of necessity, that a certain suffering of experience must continue. Unlike basics-as-breakdown, an interpretive understanding of the basics suggests that there is always a link between what we come to know about ourselves and our world and the development of *character*. Knowledge is never simply an arm's-length possession ripe for exchange (see chap. 12) but is always a mark of what we have, individually or collectively, lived through and what, individually or collectively, we have become because of our ventures.

Because an interpretive understanding of the basics necessarily links the course of experience and the formation of character, it insists that even doing the work of pursuing those forms of knowledge considered "objective" has an effect on who we become through such pursuits and how we carry ourselves in the world and in relation to others. Unlike basics-as-breakdown, which promises control over such matters and is never exactly able to deliver (a failure which simply raises the stakes and eventually the ire of the stakeholders involved), an interpretive understanding of the basics suggests that the more experienced we become in knowing our way around the disciplines we've inherited, the more we realize that our knowledge will *never be enough* to outrun their living character. Lifelong Learning means, therefore, that I am always in the midst of becoming the person I am.

Chapter 10

Landscapes of Loss:
On the Original Difficulty
of Reading and Interpretive Research

Pat Clifford
Sharon Friesen

Fifty copies of our newly purchased novel, *I Heard the Owl Call My Name* (Craven, 1973), sat in a box under the table beside our desk. It was an odd choice for a novel study. The book is nearly 30 years old. Written by a White woman, it is the story of a young priest's journey into a native village in a remote, coastal village of British Columbia. It is about dying: a dying community, a dying way of life, and a central character who has no more than 2 years of active life left. Other than the dying, nothing much actually *happens*. Not exactly the fare that comes to mind for eighth graders in a large, urban, high-needs junior high—but a book that we had nonetheless chosen with care for these students, and whose use in this setting we wanted to make an explicit part of our own action research. We let the books sit under the table for a couple of weeks, watching out of the corners of our eyes as the kids pushed at the edges of the box with their feet.

> "We're not going to read *that* book!" several kids moaned as they walked past.
> "Oh, have you read it before?" we asked, fakely innocent.
> "Well, no, but like, it's *a book*. Why do we have to do *a book?*"

To the students, this unknown text was suspect by the mere fact of its being a book purchased, in bulk, by teachers. Our students seemed quite certain of what they were in for, and just as certain that they would hate it, and detest everything we had planned to do with it. Over coffee, we talked about Pat's years as a senior high school English teacher, and her students' peren-

179

nial frustration with doing what one of them called "that shit" with books: those predictable teacher questions about plot, theme, setting, and character; about how little that shit actually had to do with the real reasons anybody reads, anyway; about the stupefying round of worksheets and teacher questions that seem to mark so many students' experience of reading. We talked, too, about what had happened in Grade 7 when we had asked this same group of students to start Response Journals when we launched into that year's novel study: "Response Journals? No way. We hate Response Journals. Why do teachers always make us do those Response Journal things?" Although our students' complaints were less scatological than those of their senior high school fellows, the grumbling was just as heartfelt, and we were taken by surprise. For our students, reading had become a school task, defined and regulated by school activities. It was what teachers expected, not what you, yourself, would choose to do. And it was so *slow*, they told us. Couldn't we just watch the video instead?

We were on dangerous ground. In opening conversations with them about school reading, which was part of our own research interest, we invoked some powerful old ghosts. It would have been snappier and trendier to have set their minds at ease with a menu of fun activities designed to deflect their attention from the difficulties of intense engagement with the text: "We'll watch the movie, we'll make posters and carve masks and have a potlatch and write song lyrics. Everyone can read a different book and dress up and do television interviews. You'll see, you'll love it."

But that's not at all what we had in mind. What we wanted to do was far more difficult: We wanted to exorcise those ghosts by moving farther into the very territory that students wanted so desperately to abandon. We wanted to take up residence together in a reading landscape whose very topography is formed by the inherent, original difficulty, not only of particular books like this one, but also of the whole business of reading, itself. We *were* all going to read the book. Together. Out loud. Twice. We were going to work with Dennis Sumara's idea of a commonplace text, "the cumulative and collective intertextual relations among readers, other texts, other experiences, and the present context of reading" (Sumara, 1995a, p. 107).

As teacher–researchers, we had already pushed our own understanding of reader response in the direction of what we were now learning to call "focal practices" (Sumara, 1995b) designed to take students beyond the teacher questions, and even beyond the more seemingly generous Response Journal into more hermeneutic, interpretive spaces where knowledge and understanding are created through the vibrant life of a community of relations (Palmer, 1993). We wanted to learn more about helping students understand that through common engagement with *this* book, *here* and in *this* place, we would come to know ourselves and one another differently. We wanted them to understand that reading together matters. We wanted them to see that their response to text was not some kind of mopping-up activity (Richardson, as cited in Sumara, 1996, p. 46) orchestrated by teachers to test whether they had somehow "got" the book. We wanted to show them that genuine understanding is always *self-understanding*, a matter of becoming worked out in relation to particular situations, particular places, in community with others.

As we began our work, that is, we thought mainly about the ways in which this novel and our approach to it would broaden and deepen our students' experience. That was the direction in which we cast our gaze, and in important ways that we are still in the process of trying to understand, we were successful. But that initial attention to the significance of focal practices for students is not the subject of this chapter. What we want to talk about here is what happened, not so much to the students, but to *us* as we came to know that what we wanted our students to understand about reading this book was just as true about our own emerging understanding of teaching and research. We came to learn that our own research and writing were not mopping-up activities added on to the end of a busy day. They were integral parts of the experience of reading *I Heard the Owl Call My Name*. A hermeneutic involvement with this text, these students, and our own situation as their teachers touched the students, certainly. More surprising to us, however, was how it touched the two of us as teachers and as researchers in fundamental ways.

LOST IN A BOOK

Right from the opening pages of the novel, there were rich moments in which many students found themselves, almost beyond their "wanting and doing" (Gadamer, 1989, p. xxvii), drawn into the dilemmas, the images, the world of this novel and of their own experience. But as we proceeded, we felt as well a strong sense of resistance, of unhappiness and complaint: "What a dumb book. When's something going to *happen*? Like, *nothing's happening in this book*. We hate it. We're lost."

Lost. That was it, exactly: In the unfamiliar world of this novel, our students were losing their way, as they so often lost their way at the start of new books. Something in the word *lost* called to us. There was something bountiful in the particular way they pleaded with us to abandon the book and return to familiar ground, something that led us to wonder whether getting lost was less a problem that we needed to solve with this book than an inherent part of the reading experience, itself. And it was this ineffable *something* that led us into unexpected places in our own research. Beginning by focusing on what happens when teachers open up an interpretive space, we had stumbled onto fundamental aspects of the reading experience, itself. While we continued to explore the themes and characters of the novel, we also began to talk with our students about how *reading* feels.

For us, as experienced readers, there was only charm in the phrase "getting lost in a book." We loved that feeling of abandoning the everyday reality of our lives, forgetting "about the doorbell, the shopping that needs to be done, the house that lies in a clutter" (Hood, 1996). We actively sought out what Birkerts calls the reading state, "a gradual immersion . . . in which we hand over our groundedness in the here and now in order to take up our new groundedness in the elsewhere of the book"(Birkerts, 1994, p. 81), a state in which time is foreshortened as if "the whole of my life—past as well as unknown future—were somehow available to me . . . as an object of contemplation" (Birkerts, 1994, p. 84).

But that is not how the kids felt. They seemed more like Hansel and Gretel, terrified in the underbrush, avoiding confrontation with the gingerbread house and the witch by refusing to move. They were like literary agoraphobics, paralyzed by fear as they ventured out beyond the confines of familiar walls of experience Their trepidation fascinated us, but so did their courage. In what at other times we might have heard as a contrary refusal to engage with the text—"We're lost and we hate it"—we began to hear a cry for direction. We took up their complaints as a serious topic. Could it be, we asked them, that as readers we are like Mark, the central character? Would it be helpful to think of ourselves, like Mark, thrust into a place we know nothing about, surrounded by strangers who make demands of us that we barely understand? Are we all like Mark, unable at first even to tell the difference between one villager and another, yet forced by chance to make sense of them, anyway? Is that what reading this book is like? We discussed the only other White person in the village, a teacher "serving time" for 2 years, and hating every minute of it. Was there any difference, we wondered, between Mark's dilemma, which seemed to be to find a way *into* the life of a village he understood so little, and the dilemma of the teacher, which was clearly to *get out* as soon as he could? Might those two characters might tell us something about different kinds of readers?

As experienced readers, we knew and delighted in the necessary sense of loss that accompanies the opening of any new book. We read *for* exactly the kind of experience our students were finding so difficult to endure: the vertiginous sense of alienation and self-loss that permits the boundaries of the familiar to "waver and tremble" (Caputo, 1987, p. 7) as we enter into other worlds. We knew, because we had done it so many times before, that the adventure of reading books in this way always holds, ironically, a promise of self-discovery. Letting go of the hard-edged protocols of the normal, of the taken-for-granted, of the ordinary aspects of everyday life, we had learned, through imaginative engagement as readers, the hermeneutic lesson that the world is interpretable; that things can be other than they seem; and that "when we read we not only transplant ourselves to the place of the text, but we modify our natural angle of regard upon all things; we reposition the self in order to *see* differently" (Birkerts, 1994, p. 80).

As experienced readers, we knew that the other-wise space of imaginative possibility was a space in-between: in between the familiar and the strange; in between self and other; in between the text of the story and the texts of our lives. We knew that one of the addictive delights of reading is its power to invite us, "without expectation into one of those moments that is suspended between time and space and lingers in the mind" (Craven, 1973, p. 58). As teachers, we knew as well that letting go and learning how to live in between can be very scary, indeed, for a change in the natural angle of regard holds always the terrifying, exhilarating possibility that *everything* will be different because we have read.

As teachers, then, we knew that part of our task had to be to help students give themselves over to the world of the text. We did not want to abandon those scary, in-between places by reducing our explorations of the story to the grotesque certainties of worksheet questions that treat the landscape of text as inalterably given: "Is . . . [the author] using metaphors or similes? Define each term. Why did . . . [the author] choose to use metaphors instead of similes, or similes instead of metaphors?" (Postman, 1995, p. 173). Neither did we want to substitute the seemingly open-ended and seemingly more generous version of stock questions that appear in as Reader Response posters and Journal prompts: "I think . . . , I wonder . . . , I feel. . . ." The banality of such questions seemed to us to be an abandonment of another kind: not to the intractability of text-as-given, but to the "chill structures of autonomy" (Greene, 1988, p. 478) that erect "shells of privatism" around the experience of reading, reducing it to a private, interior interaction between the solitary reader and the personally constructed text.

We wanted questions that were more true to that in-between space: questions that required conversation; questions that demanded both a careful attention to the text, an exploration of self, and attentive listening to the voices of others. We wanted our students to begin to see light filtering through trees—both the trees on their own street, and in the park across the way—as well as trees on the page "that take on outline and presence" (Birkerts, 1994, p. 81) as they read. We wanted students to experience the ways in which small details and large events could speak directly and powerfully to them, not as *what* they were, Grade 8 students in our classroom, but as *who* they were: diverse, unique individuals bound together in a web of relationships created through the work that we did with one another. And so, in all our talk and writing about the novel, we asked them to pay attention to "good bits": lines, images, and phrases that called out to them, for whatever reason. In conversation and in our response to their writing, we helped them learn how to explore those good bits, connecting them with feelings and ideas, asking questions, drawing parallels between passages in the novel and issues in the world around them; listening for echoes of other books they had read; arguing with the text and with one another whenever they took issue with the point of view of one of the characters, of one of their fellows, or of the author, herself.

And we let the good bits from one day's conversation propel the next day's work so that their talk made a difference. It worked. We found increasing numbers of our students coming to care about what happened to Mark and the villagers, and more and more of them willing to enjoy the time it was taking to read to the end of the book. We delighted in *their* delight in compelling passages, and we enjoyed our explorations with them.

For many students, the reading space opened up a more reflective, inwardly directed part of themselves. But what we want to pay attention to here is that we found the same thing happening to us. Parts of the book began to open unresolved dilemmas in our own lives that we had not expected to see addressed in a school book. And that opening helped us understand our own action research as a quality not only of teaching, but also of living.

Even as we write that we had not expected to see parts of our own lives as teachers addressed in this novel, we know that is not quite what we mean. In learning, over the years we have taught together, to pay attention to our choice of books, we have learned that the best choices are those that contain, usually without our knowing it, lessons that we, ourselves, need to learn. Again and again, we have found ourselves, with one book or another, stopping dead in our tracks. "Oh my God," we would say, "is *that* what this is all about?" And we would talk and talk about what this new book told us about our lives as teachers. We would read parts of the stories over and over again to one another. And on bad days, long after all the children and all our colleagues had gone home, we would sometimes cry.

Being touched in particular and powerful ways by stories and by students' questions that created connections and touched parts of our lives that they could not know, we had experienced many times before the generosity of those in-between spaces: in-between us and the story, in-between the story and our engagement with our students. And here we were, once again, moving into spaces where we, as teachers, were most strongly addressed (Gadamer 1989, p. 299) by the text. Teaching the novel, we were once again claimed by the work we were doing. Writing about that teaching, the book came alive for us. It spoke directly to us and to our engagement with the classroom, the school, the community in which we had come to live: the hardest school in the city, the poorest community, the most difficult and chaotic of children.

Until we began our work in this junior high, we had always worked in middle-class schools. As we read about the central character, Mark, being sent to Kingcome, to the hardest parish in the diocese to learn what he needed to know in the time that remained to him, we realized that, like Mark, we had come to a difficult place, to one of *those* schools that people often try harder to get out of than to move into.

SO SHORT A TIME TO LEARN SO MUCH . . .

In *I Heard the Owl Call My Name,* characters wait. From the beginning we puzzled over passages like this on page 37: "It was always the same. The sad eyes. The cautious waiting. But for what? How must he prove himself? What was it they wished to know of him? And what did he know of himself . . . ?" From the beginning, we tried to get our students to talk about all this waiting. They were not interested. What puzzled us, made us highlight our own copies, and raised questions for us did not speak at all to them. For them, waiting was not an issue.

But it was for both of us. Here we were, in our difficult parish, teaching the same group of students with whom we had begun the year before. What was there in *our* situation that made waiting such a puzzle? As we talked about the story with the students, with colleagues, and between ourselves, we recalled how we had arrived, committed, eager to make a difference in a school most defined in the public mind by its needs. Two years have gone by, and we are only now able to face squarely the dark side of the missionary-like zeal that had fueled some of our early months in the school: our determination to give the best of what we had to offer, our hopes that we could make a difference with these students, make their lives richer, our good intentions to involve them with us and with each other in compelling work.

And when, by October of the first year we had made almost no headway at all, we were devastated. Going head-to-head with angry, rebellious teenagers who refused to follow our plans for them, we learned the awful power of Mark's observation about the Kwakiutl: Our students had no word for thank you in their language. Even if we left the classroom, broken, they would not thank us for our coming. Teachers come, teachers go, they had learned, and there was no reason to think that we would be any different from any other. We offered story after story, problem after engaging problem, and they refused all of it. They fought with us and with each other, turning whole days upside down with an awful, defiant energy. "Where on earth are we?" we asked ourselves again and again, "and why the hell do we think we belong here?"

In retrospect, we think we were like Mark, wondering what we could possibly do to prove ourselves. It was such a difficult, difficult time. We desperately wanted to break through the hard shell of rebellious indifference that met us day after day. We wanted to re-create what we had had before, a classroom community sustained by work that was rich enough to encompass all. We had no way of knowing then what students have only decided to tell us now, a year and a half later: They had no intention at all of being saved by us or by anybody else. Only after all this time will they talk to us about their previous school experiences. Only now will they tell us their stories, the myths that were the village of their experience. When we breezed into their lives, sitting them at tables, reading stories out loud, coaxing conversations and exploratory writing and problem solving, they were sure it would never last, and neither would we. They knew they could wreck every single thing because they had done it before. In elementary school they had sat at tables for a couple of days once, they now tell us. Their teacher had been so horrified at how they behaved when they were let out of straight rows that he quickly moved all the desks right back again. They had already plotted successfully how to do teachers in. We remembered their boastful warnings from the year before: this teacher had had a heart attack, that one had had a nervous breakdown. "We caused it, you know," and they looked us straight in the eye.

As we sat with the novel and with these students well into our second year together, we read words like these in a way made possible by the trials we had all endured together: ". . . You'll see a look that is in the eyes of all of them, and it will be your job to figure out what it means, and what you are going to do about it. And . . . [they] will watch you—they will all watch you—and in . . . [their] own time . . . [they] will accept or reject you" (Craven, 1973, p. 11).

As we look back to those first difficult months, we see written here the truth of our experience with these students: It was in their hands to accept or reject us. They would do it on their own terms, and we could not know in advance, could not even know in the present moment of any action, any decision, whether we were making ourselves more or less acceptable to them. We dug in our heels in the face of their intractability. We refused to bring in desks and straight rows. We refused to run off worksheets or dictate pages of notes to keep them busy and quiet. We insisted, day after day, of meeting as a full group to talk. We tossed them out of class for fighting, would not let them swear or scream. And we insisted that they do good work, turning back half-hearted and slap-dash attempts and insisting, instead, that they take their time, rewrite, plan. We would sit with first one and then another, revising, talking, taking their reading and writing seriously. Met with fierce adolescent stubbornness, we gave as good as we got most days. It was as we remember it now, an ugly battle of wills, waged without the least assurance that we were even doing the right thing fighting fire with fire and insisting on having our own way in creating a workspace dedicated to thought and genuine exploration.

And yet there was more to it than just stubbornness, for even in the early, difficult days we knew that what we had been told about these kids was somehow very wrong.

> "They're experience deficit," some would say, meaning that the kids knew little of middle-class virtue.
>
> "They haven't got any work ethic," others would insist. "Don't expect any homework out of them. They'll never do it."
>
> "Fully a third of them are functionally illiterate. They need remedial work, basic skills to build a foundation."
>
> "Aw, fuck the curriculum when you work with these guys. They can't learn anything until you civilize them."

Even then, we knew that all of this was wrong, for through all the struggles we also saw glimmers of something different, something breathtaking breaking through in odd moments and small, precious ways. We knew, that is, what Mark himself had learned when he wrote to the Bishop:

> "I have learned little of the Indians as yet. I know only what they are not. They are none of the things one has been led to believe. They are not simple, or emotional, they are not primitive." The Bishop wrote back: "Wait—you will come to know them." (Craven, 1973, pp. 55–56)

Cast so often as problems, our students reminded us about the *true* nature of pedagogical problems. They were on sure and certain ground in their dealings with us. They knew what they wanted to do and how to do it. It was *we* who actually had a problem; we who were uncertain about whether it was possible to make any headway at all in this strange, new place. It was we who would have to wait to see whether it was possible to know them differently, to know them as we now do, as people who write wonderful things like this:

> When Mark says the old ways are reflected on the faces like the glow of a dying campfire, it shows that he can sense the joy and importance of the old ways. Yet he knows that it is only a faint glow and it flickers on and off. He knows that one day it is going to die out unless someone lights it again. (Student response)

Or, in response to their own "good bits," this:

> "They were six years old perhaps, a little girl and boy. They had entered without knocking and they stood like fawns, too small to be afraid. They stood absolutely still, and they smiled, slowly and gently." When I read this passage I . . . thought about a little girl and a little boy with large, wide-open eyes. They

stood still to look at strange things. How beautiful it was! I like the sentence "They had entered without knocking." I do not think that this means they are bad kids. It just means they do not know that they should knock because no one had taught them. In the Indian land, there is probably no one who knocks. . . . The kids have grown up in the Indian land and have been taught the Indian ways. People here are probably shy. I remember my country, Vietnam. The kids who live in the country, not in the city, are very shy. They are afraid of everything. Whenever you talk to them, the first action you get is a smile, a shy smile. They use the shy and gentle smile to begin a dialogue with strangers.

Or this:

"The young women found an imminent need to exchange crochet patterns, and they met like a huddle of young hens and whispered about his looks, his manners, even his clean finger nails." Whether or not this is meant to be a good passage, it reminds me of my friends and I checking out the new guys . . . or still looking at the old guys from last year. We all make our huddles and whisper, and look at their bums. All the little things we girls do. I kind of laughed to myself listening to this.

We are not sure that we could have identified what we were doing as a kind of waiting if we had not read *I Heard the Owl Call My Name* with these students, in this place. Were we waiting for these students to reveal their true, but hidden, selves to us? Not really, for what we saw emerging in their engagement with the novel, with us and with one another were selves constituted and known in the particularity of our situation, studying this book, at this time, in the second year of teaching and learning together. The character of who we became to one another through the reading of this book was not lurking in the underbrush awaiting discovery. The distinctiveness of the complex web of relations that connected us through this book would have emerged differently if we had chosen a different novel, or if we, ourselves, had been claimed by a different set of issues and ideas. The novel mattered. The good bits the students chose mattered. It mattered that the issue of waiting called to the two of us from start to finish. And it mattered that all of the strands of our knowing took time to weave.

"Wait," we remember the Bishop saying to Mark, "you will come to know them." What Mark is left to figure out for himself is the tactful, mindful quality of the waiting that will make it possible to weave a fabric of care with the people in his charge. It is, we think, precisely the kind of waiting and weaving that teachers must learn to do.

But if, while we were struggling to get to this point with our students, someone had said to us, "Just wait, it will be all right," we would probably have become quite angry.

"Wait?" we might have shot back. "We can't afford to wait. There's too much to be done. We don't have time to wait."

In the ordinary, passive sense of waiting, we would have been right.

We have learned, certainly, that waiting is not a kind of idleness. If, for example, we had sat on our hands, had given in or fallen apart in those early, difficult days nothing at all would have happened. Things would have been, if not well, at least ordinary and recognizable to the students. And we would have left the school as Mark knows he might well have to leave the village, broken and soon forgotten.

There *was* much to be done, and we set about doing it regardless of whether anyone would bless our efforts or not. We mobilized caretakers, tossing out broken chairs and insisting on tables rather than the slant-top desks that made group work impossible. We painted all the bookshelves, scrubbed the carpet and washed stains off the cindercrete walls. We lugged in more than 50 cumbersome boxes of books and four computers by ourselves, covered bulletin boards and bought flowers. We could not have known it then, but we were like Mark who, faced with a falling-down church and vicarage, rolls up his sleeves and fixes things up himself, prepared to accept help if it were offered and prepared to do without if it were not.

Mark recognizes the seductive danger of beginning "where every man is apt to begin who is sent to hold some lonely outpost. He was going to begin by begging, 'I want this. I need that . . .' " (Craven, 1973, p. 35). In fact, he sees exactly this kind of begging in the school teacher, the only other White person in Kingcome, who "accosted him on the path, asking that he intervene with the authorities, that he be given proper supplies. Even the smallest villages were given more pencils and pads. Also, he was expected to pay for the paper tissues which he dropped so generously for the sniffling noses of his pupils" (Craven, 1973, pp. 38–39).

We have thought a great deal about that teacher and his vast unhappiness in the village of Kingcome. Having chosen to come there solely for "the isolation pay which would permit him a year in Greece studying the civilization he adored" (Craven, 1973, p. 33), the teacher is miserable. "He did not like the Indians and the Indians did not like him" (Craven, 1973, p. 33). Nothing suited him. The children, runny-nosed and inalterably *other*, were a constant disappointment. There wasn't enough of anything: not enough money, not enough pencils, not enough resources, not enough support, not enough recognition. His litany of complaint was uncomfortably familiar to us. Was that what we were doing when we said, "These broken chairs have to go. No rich kid in this city has to sit on a broken chair." Or, "We won't have these desks in here. They're no good. How can anybody do lab work on these things? Their stuff will slide right off onto the floor." Were we being as whiny and obnoxious as that teacher? Is that how our insistence on better chairs, better tables sounded to others who had lived for so many years without? We were tempted to read fast over these bits about the teacher, tempted to peek at him only between our fingers, for he warned us of the seductive *hubris*, of the dark side, the shadow of our own commitment. In some way, the teacher is on a colonial mission to the village, a mission on whose edge the two of us often skated.

Mark is different from that teacher, and we sensed a lesson in his difference. For Mark, the derelict church and vicarage are, indeed, unacceptable. He does not expect the villagers to worship in filth and neglect, nor is he, himself, prepared to live that way. But neither does he expect another person in the village to do for him what he refuses to do for himself. While the villagers look on in amusement (and while our own colleagues dropped by to comment on the domestic enthusiasm of the new guys on the block) Mark simply does what he does, expecting nothing in return. We sensed in him a subtle tact needed by all of us who move into the lives of others. Throughout the novel, the teacher remains aloof, apart from the village and its essential life. He lives like a colonial expatriate, like the British of the Empire among whom it was a virtue not to feel touched by the natives. Even at the very end of the novel, when Mark's body is brought home to the village for burial, the teacher stands behind his closed door, refusing to make himself part of the funeral procession, for "to join the others was to care, and to care was to live and to suffer" (Craven, 1973, p. 158).

TO JOIN THE OTHERS

To care is to live, and as we think about how we have come to care for the students we teach, we realize in ways that would have been impossible without the experience of reading this novel with them, how fully we have come to live in our work with them. Now, years after all the furious scrubbing and cleaning, after the battles and the relentless insistence, day after day, of doing things other-wise, after the joys of precious moments when we broke through the walls that had been keeping us apart, we overhear one of the girls say to a friend in another class, "Look, if you want to talk, you've got to come to this room. I'm not going to your classroom. I like my own room." We grin because we know her stubbornness is only partly about paint and wallpaper and the sun streaming through the window. It is also about the spirit of the place, about the sense of belonging to one another through the hard work and, indeed, the suffering, we have endured together.

We asked a great deal of our students when we asked them to read *I Heard the Owl Call My Name*. We asked them to lose themselves so that they could find themselves transformed by the experience of reading. We worked with them to make the edges of their known worlds waver and tremble. And we did that with a particular kind of mindfulness, we think, because what we asked of the students we also demanded of ourselves.

We said to the kids at the very beginning that teachers could be guides through the mysterious forest. "All the trees are going to look the same for a while," we told them, "but we will help you learn to tell oak from aspen. It will be okay." What we now know is that there are at least two kinds of guides. There is the guide who can show a path because she had traveled it many times before. This is the kind of teacher–guide who has puzzled through all the known difficulties of the text and can help students shortcut or at least endure the underbrush.

But there is another kind of guide, we think, and that is the kind of guide we strive through our research, to become.

Connected to the landscape of loss, we want to be like Mark, doing our own work even as we wait for others to begin theirs. Asking students to immerse themselves in the difficulty of the novel, we ourselves embraced anew the original difficulty of all reading. Refusing to remain aloof, imprisoned behind the closed door of pedagogical certainties, we ventured out with them, experiencing in our own ways how bloody hard it is to do the work that we daily ask of them. We promised not only with our words to help them find their way. We also promised with the deepest possible commitment to stick with them as they—and as we—lost our selves together.

And somehow, even though we never talked to them about the specifics of our own struggles to understand what waiting is all about, they seemed to know that we *were* with them in powerful ways. Less strange to one another than when we began, we came to know each other through reading this book together. Less strange, we all were better able to understand more about the place we inhabited together, about its beams of light and dark, frightening shadows. Less strange even to ourselves, the two of us came to know more deeply and more fully who we are in this world.

For us, action research is not just one more thing to add to our lives. It is, instead, a layered way of living that embraces the very difficulties, ambiguities, and suffering that so much teaching practice seems determined to eradicate. We began with a practical concern for teaching students through a more interpretative approach to shared texts and experiences. However, our own thinking, reading, and writing about these particular texts and experiences soon became far more than a report on what we did with the novel. Rather, our own interpretation, itself a hermeneutic act, moved us, as teachers, into new spaces in which epistemology and ontology, knowing and being, lost their distinct and sometimes lonely character. It moved us into a space in which the *teaching* of a novel became the text, itself, of our *lives* as teachers.

Preamble 11

I haven't got time in my class to spend three weeks making papier mache igloos. We've got exams coming.

These words of a local elementary school teacher are very important and they reveal a truth about how the debate about the basics tends to live itself out in the atmosphere of schooling. One of the difficulties that arises in attempting to question basics-as-breakdown is that, as with any dominant discourse, the discourse of breakdown tends to define what alternatives to it might look like.

Thus the sort of caricature we find in that elementary school teacher's words. Alternatives to the regimes of breakdown and its consorts (forms of testing, monitoring, management, control, and so on) are commonly characterized as soft-headed, unrigorous, touchy-feely, frivolous, personal, subjective, permissive, overly emotional, all about self-esteem and feeling good about yourself.

If we concede to the (we believe outdated) version of the empirical sciences that underwrites basics-as-breakdown, we concede as well that it describes the "objective" world that can be rigorously, methodically known. And if we concede this, then we concede that "knowing" means "controlling, predicting, and manipulating" and the "objective world" means "that world that can be controlled, predicted, and manipulated." And if it describes the "objective" world that can be rigorously known, *of course* alternatives to it must be described as "subjective." Once we concede that basics-as-breakdown describes objective realities, all we are left with are feel-good activities like making papier mache igloos.

This is the most pernicious effect of a dominant discourse: not only that it tends to define what alternatives to it can be, but that, more often than not, those who wish to pursue such alternatives tend to fall into precisely this logic. Educational theory and practice are full of "alternatives" that are defined by what they wish to replace. The following chapter takes up one of these phenomena: the idea of "curriculum integration" in elementary schools.

One of the telling threads here is that the versions of curriculum integration widespread in educational theory and practice are premised upon breakdown. That is to say, curriculum integration is something we might have to *do* only in a dis-integrated world, where the relations have been severed and dispersed and must be concertedly re-gathered. The forms of curriculum integration that are considered in the following chapter are thus *consequences of basics-as-breakdown* rather than alternatives to it.

Stepping away from this situation—stepping away, that is, from how basics-as-breakdown and the alternatives it allows orbit each other and, in some sense, require and feed off each other, is a difficult task. Just consider how well-oiled are the educational debates between child-centered and teacher-centered, between theory and practice, between whole language and phonics, between esteem and assessment, between open- and closed-classrooms, and other so-called "pendulum swings" that make for cynicism and exhaustion regarding educational change.

It is difficult to understand why Gadamer (1989, p. 276) would say that, in interpretive work, "the focus on subjectivity is a distorting mirror," given the alternatives to basics-as-breakdown that seem to be available. Interpretively understood, stepping away from this situation is never accomplished once and for all. We always find ourselves living in the world and living out and living with the logics that world presumes as obvious. Interpretive work therefore always involves the task of *application* (Gadamer, 1989, pp. 307-334). This classroom, this child, that comment or question, that curriculum demand, that upcoming test, that papier mache igloo caricature—each individual case will have something to say about what calls for interpretation. Interpretively treated, each case *demands something of us* and, as such, a focus on subjectivity is necessarily inadequate.

But the opposite is also true: Each case, interpretively treated, is also not objective because, so to speak, each case *faces us* and *demands something of us*, rather than simply *us* making methodologically controlled demands of *it*. This is why it is commonplace in interpretive work that the nature of interpretive work itself is constantly being re-addressed. This is not because it is new-fangled and perhaps unfamiliar, so that it is necessary to explain what it is over and over again. Rather, it is because, in interpretive work, each case is not only treated interpretively but is allowed to make its own case for what an interpretive treatment might be in this case. Interpretive work, therefore, only works in the face of the case that calls for its peculiar form of attention.

This is why it makes some sense to say that interpretation is not a "method" that can simply be pointed at a particular topic. Interpretive work is always finding that its topics are telling of it as much as it is telling of them. This is why it is so unerringly annoying to try to describe interpretive work in general. Without a substantive and demanding topography in which to show itself, interpretation becomes overly philosophical and vaguely incomprehensible. This is why, in the area of educational research and in "research methods" classes with graduate students, the first question is never "what method are you using?" but rather, "*where* does your interest lie?" This is why, as well, in our undergraduate teaching methods classes, we always attempt to stick with the difficult work of opening up the rich topographies we have inherited, and avoid the pre-emptive questions of "how do I teach this?" It is not that the question of how to teach something never arises, but when it arises as an outcome of the interpretive exploration of ancestries and bloodlines and relations, it necessarily arises within a context in which children and their questions and experiences are *already present.* The question of "how to teach" something therefore changes tone under an interpretive treatment of the basics. Interpretation allows us to see how things are, so to speak, "already underway," both for us and for our students, before our concerted efforts at teaching ensue.

So, on to the case of "curriculum integration." As will become evident in the chapter that follows, even "curriculum integration" ends up having something to do with the case of a particular pair of *someone's* shoes. Because of its dominant nature, breaking the spell of basics-as-breakdown necessarily requires a sort of interpretive "exaggeration" (Gadamer, 1989, p. 115). We will have to leave it to others to decide the extent to which we ourselves have been guilty of precisely the same sort of caricaturing-the-opposite that we are attempting to move away from. Setting up nothing but a weakling version of basics-as-breakdown only to knock it over is always to some degree cowardly.

Chapter 11

"In These Shoes Is the Silent Call of the Earth": Meditations on Curriculum Integration, Conceptual Violence, and the Ecologies of Community and Place

David W. Jardine
Annette LaGrange
Beth Everest

INTRODUCTION: "SOUNDS LIKE AN INTERESTING UNIT"

The following is a portion of a recent e-mail exchange:

> Forgive the cross posting; I'm looking for a variety of points of view. I'm looking for lesson plans (or ideas that I can make in to lessons) for teaching art in math (or math in art). Specifically, what math can I see in any work of Van Gogh? This will be a workshop for 5/6th graders.

One response received to this request was:

> How about the spirals in Starry, Starry Night and the sunflowers in picture of same name? Both can be connected to math and/or science. Spiraling procedures can be written in Logo teaching the concept of stepping. Estimations of number of sunflowers in head as well as patterns created by seeds while still in head are other ideas. You could sprout sunflower seeds and collect data: How many days average to sprout? What percentage of seeds sprouted? Does size of seeds affect sprouting speed? etc. etc. Sounds like an interesting unit. (Lugone, 1996)

The authors' interest in curriculum integration is, in part, a response to an unsettling sense of fragmentation that can be found, not only in this example, but in much of our work with teachers, student–teachers, and schools. We believe that the opening citation is typical of what counts as thinking about curriculum integration in elementary schools. It betrays an almost random surface skittering over topics which casts the oddest of things together. The brilliant sunflowers in Arles in the south of France and how they bore Van Gogh's agonized attention in his final years are linked, in the imagination of those who frequent early elementary classrooms, to rows of white Styrofoam cups with masking-taped names and dried soils and neglected, dying sunflower seedlings drooped on hot Grade 1 classroom sills. Reading this e-mail exchange produced in us a strange sense of restlessness, displacement, and homelessness, a sense of no longer knowing where we are or what is required as a proper, generous, but honest response to this well-meant pursuit of "curriculum integration."

Curriculum integration poses hard questions to those involved in the educational endeavor. What does it mean to teach with integrity? What does it mean to treat one's topic of study with integrity? How might school classroom and university teachers alike teach in a way that respects the character and integrity of the lives and experiences of children and the work undertaken with them?

We suggest that part of the answer to these far-too-large questions is ecological in character. Curriculum integration has to do with keeping things in place, nested in the deep communities of relations that make them whole, healthy, and sane. We are intrigued by Berry's (1986) reminder that an orientation toward integrity and wholeness has something to do with health, healing, and the mending of relations, and, therefore, that pursuing curriculum integration in our classrooms has something to do with "choosing to be healers" (Clifford & Friesen, 1994) in relation to ourselves, the Earth, the topics taught in our schools, and the children invited into those topographies. We are intrigued as well by how such difficult, disciplined work is much more deeply *pleasurable* (Berry, 1989) for adults and children alike than the panic of "activities" that consumes so much of educational practice.

We must be generous enough to hope that the clashing together of Van Gogh and mathematics in this e-mail exchange was done in good faith, and that real, substantial, integrated, heartening work has resulted. Even if these teachers did not find their way into such work, we cannot deny that the oddness of this example is not precisely *their* problem. School teachers and university teachers all, in their own ways, are living out a deep cultural logic of fragmentation and we (for we must include ourselves here, as the authors of this chapter) have all participated, directly or indirectly, in the strange efforts at curriculum integration that sometimes result.

This exchange still stands, however, as a sign or a warning that issues of curriculum integration still need our attention. This continuing need for attention is almost too obvious: In a living system, health and wholeness and the cultivation of good relations are never simply givens, because the young are always still arriving again, ready to call what we have taken as given to account in their own lives. The Earth, too, is beginning to have its say about our character and our conduct and our ignoring of its ways.

"ONE AFTER THE OTHER"

A teacher recently mentioned on an Internet listserve called "Kidsphere" that she was thinking of doing "shoes" as a theme or a unit in her classroom. Over the course of nearly 2 weeks, the Net was inundated with dozens of responses from all across North America—different types of shoes, different styles and preferences, different materials that shoes are made of: "There was an old woman who lived in a shoe," indoor and outdoor shoes, Hans Brinker's skates, shoes and boots, cobblers and elves, different professions and their footwear, snowshoes, skis, and such, different countries and their shoes, different ways to secure them (laces, velcro, buckles, slip-ons—leading to numbers of eye-holes and lengths of laces and the idea of "pairs"), Puss and his boots, sizes of shoes, graphs of shoe sizes, graphs of shoe colors, graphs of shoelace colors, dismissing children by shoe color as a management technique, shoeprints and footprints in paint, tracks and animals in science, and perhaps a detective game that has children tracking something by its prints.

And so on.

We can all understand the giddy rush of such exchanges, and we have all participated and taken some pleasure in them. However, despite their earnestness and good will, and the conviviality with which they occur, such exchanges seem to treat each moment, each particular, with haste and a lack of careful attention. Of course, such a "continuity of attention and devotion" (Berry, 1986, p. 13) to particulars is not what such brainstorming sessions and subsequent "webbings," "mappings," or "theme-ings" are for. They are intended to give a broad and quick picture of surface similarities, surface connections, surface relations under the name of *shoes*.

However, because none of the nodes in the web is read for its rich textures and patterns and hidden discourses, none of the connections seem especially strong or robust or well-rooted. What result are connections that sometimes seem forced and trivial, betraying a rushed, ultimately unsatisfying lack of attention and care to anything in particular. Rather than providing a picture of some integrated patterns of the world or serving as a prelude to the work of settling oneself somewhere, it is as if these themes or webs of ideas concede, aggravate, or even sometimes create the very situation of fragmentation and alienation that they are meant to remedy.

Consider these words of a sixth-grade teacher:

> When you mention an idea, it's so typical of teachers to graciously share every-
> thing they can. And they start throwing ideas at you, all meant to help out.
> You really don't have time to think about anything. Nothing gets a chance to
> soak in. You get so overwhelmed by all the bits, and, after all, you don't want
> to leave any out now that people have offered them, so that all you can do is
> just present them one after the other. (Research note, December 1996)

In their own way (and this may be especially aggravated by the existence of
Internet and the possibility of hundreds of comparatively instantaneous responses), such brainstorming flurries seem to work against, or at least make
more difficult, settling down *somewhere*, doing *something* well, treating *something* with the integrity it warrants.

It is as if these flurries start out as emulations of the giddy rush of life, of
newness, freshness, and ebullience that we find so pleasing in our children.
However, in many elementary school classrooms (and so much of the work
done in Faculties of Education), we let loose rushes of thin, restless activities not one of which warrants much attention or work. We then end up
producing, in turn, fading attention-spans both in our children and in ourselves. And such a loss of attention is most frequently then blamed on our
children. We call their shortness or lack of attention "a characteristic of
young children" and we excuse our own lack of attention to the work at
hand by citing the attention each individual student needs from us.

After witnessing the activity of her cooperating teacher for a semester,
one student–teacher recently said something we found quite telling regarding the tempo, attention, and activity level in elementary school classrooms:
"My teacher is busy all the time but she never seems to do any work" (Research note, December 1996).

CURRICULUM INTEGRATION AND CONCEPTUAL VIOLENCE

What is lost in many efforts in curriculum integration is precisely the *topography*, the *ecos*, the place of any particular thing. Many webs or themes proceed in a "heady" fashion: Each particular gains "wholeness"/integration
only through the concerted intervention of a *concept* (e.g., the *concept* of
"shoes"). It is the *concept* that brings the particulars together.

Pursued in this way, curriculum integration can become a sort of *conceptual violence* that tears particulars out of their intimate, particular places and
re-sorts them "away from home" under general, abstract, anonymous categories. These categories are not sensuous, bodily, indigenous, and immediate, but oddly cold, ideational, fleshless, and alien. The very act meant to
heal and restore communities of real, integral relations and patterns thus

becomes complicit in their unwitting destruction and replacement with conceptual structures that are cleaner, clearer, and less Earthy and alluring than those living communities. The very act meant to help us attend to the integrities of our experience in a whole and healthy way becomes a form of interpretive deafness, an inability to hear what words and worlds of implication might be *already at work* in the stubborn particulars (Wallace, 1987) that come to meet us, before our conceptualizations take hold. As one teacher put it so poignantly, "the water of chemical composition and the water in which my child has drowned *don't belong together*" (Research note, December 1996), in spite of their conceptual affinities. The *world* of hydrogen, oxygen, and their combinations is not the same world as the agonies of the loss of a child, or the mysteries of the water that washes away sins, or a tall cool glass stippled with condensation on a hot summer's day. Each of these bears *its own* memories, relations, obligations, its own tales and topographies that make it whole, healthy, and livable.

The intervention of a *concept* of "water" into these worlds in order to "integrate" them is simply tactless and unbecoming—disintegrative, in fact, of the integrities of experience that are already at work without such intervention.

NARRATIVE INTEGRATION AND THE RECOVERY OF THE PARTICULAR

Our growing concerns over this portrayal of the situation of curriculum integration as a sort of thin, conceptual surface picture and the ensuing loss of the topographies of the particular, gave way to the recollection of a passage in Martin Heidegger's (1971) *Origins of the Work of Art*, in which he meditates on a Van Gogh painting of a peasant woman's shoes. This meditation, in all its convoluted twists and turns (and despite its tone of high German Romanticism), provided us with a way to begin reconceptualizing the nature of curriculum integration:

> As long as we only imagine a pair of shoes in general, or simply look at the empty, unused shoes as they merely stand there in the picture we shall never discover [them]. A pair of peasant shoes and nothing more. And yet from the dark opening of the worn insides of the shoes the toilsome tread of the worker stares forth. In the stiffly rugged heaviness of the shoes there is the accumulated tenacity of her slow trudge through the furrows of the field. Under the soles slides the loneliness of the field-path as evening falls. In the shoes is the silent call of the earth, its quiet gift of the ripening grain and its unexplained self-refusal in the fallow desolation of the wintry field. This equipment is pervaded by uncomplaining anxiety as to the certainty of bread, the wordless joy of having once more withstood want, the trembling before the

impending childbed and shivering at the surrounding menace of death. (pp. 33–34)

There is a profound familiarity in these words, one that recalls all the years of early childhood. Stopping, with a sort of interpretive mindfulness, over *this* pair of shoes (and not skittering past it in a brainstorming session) might itself reveal a way that our course (*currere*/curriculum) is whole/integrated in some deep, ecologically sane and sustainable way.

We can recall moments of passing by our father's or mother's or grandfather's shoes tucked by the front door or left tumbled on balconies or verandas, seeing the deep imprint of their tracks inside, the places of shiny imprint, traces of the lives they have lived and the work they have done, and how, in slipping these on our own small feet, it was not just these particular things that we engaged but a whole world, their world and its deep familial intersection with our own. We can all recall, too, how we may have warily avoided those shoes and the life they stamped on us or others.

All of us understand, somehow, that *these* shoes are not capturable with any integrity and wholeness on a web under, say, "different types of shoes" or "shoes and types of work." Rather, *these* shoes gain an integrity and place in a world full of rich memory and familiarity and use, a world full of the intractable particularities of experience, whether for good or ill or some troubling mixture of the two.

These shoes—the black boots my neighbor Harry wore in our trudging work of installing furnaces in people's basements—are not understandable in an integrated way by simply placing them alongside others in a list of different types of shoes from around the world. They do not belong alongside others, except perhaps those of his wife when he arrives home, or mine as we rested at lunch, and then how those age-old boots fit with the Thermos and lunchpail worn thin from use, like his tools, bearing the marks of his hands and the marks of age and work and craft. The world in which one might produce a web of different types of shoes is a different world than the world evoked by dark stains and smells of oil and coal dust, or the knotted pieces of broken lace as signs of Harry's odd frugality.

Understood conceptually and in general, *shoes* bear no history, no memory, no continuity, no dependencies, no place, no communities of relations. They are not *someone's, here, in this place*, and, in this sense, they are simply an *idea* of shoes, not fleshy and warm and curved just so. Despite all its calls to integration, categorizations, or thematizations such as "different types of shoes" breaks apart the very small, intimate threads of familiarity, obligation, and relation that actually hold *these* shoes in a real, integrated place. Such small, intimate threads and the worlds they evoke get replaced with a concept which cannot provide any of the comforts, the common strengths, of the place the particular has left behind in such severances.

Sticking with such particularity has an interesting effect. Rather than simply bogging us down in the burden of specificity (Smith, 1999), the particular takes on a certain buoyancy and lightness. It becomes a node on a web of real sustenance and import.

What emerges from taking these particular shoes seriously in their wholeness is a sense that things have integral places. Things themselves, in their very particularity, issue a sense of belonging somehow, in intractable relations of materiality, obligation, community, history, memory, and so on. The integration or wholeness that ensues, therefore, is not just about these particular shoes. Rather, the phenomenon of integration or wholeness itself, as involving an attention to place and memory and relations and community, starts to come forward.

What starts to come forward is not a bluster of activities for the classroom, but a way of taking up the world that breaks the spell of the consumptivism, exhaustion, and the panic of activities into which so much of our lives is inscribed.

This does not leave us with a "great idea" that we can now directly address or directly "apply." We now have, in its stead, *a serious, immediate, ecological obligation,* to treat things that come to meet us with integrity, to heal the ways that things have become fragmented and displaced and unsettled and dispersed into the ethers of goodhearted but ecologically suspect Internet exchanges.

ENDBIT: PARTICULARITY AND DE-ROMANTICIZING "PLACE"

In circulating the idea of this chapter to colleagues and students and friends, an odd thing began to emerge, something typical as a response to interpretive work. What arrived were particular tales of particular shoes that were, in each case, wedged deeply in the flesh and breath of the teller. As this paper proceeded, it became clear—although still somewhat mysterious—why shoes are so frequently a topic in Early Childhood Education. It seems that they always already bear a fleshy familial intimacy that we all recognize at some deep, gutty level and that belies and resists our efforts at conceptual thematization. It may be that our initial attraction to shoes reveals some mute recognition of an integrity of children's (*our* children, and therefore our own) experiences that is then unwittingly betrayed in our subsequent conceptualizations.

It may be that our curriculum integration conceptualizations are unintentionally teaching a horrible lesson.

Consider one particular response we received as we wrote and spoke of shoes and curriculum integration. A poem that brings particular shoes to life:

David is talking about shoes, about some
paper he is writing about shoes, & I am
thinking about Dad's rubbers, the black
rubber oversoles/overshoes that he always
wears in the rain & the snow. old man's
shoes. things that he must wear. the stamp of
him. the mark that he makes in the snow, in
our lives, in my own life. his father wears
them too

& I think that i cannot really find the shoe
that fits my mother; perhaps it could be the
high heels that are in the dressup box, the
things that are left over from some other
life that we as children never knew, can
never know. but she does not wear these now &
i must imagine her long legs sliding into
white silk stockings. the garter belt that
she throws on her wedding day

all of these scenes i must imagine, as now
most often i remember her in sneakers, but
this is not the right word to describe my
mother's footwear. ked's? tennis shoes? sensible
flats? the glass slipper?

my father wears rubbers, overshoes, like he
has always done because he has always been
old, but my mother i cannot define so simply.
nor can i explain her passion for shoes, stored
in her closet. winter shoes: oxfords, smooth
soled, vibram soled, patent leather, navy, black,
brown, dark green, khaki. summer shoes:
red, white, yellow, orange, stored in boxes

I hear the water running for her bath. imagine
the dressing gown folded. her blue
nightie. the large white towel. a new bar
of soap. her legs. still slender, she
steps into the bubbles. her feet, narrow,
bumpy. her voice is soft.
i cannot hear her step
on the stair.

—Beth Everest (1996)

We wish to end with a plea for forgiveness that we ourselves require. We are
all living out a deep cultural logic of fragmentation that distracts attention,
that is cynical about devotion or depth, and that mocks any talk of good

work, that identifies settling and quiet and meditation with passivity, and that cannot imagine how one could want anything but business in our classrooms.

What we are alluding to here is not simply another great idea for the classroom. It is not merely an issue of *teacher knowledge* or adequate *information* about a topic or a child:

> One thing we dare not forget is that better solutions than ours have at times been made by people with much less information than we have. We know, too, from the study of agriculture, that the same information, tools and techniques that in one farmer's hands will ruin land, in another's will save and improve it. This is not a recommendation of ignorance. To know nothing, after all, is no more possible than to know enough. I am only proposing that knowledge, like everything else, has its place, and that we need urgently now to *put* it in its place. (Berry, 1983, pp. 65–66)

This place into which knowledge must find its way, Berry suggests, has to do with care, character, and love—surprisingly antiquated words in the current educational milieu. Integration and wholeness have more to do with the *way* one knows, the *way* one is, the *way* one hopes children will become and how we and they will carry ourselves, and how light and careful our footfalls will be on this Earth.

The examples we have cited are from the good-hearted work of teachers who are bearing an old logic of fragmentation and distraction on our behalf. We cannot pretend that their distraction is simply *their* problem, as if our own lives were somehow precious and exempt from questions of how to proceed with integrity, as if we might pretend to have somehow solved this problem in our own lives. Each new topic we address in our work with colleagues, with children and with student teachers requires that we raise these questions of integration all over again. Although it might initially result in frustration, we have deliberately resisted the false promises of "yet another model" of curriculum integration sold to the highest textbook bidders.

One thing, however, is certain. We, as teachers, as parents, find ourselves at an especially difficult juncture in this cultural logic that we are all living out, facing the possibility, but not the necessity, of passing it on to our children.

Preamble 12

It is its love of . . . generativity and its longing to open up inquiry to such generativity that makes hermeneutics appear so negative in regard to certain forms of inquiry and discourse. It is this love that undergirds hermeneutics' intolerance of those who would traffic in the business of education as if it were as meaningless, as deadened, as unthankful and unthinking, as despising of children, as they propose it to be.

—Jardine (2000, p. 132)

Now, at this tail-end of our text, two themes emerge which at first seem new, but have been hidden there all along: the excessiveness of the gift and the idea of movement both as fundamental to an interpretive treatment of the basics in education.

At first, of course, the idea of "excessiveness" seems to be precisely the opposite of "the basics" and the idea of "the gift" does not fit at all with basics-as-breakdown.

In this last chapter we link up the idea of basics-as-breakdown to the commodification of knowledge as something to be exchanged, in a highly monitored, zero-sum fashion, for marks, for employment, for promotion (in school or otherwise), and profit. That we might profit from knowing, as an allusion to character, has been replaced with images of a "knowledge-economy" in which character is simply not at issue.

Thus, basics-as-breakdown sets in motion a peculiar form of panic that we find to be endemic in so many schools: There is so much to "cover," there is so little time, students are in constant competition for marks and their value as market-exchange items. Knowledge becomes strangely characterized under this panic: There is not enough to go around, hoarding it for personal gain is essential, and controlling it, owning it, and dispensing it only for profit is all there is to the adage of Lifelong Learning (see Preamble 10).

When any of us think of those things in the world that we dearly love—the music of Duke Ellington, the contours of a powerful novel and how it envelops us if we give ourselves over to it, the exquisite architectures of mathematical geometries, the old histories and stories of this place, the rows of garden plants that need our attention and devotion and care, varieties of birds and their songs, the perfect sound of an engine that works well, the pull of ice under a pair of skates, and on and on—we understand something in our relation to these things about how excessiveness might be basic to such love. We do not seek these things out and explore them again and again simply for the profit that we might gain in exchanging what we have found for something *else*. What we have found, in exploring and coming to understanding, to learn to live well with these things is not an arm's-length commodity but has become part of who we are, and how we carry ourselves in the world. We love them and we love what becomes of us in our dedication to them. And, paradoxically, the more we understand of them, the better—richer, more intriguing, more complex, more ambiguous, and full and multiple of questions—*they* become and the more we realize that gobbling them up into a knowing that we can commodify, possess, and exchange is not only undesirable. It is impossible. We realize, in such knowing, that the living character of the things we love will, of necessity, outstrip our own necessarily finite and limited experience and exploration. To know about a living discipline, then, means, in part, to recognize the inevitability of its excessiveness. To the extent that, for example, mathematics remains a living discipline, nothing we individually or collectively do will be able to control, predict, and manipulate its course. It is one of the bloodlines to which we belong, for good or ill. To the extent that we can control, predict, and manipulate it, it has ceased to be a living inheritance to which we belong and has become an arm's-length object which now belongs to us.

This is why, in hermeneutic work, knowledge is inevitably linked up with the "experience of human finitude" (Gadamer, 1989, p. 357). Rather than being a form of morbidity, this simply means that the experience I have gained regarding the belonging together of addition and subtraction is necessarily open to the arrival of an unforeseeable future that will inevitably have something to say about this topic, this topography. And, more than this, it means that my experience is the experience *of* features of a living discipline that *does not belong to me*. Rather, in knowing it, I belong to it and add my voice to the "multifariousness of voices" (Gadamer, 1989, p. 284) in which it exists. Thus knowing it is not "owning" it but participating in transforming and re-vivifying its questionableness by handing it down (p. 284).

Therefore, it is not that interpretive work, in resisting basics-as-breakdown, offers a Romantic alternative to the idea of knowledge as an exchangeable commodity. Rather, it points to the fact that my experience, for example, of the inverse character of addition and subtraction (my "knowing my way around" this phenomenon) will, paradoxically, only *increase* if I give it away. In listening to that Grade 2 girl's questions, in treating them as addressing the character of mathematics, not only does her knowledge and my own knowledge perhaps increase. What also increases is the living complexity of the place in which we come to know our way around through our conversation. Something is set in motion that seemed previously fixed and given. We glimpse that addition and subtraction had both been isolated from each other, commodified, one might say. We found that, without each other, neither can, so to speak, "move." And, finally, we found that, without the possibility of such movement, neither makes much mathematical sense. Thus, what we get a small glimpse of is that, as a living place, mathematics is, in part, defined by its *movement,* by the way in which, for example, addition gives itself over to subtraction and only properly is itself if it gives itself away in this manner.

In this way, whole new parts of *this living place* open up that were heretofore closed by the breakdown–isolation of addition and subtraction. This is why, in Preamble 6, we mentioned the hermeneutic idea that living inheritances undergo an "increase in being" (Gadamer, 1989, p. 140) in being understood and furthered in such understanding. As living disciplines, things *are* their complex, contradictory, multifarious movements of opening and furtherance. This is their "generative" character, and this is why, so often in this text, we have insisted that the questions that come from our children about what we took to be no longer in movement, no longer open to question, are basic to their living character. Differently put, because mathematics, interpretively understood, *is* how it has "gathered and collected itself" (Gadamer, 1989, p. 97; see Preamble 6), what our students gather about mathematics *is* mathematics itself. All of the questions our students ask, which would seem so very excessive if we thought mathematics was a given, are interpretively insinuating into its being a living inheritance.

This is why we were attracted to the idea of the gift and its excessiveness and why we make the audacious claim in the following chapter that it is precisely *the excessiveness and abundance of the disciplines we have inherited,* their *living* character, that is most "basic" to them. And, as we have detailed all along, entering into this living character with students is far more difficult that the regimes of control, prediction, and manipulation requisite of basics-as-breakdown. But is also far more pleasurable, far more inviting, far more generous to our children and to ourselves, far more concerned with the living continuance of the life of such inheritances, than the panics induced by breakdown.

We hedged our bets in our Introduction and we need to do so again as we conclude this journey for now. An interpretive treatment of "the basics" is not put forward as somehow *really* the basics, whereas basics-as-breakdown is not. Rather, as we have been exploring throughout this book, "the way we treat a thing [like the basics] can sometimes change its nature" (Hyde, 1983, p. xiii). And let us recall the questions we posed: What might seem most important to us? How might we talk differently? How might we act differently? What new or ancient roles might we envisage for ourselves and our children in the teaching and learning and understanding of the disciplines that have been entrusted to us in schools? What, in fact, might "understanding" mean, given this alternate image of "the basics"?

So the question to be posed to an interpretive treatment of the basics is not "Are ancestry, memory, character, interrelatedness, tradition, new blood, generativity, inheritance, excessiveness, movement, and love *really* 'the basics'?" The question to be asked is, "What difference does treating the basics interpretively make to how we live out the life of education with our children if we treat 'the basics' this way?"

And, equally important and equally difficult is this. In such interpretive work, we "must accept the fact that future generations will understand differently" (Gadamer, 1989, p. 340). Therefore, the question of what difference it makes to treat the basics interpretively hides ethical questions: Here, now, in the circumstances we face in the everyday life of schooling, can we live with basics-as-breakdown, or is something else called for in these difficult times? Given that we can treat the basics as we see fit, what shall we do, what might be best, who should be party to such questions, and how shall we properly and gracefully decide? These questions will, of necessity, have to be "kept open for the future" (p. 340).

Chapter 12

Scenes From Calypso's Cave: On Globalization and the Pedagogical Prospects of the Gift

David W. Jardine
Patricia Clifford
Sharon Friesen

> *Beginning . . .*
> *We will try to understand why our society, which, more than any other, insists
> that each individual is unique, systematically tends to dismiss those primary so-
> cial ties that enable people to affirm and shape their uniqueness and promotes
> those abstract and secondary ties that, at least in theory, make people inter-
> changeable and anonymous, only to later create an ersatz personalization
> through identification with work or the state.*
> —Godbout, with Caille (1998, pp. 19–20)

The economy of the gift is a knitting of such primary social ties, an exem-
plary form of which is our relation to our children (Godbout, with Caille,
1998, p. 27), because it involves one of the most intimate ways a living community of relations "renews itself in renewing the pact with every 'generation' " (p. 30). The character of the gift is in its movement (Hyde, 1983, p.
16), in its being handed along (Gadamer, 1989, p. 284) and, in such movement, in the forfeit of its measure and the forfeit of the expectancies of return.

It is giving up.

It is always and necessarily unnecessary. It is excessive (Schrift, 1997, p.
7). It is an abundance (Hyde, 1983, p. 22) that does not diminish but increases in the giving away.

It is a form of love because, "as in love, our satisfaction sets us at ease because we know that somehow its use at once assures its plenty" (Hyde, 1983,
p. 22).

INTRODUCTION

> *Borders have been crossed and re-crossed since the dawn of human civilization. If globalization is something new, it must involve more than a series of proliferating cross border exchanges. As people have thought about the contemporary period, it is not so much that borders are crossed or even opened up. Rather it is that they are* transcended. *Global phenomena are those that extend across widely dispersed locations simultaneously and can move between places anywhere on the earth simultaneously. Hence, we often speak of globalization as a matter of* compressing space and time. *So territorial distance and borders have limited significance; the globe becomes a single place in its own right.*
>
> —McMaster Website

Our conversations about globalization and the pedagogical prospects of the gift began with the recognition of the ambiguous and alluring power released in our classroom conversations and work through the use of the Internet. Our beginning questions turned out to be deceptively simple: "Why do people put up all these great papers and links and sites for nothing?" "Why are all these people just giving away their stuff?" The three of us had been struck by the generosity of scholars, researchers, and amateurs in sharing freely the fruits of their labor on what appeared to be every imaginable topic.

Such free and generous arrivals were not without risk. What is transcended first and foremost with the onrush of Internet possibilities is the taken-for-grantedness of the warrant of what we receive in such gifts. As Hillman (1979, p. 157) suggested, "opportunities are not plain, clean gifts. They trail dark and chaotic attachments." They are thus inherently ambiguous and tricky: "reciprocity as rivalry, generosity as interested, the free return as obligatory" (Schrift, 1997, p. 9) always remains a series of open possibilities, since the economy of the gift "refuses to attend to egoistic and interested calculations of exchange while at the same time remaining aware of that very logic of exchange" (p. 14).

Therefore, the phrase "given away for nothing" has stayed with us, because it still rings of a proximity to commodified forms of exchange that have been, somehow, for some mysterious, dark and chaotic reason, transcended, even though it is not yet quite plain and clean what has arrived through such transcendence. Therefore, also, we have begun to read the movement from commodified relations toward the economy of the gift as a way of understanding the transcendence of boundaries characteristic of the phenomenon of globalization.

These beginning questions helped us to listen differently to the roiling conversations in the classroom as one child or another would grab the whiteboard marker to insist on showing another, better way of thinking about a problem; as one or the other of them would follow University re-

searchers around the classroom, arguing the fine points of distinction between human and natural structures. Again, similar questions arose: "Why
did they bother, these children, to argue pink-cheeked in favor of their pre-
ferred solutions?" "Why did they care to be clear or controversial or interesting?" "What were they giving us in these exchanges?"

Why don't they just *stop*?

And what of that experience of standing stockstill in the middle of 60
seventh-grade students and feeling the propulsive movement of one utterance on top of the other, with waves of dissent from this corner or that issued to each pronouncement, clearly giving the feeling of a sort of "surf-
ing" more bodily, grounded, work-like, and generous than the panicked
rush from one thing to another that underwrites many postmodern love-
laments about such issues? It may be that:

> the subject of postmodernity is best understood as the ideal-type channel-
> hopping MTV viewer who flips through different images at such speed that
> she/he is unable to chain the signifiers together into a meaningful narrative,
> he/she merely enjoys the multiphrenic intensities and sensations of the sur-
> face of the images. (Usher & Edwards, 1994, p. 11)

Even though such "flipping" was occurring here and there in the middle of
this classroom movement, those who "flipped out" were more often than
not overwhelmed when their flip answers were taken seriously, were taken
up, were sometimes read as more generous gifts than the giver could have
imagined alone. How they were taken, then, moved them into the movement that underwrites a gift economy. "Gift" is thus not an objective property of something. Rather, "the way we treat a thing can sometimes change
its nature" (Hyde, 1983, p. xiii) from gift to commodity to gift and return.

"If we are so bold to affirm [the image of the gift], it can only mean that
we are incapable of penetrating the veil. For the modern sophisticate . . . innocence is no longer possible unless leavened with irony" (Godbout, with
Caille, 1998, p. 3). We affirm this image of the gift as essential to pedagogy
and especially essential to understanding the place of new technologies and
the moving, gifted "chaos of possibilities" (Hillman, 1979a, p. 157) they can
release into the work of pedagogy. These children—sometimes unwittingly,
sometimes even unwillingly—were giving us something for nothing, something that sidestepped the venerated irony, cynicism, withholding, anger,
and urban(e) hyperliteracy (Smith, 1999) that some postmodern accounts
of this phenomenon might sometimes require. And, in engaging them in
these conversations, it seems that we were doing the same, all of us now
caught up in the play, caught up in the *Spiel* (Gadamer, 1989, pp. 101–134),
caught up in the "circular movement" (Hyde, 1983, pp. 11–16) of something playing itself out all around us, something moving in wider and richer

arcs than the commonplace boundaries and borders of seemly schooling often allow.

THE LANGUAGE OF PEDAGOGICAL COMMODIFICATION AND THE INTRANSIGENCE OF ITS BOUNDARIES

> *Could we escape the limits of the . . . ideal of autonomy—the* nomos *of the au-tos—as a law of the self, which might make it possible to exceed the limits of our-selves and enter into the between of self and other without losing ourselves in the process? To free ourselves from the oppositional logic of "self vs. all others" might allow for our self-construction as something other than isolated and atomistic subjectivities. Freed from the constraints of an atomistic and autonomous indi-vidualism, might possibilities be opened for establishing nonproprietary relations . . . in which a fully intersubjective self could be at home in the between of self and other? And might such . . . relations facilitate the formulation of an alterna-tive logic of the gift, one liberated from the presuppositions of more classic exchangist logics that imprison gift giving within the constraints of the economic assumptions of commodity trading?*
>
> —Schrift (1997, p. 20)

> *(The true locus of hermeneutics is this in-between. [Gadamer, 1989, p. 295])*

Much traditional educational research and classroom practice can be un-derstood as operating within the borders and boundaries of the language of commodity-trading, and therefore within the language of a sort of atomistic individuality that cannot envisage any in-between other than dis-tanced, monitored forms of anonymous, zero-sum exchange.

Such commodification of pedagogical relationships is part of the deep malaise we as educators experience in our daily work and in our scholarly efforts to understand the logic we are living out. Images of commodifica-tion, their premises and their consequences infest the classroom with the most intransigent of boundaries. In this imagining, the "to and fro motion" (Gadamer, 1989, p. 104) of the gift disappears and with it, we suggest, the very possibility of pedagogy.

Without the free and un-self-conscious (Hyde, 1983, p. 152) movement of the gift, education loses its abundance. It loses its love, not only of chil-dren, but also its love of the ways that the worlds we are entrusted with (mathematics, language, and so on) are themselves great and ambiguous gifts, great movements into which we might step. Things become leaden. Things stop and take on the measured click of the machine, where "time is always running out" (Berry, 1987, p. 44) and where knowledge becomes scarce and there is never enough for everyone. Without the movement of the gift, we live, in our classrooms, unable to be moved or to feel the movement of the living disciplines of the world.

There are many faces to this pedagogical commodification, both in educational theory and educational practices: it begins, first, with an image of "the individual" as separate and autonomous, and, therefore, an image of interrelatedness as a matter of optional, discretionary, wilful, withholdable exchanges with other equally autonomous individuals. Thus education becomes full of a language of cross-border exchanges between teacher and student, between student and text, between consuming knowledge and reproducing it on tests, between the accumulating and hoarding of knowledge and the exchange of such knowledge for marks. Commodification marks the break-up of the living disciplines of the world into carefully packagable, dispensible, consumable, and managable curriculum resources and such a break-up lends itself perfectly to talk of the marketability of skills and widespread images of accountability and monitoring. Knowledge begins to appear to be scarce, something hoarded by teachers and dispensed in developmentally graded increments. And this reproduces images of second and third worlds, of underdevelopedness and of the desire of development as underwritten by the opening of new markets: a horrifying image of educating our children in order to open up them to being new markets for our own profit. Of course we do this "for their own good" (Miller, 1989) because they, too, *if they make the grade, if they measure up*, will become autonomous producers and consumers along with us, able, like us, to survive and profit.

Since the premise of these moves is what could be called a "metaphysics of self-containment" (and therefore subsequently containable exchanges between "individuals"), such exchanges must commodify the "worth" of those exchanges such that no self-contained individual loses out in the rounds of exchange. The space "in between" individuals thus becomes "the market" where exchanges occur.

Moreover, those exchanges that become most "valued" are those that *allow* such commodification. It is therefore interesting to note how images of "the basics" in education are themselves produced out of this logic. It turns out that "the basics" are those elements that can be most easily packaged and delivered in discreet, sequenced, monitorable exchanges; they are also those elements that can be most easily tested and assessed by having children give back to us what we have given them. They are also those elements that can and must be learned and understood "individually." There is no need for one child to converse with another about a "basic math fact" question on a test. In fact, this would be "cheating."

Another buried consequence of this logic is evident in how so much of the discourse of beginning teachers begins by revolving around issues of "management." If classrooms are ideally/ideologically constituted by the logic of containable exchanges, and teachers are those entrusted to monitor and facilitate such exchanges in ways fair to each "individual child," then *how to manage this* becomes paramount. Teachers become "good facilitators" of seemly exchanges. Add to this another odd logic we are living out and a great deal of classroom turbulence is laid out.

From our inheritance of late 19th century pedagogies (Miller, 1989), children are understood to be the uncivilized, the wild, those who will wilfully attempt to despoil civil, commodifiable, and containable relations. Thus, classroom management becomes even more central to our ability to imagine the contours of educational theory and practice. Worse yet, the much heralded arrival of constructivism becomes visible as a way to co-opt the wilderness/wildness of children by offering them a part in the dampening down of their own audacities, a part in their own "civilization," a part in their own self-containment: They now produce knowledges that are already and ahead of time co-opted in the rounds of exchange that constitute schooling and school success and future employment prospects. The invitation that constructivism thus offers children is one that keeps in place their diminishment but now lures them into doing it to themselves. Perfect: Children, as reflective-constructive participants in their own education, become self-monitoring, self-assessing, self-managing, self-containing.

And we end up, in a weird and horrifying ecological backspin, calling wilderness forests "natural resources" and calling our children "our *greatest natural resource.*"

In such an imaginal space, the idea of "globalization" gets collapsed into a happy gloss for the colonizing imposition of marketspeak in all aspects of our lives. The language of the market, the language of commodity, has become the only warranted form of publically speaking. And, as educators, we have all experienced how knowledge has become a commodity, students and parents have become "stakeholders" and customers, and teachers have become "accountable" in ways that no longer have any hint other than "are we getting our money's worth?"

All else seems merely naïve, unable to understand "the realities" of things. And, although it might seem naïve to suggest otherwise, this is not the sort of transcendence of boundaries that globalization can portend.

THE LANGUAGE OF THE GIFT
AND THE TRANSCENDENCE OF BOUNDARIES:
GLOBALIZATION AS WORKING IN THE ECONOMY
OF THE GIFT

A brief entry in a mid-nineteenth-century collection of English fairy tales tells of a Devonshire man to whom the fairies had given an inexhaustible barrel of ale. Year after year the liquor ran freely. Then one day the man, curious to know the

> *cause of this extraordinary power, removed the cork from the bung hold and looked into the cask; it was full of cobwebs. When the spigot next was turned, the ale cease to flow.*
>
> *The moral is this: the gift is lost in self-consciousness. To count, measure, reckon value, or seek the cause of a thing, is to step outside the circle, to cease being "all of a piece" with the flow of gifts and become, instead, one part of the whole reflecting upon another part. We participate in the esemplastic power of a gift by way of a particular kind of unconsciousness.*
>
> —Hyde (1983, pp. 151–152)

Just as the relation between the speaker and what is spoken points to a dynamic process (a "to and fro motion" [Gadamer, 1989, p. 104]) that does not have a firm basis in either member of the relations, so the relation between the understanding and what is understood has a priority over its relational terms. Understanding [thus] involves a moment of "loss of self" (Gadamer, 1977, pp. 50–51).

In some of our earlier work (Jardine 1990, 1998), we have already explored some of the philosophical underpinnings of the image of the gift and its pedagogical character. We suggested that the idea of data or a datum is defined as that which is freely given and therefore, following Heidegger (1968) in one of his wonderfully wild etymologies, *thinking* (*Denken*) about the living realities of classroom events might best be described as a form of *thanks* (*Danken*) of the gift of the given. This line of thought provided us with a wonderful way of thinking through Gadamer's (1989) idea of taking up what is freely given in a classroom conversation. He suggests that, rather than combatting what has been offered up in argumentative ways in order to weaken it in favor of something else, one might rather attempt to strengthen it (p. 367) by taking it up by taking seriously its claim (pp. 126–127) on us, taking seriously its claim to be, in some sense, true of something. It should, that is, be taken up as a gift and read back perhaps more generously than the giver intended or knew or desired.

This is especially evident in one of the most telling passages in Gadamer's *Truth and Method* (1989, p. 294) where he stated that "it is only when the attempt to accept what is said as true fails that we try to 'understand' the text [what is written or said] as another's opinion." Understanding what a child offers in a classroom conversation as "their opinion" might be intended well, but it is also understandable as a refusing of the gift that is offered by handing it back to them as belonging to them. It is refusing to let it lay claim to us, to address us, to obligate us by its arrival to enter into the movement of thinking it sets forth. It is, however much unwittingly, a re-invoking of the whole metaphysics of commodification where experience is something an individual *has* (think of all the rhetoric of "ownership" in educational discourse) and conversation is something where individuals simply enter into relations of exchange. Forcing the gift back into "another's opinion," although it is meant as a way of honoring each child, in fact reinforces a zero-sum game in which every utterance rests inert beside any and all others, each having lost its power of address (i.e., its power to draw us into some larger, richer, more mysterious movements of ancestry and obligation than the narrows of owned-and-exchanged subjectivities). In fact, we begin to glimpse that "the focus on subjectivity [and its reliance on images of autonomous individuality] is a distorting mirror" (Gadamer, 1989, p. 276).

All of this came home to us when we began to think of our recent experiences in studying a version of Homer's *Odyssey* with a group of 50 Grade 2 children. We had chosen the *Odyssey* deliberately, as a tale we knew to be full of wondrous images, wondrous questions, wondrous topographies. We had taken several other groups of children into this place before. We knew, as Gadamer (1989, p. 21) has noted, that "youth [in fact, anyone "new" to something] demand images for its imagination and for the forming of its memory. [We must, therefore] supplement the *critica* of Cartesianism [i.e., methodological issues of *how* to teach children to read] with the old *topica*" [imaginal topographies that involve issues of what is worthy of the imagination and involvement of teachers and children alike, where is a rich, recursive, rigorous, interrelated (Doll, 1993) place in which we might meet?]."

We did invite these children to read in a particular way that we also expected of ourselves. We enticed them to "give their hearts away," to find in the tale the images, characters, words, (the "good bits" as we and the children called them) that really spoke to each one of them and that were the opening or portal or door into what this tale might help us understand about ourselves and the great, mysterious arcs that tether us to this alluring place. Pairs of children carefully mapped out elaborate illustrations to different moments in the story that had for them a special hesitation. These pictures were sweated over for weeks, and the classroom became simply filled up with the images the children carefully, thoughtfully, diligently labored over. These pictures, with the appropriate re-telling by each child, were posted on the school's Internet site. Part of the labor of understanding this tale, then, involved all of us giving away what each of us found in favor of wider, more generous, more worldly rounds of movement in which each of us were intimately involved. We each found ourselves involved in the movement of "primary social ties that enable[d each of us] to affirm and shape [our] uniqueness" (Godbout, with Caille 1998, pp. 19–20). This was no longer part of the curriculum that had to be "covered" and, in such "covering" "promotes those abstract and secondary ties that, at least in theory, make people interchangeable and anonymous" (Godbout, with Caille, 1998, pp. 19–20) and subject to "ersatz personification" (p. 20) through an anonymous identification with Grade Level Expectations.

Hyde (1983) mentioned that a peculiar characteristic of the gift and its movement is that it always, so to speak, has to go around a corner, out of sight. The movement set in motion by the gift always just might re-turn, like the unanticipated converses of a good conversation, drawing us out of ourselves into a movement greater than we could have experienced alone. The gift is always experienced as arriving from elsewhere, somewhere unexpected, undeserved, unearned. It is impossible to know in advance how it will be taken up, just as Homer himself could not have imagined that these children, here, in these times, would give their hearts away like this.

Three years after the second graders completed their work, the following (excerpted) letter arrived at the School Division Office and was eventually directed to us and, through us, to the children and parents involved:

> *I am a Professor of Nuclear Engineering, Purdue University, and write to you from Athens, Greece, where I am spending the current semester.*
>
> *I have translated the first rhapsody of Homer's Odyssey into modern Greek and am in the process of publishing it in Greece. This translation differs from others in the sense that I use all the words of Homer that are still in use today even though the modern Greek reader might have difficulty in recognizing some of them as they have changed over time and only the root of the word remains. These words (more than forty percent of the original dates to ca. 800 BC), are printed in the old and modern Greek in red.*
>
> *For some time I have been in search of an appropriate cover for my translation. It was my good luck to find via the Internet the beautiful drawings of the Grade 2 class of Banded Peak School as they retell the Odyssey in words and pictures.*
>
> *I am considering using one of the following two:*
>
>   **Calypso's Cave** *by A. and A.*
>   **Odysseus Escapes** *by M. and M.*
>
> *Will you please grant me the appropriate permission to do so? Looking forward to your reply.*
>
>   *Sincerely, (signed) Paul S. Lykoudis, Professor Emeritus*
>   *Purdue University, West Lafayette IN.*

Teachers, children, and parents alike experienced the vertigo rush in this wonderful, unexpected arrival. Because the children had accepted the gift-movement of Homer's work, their pictures that were themselves given away set in motion a cascade of transcendences: between school-work and the work of the world; between children's work and the work of adults; between the work of careful illustration and the ebullience of the playful pleasures of real work; between teachers and learners, between the cultural boundaries of Canada and an American scholar now working in contemporary Greece; between "Ancient Greece" as a mandated curriculum demand and "Ancient Greece" as a living place inhabited by children's and teachers' imaginations; and, from Lykoudis's letter, between ancient and contemporary Greek words and the fact that his translation is premised precisely on long-forgotten rootednesses of contemporary terms and their origins. So his reading of the *Odyssey* in this way is itself in part a releasing of the gift-movement of contemporary usage back into its living inheritance.

The image of the gift helped us glimpse something we had taken for granted in this work and the rounds it seemed to take. We found that we had been deliberately taking up those things entrusted to us as teachers of young children as living gifts, living inheritances, rather than as commodifiable, inert, exchangeable objects. We had been acting on the belief that, for example, the tales and images of Ancient Greece are not simply deadened curriculum mandates that have to be somehow "covered." Rather, they "possess [their] own original worldliness and, thus, the center of its [their] own Being so long as [they are] not placed in the object-world of producing and marketing. Our orientation to [such things, unlike our orientation to the object-world] is always something like our orientation to an inheritance" (Gadamer, 1994, pp. 191–192). We chose it, therefore, not because it is some sort of "great book" but because it is *already on the move* in our culture, in the imaginations of children, in our images of journeys, in tales told and monsters imagined, in ideas of travel and home and family and fates and return. We had been reading a version of Homer's *Odyssey* with a group of second-grade children with an eye to its movement in our lives as a gift, as an arrival, not, then, with an eye to what we might get from it, but with an eye to how we might give ourselves to it and, in such giving of our attention and love, keeping in motion its character as a gift.

Commodification stops the movement. It stops things from being "moving" and makes it possible to understand "being moved" as little more than being emotional, subjective, idiosyncratic, and personal and therefore dismissable in light of more cynical, more "realistic" insights. This relationship between the movement and the stopping has always been a topic for us with the children and student–teachers we engage. What is becoming clear is that questions of how to motivate children have disappeared in favor of questions of how to find what is moving, how to find the movement, the living generosity, of the subjects we teach. We are finding that *this movement is what defines for us the idea of what is "basic" to any discipline with which we have been entrusted.*

The *Odyssey* is thus not some "thing" whose characteristics can be hoarded in the back of some seminal text and withheld and then dispensed for marks. Unless we enter wholeheartedly into the movement of thinking that it offers us, it remains anonymous and dead and takes on all the deadliness of school-as-consumption-and-production.

The conversations that interest us are not part of this zero-sum game of monitored dispensation. The conversations that interest us and that take our breath away are purely and clearly *excessive*. We are suggesting that what is "basic" to any of the work we do in education is *precisely in such excessiveness.* What is basic is the abundance, the gift in what we teach.

ENDBIT

Back, at this tail-end, to our fascination with the gift-character of the Internet. We cannot avoid the fact that, in the midst of all this joyous transcendence and excessiveness, other, more silent borders are heightened in such a way that *their* transcendence becomes even less likely than before. As Ivan Illich reminds us, "every technological response to a deeply human need creates a new level of poverty" (Godbout, with Caille, 1998, pp. 19–20). Every gift can also sometimes subtly, sometimes grossly and intentionally diminish those outside the circles of its movement. We know that we have come upon "something else" (Godbout, with Caille, 1998, p. 3) here and we understand the terrible dangers of treating such matters naïvely, as if the political and economic forces at work in the new globalization were all somehow either nonexistent or beneficent.

Without a careful critique of commodification, globalization turns out to be nothing more that the new colonialism. But without imagining "something else" than such commodification, such a critique is ripe and ready for the sort of cynicism, paranoia, and exhaustion that, as teachers, we cannot readily afford.

References

Aardema, V. (1981). *Binging the rain to Kapiti Plain*. New York: Dial.

Abram, D. (1996). *The spell of the sensuous: Language in a more-than-human world*. New York: Pantheon Books.

Abram, D., & Jardine, D. (2000). All knowledge is carnal knowledge: A conversation. *Canadian Journal of Environmental Education*, (5), 167–177.

Arendt, H. (1969). *Between past and future*. New York: Penguin Books.

Atwell, N. (1990). *Coming to know: Writing to learn in the intermediate grades*. Portsmouth ME: Heinemann Books.

Barlow, M., & Robertson, H.-J. (1994). *Class warfare: The assault on Canada's schools*. Toronto: Key Porter Books.

Bass, E. (1989). Tampons. In J. Plant (Ed.), *Healing the wounds: The promise of ecofeminism* (pp. 33–36). Toronto: Between the Lines Press.

Beck, D. (1993). *Visiting generations*. Bragg Creek, AB: Makyo*Press.

Benso, S. (2000). *The face of things: A different side of ethics*. Albany: State University of New York Press.

Berk, L. (1985). Back to basics movement. In *The international encyclopedia of education: Research and studies* (Vol. 1, pp. 223–225). Oxford, England: Pergamon Press.

Berman, M. (1983). *The reenchantment of the world*. Ithaca, NY: Cornell University Press.

Berry, W. (1983). *Standing by words*. San Francisco: North Point Press.

Berry, W. (1986). *The unsettling of America: Essays in culture and agriculture*. San Francisco: Sierra Club Books.

Berry, W. (1987). *Home economics*. San Francisco: North Point Press.

Berry, W. (1989). The profit in work's pleasure. *Harper's Magazine*, March, 19–24.

Berry, W. (1990). *What are people for?* San Francisco: North Point Press.

Birkerts, S. (1994). *The Gutenberg elegies: The fate of reading in an electronic age*. New York: Fawcett Columbine.

Bly, R. (1988). *A little book on the human shadow*. New York: Harper & Row.

Bly, R. (n.d.). *When a hair turns to gold.* St. Paul, MN: Ally Press.

Bogdan, D. (1992). *Re-educating the imagination: Toward a poetics, politics and pedagogy of literary engagement.* Portsmouth, ME: Heinemann Educational Books.

Bohm, D. (1983). *Wholeness and implicate order.* New York: Ark Books.

Bright, W. (1993). *A Coyote reader.* Berkeley & Los Angeles: University of California Press.

Bruner, J. (1990). *Acts of meaning.* Cambridge MA: Harvard University Press.

Calkins, L., with Harwayne, S. (1991). *Living between the lines.* Portsmouth, ME: Heinemann.

Calusso, R. (1992). *The marriage of Cadmus and Harmony.* New York: Knopf.

Caputo, J. (1987). *Radical hermeneutics.* Bloomington: Indiana State University Press.

Caputo, J. (1989). *Against ethics: Contributions to a poetics of obligation with constant reference to deconstruction.* Bloomington: Indiana State University Press.

Carroll, L. (1966). *Alice's adventures in wonderland, and Through the looking glass.* New York: Macmillan. (Originally published 1865)

Clifford, J. (1986). Introduction: Partial truths. In J. Clifford & G. Marcus (Eds.), *Writing culture: The poetics and politics of ethnography* (pp. 1–26). Berkeley: University of California Press.

Clifford, P., & Friesen, S. (1994, October). *Choosing to be healers.* A paper presented at the JCT Conference on Curriculum Theory and Classroom Practice. Banff, Alberta.

Coles, R. (1989). *The call of stories: Teaching and the moral imagination.* Boston: Houghton Mifflin.

Crapazano, V. (1986). Hermes' dilemma: The masking of subversion in ethnographic description. In J. Clifford & G. Marcus (Eds.), *Writing culture: The poetics and politics of ethnography* (pp. 51–76). Berkeley: University of California Press.

Craven, M. (1973). *I heard the owl call my name.* New York: Dell.

Doll, W. (1993). Curriculum possibilities in a "post"-future. *Journal of curriculum and supervision, 8*(1), 277–292.

Dressman, M. (1993). Lionizing lone wolves: The cultural romantics of literacy workshops. *Curriculum inquiry, 23*(3), 239–263.

Egan, K. (1986). *Teaching as story telling: An alternative approach to teaching and curriculum in elementary schools.* London, ON: Althouse Press.

Egan, K. (1992). The roles of schools: The place of education. *Teacher's College Record, 93*(4), 641–645.

Eliade, M. (1968). *Myth and reality.* New York: Harper & Row.

Eliade, M. (1975). *The quest.* New York: Harper and Row.

Estes, C. P. (1992). *Women who run with the wolves: Myths and stories of the wild woman archetype.* New York: Ballantine Books.

Everest, B. (1996). [Untitled poem]. Calgary, Alberta.

Evetts-Secker, J. (1994, June). *In being able to imagine.* Paper presented at the Early Childhood Education Conference, Calgary, Alberta.

Fainlight, R. (1991). Lilith. In V. Green (Ed.), *Rhythm of our days: An anthology of women's poetry.* Cambridge, England: Cambridge University Press.

Field, J. C. (1991). *Educator's perspectives on assessment: Tensions, dilemmas, contradictions.* Unpublished doctoral dissertation, Faculty of Education, University of Victoria, Victoria, British Columbia.

Fischer, M. (1986). Ethnicity and the post-modern arts of memory. In J. Clifford & G. Marcus (Eds.), *Writing culture: The poetics and politics of ethnography* (pp. 196–233). Berkeley: University of California Press.

Freedman, J. (1993). *Failing grades.* Red Deer, AB: Society for Advancing Educational Research.

Fulwiler, T. (Ed.). (1987). *The journal book.* Portsmouth ME: Boynton/Cook.

Gadamer, H.-G. (1977). *Philosophical hermeneutics* (D. E. Linge, Trans.). Berkeley: University of California Press.

Gadamer, H.-G. (1983). *Reason in the age of science* (F. G. Lawrence, Trans.). Boston: MIT Press.

Gadamer, H.-G. (1989). *Truth and method* (J. Weinsheimer, Trans.). New York: Crossroads.

Gadamer, H.-G. (1994). *Heidegger's ways.* (J. W. Stanley, Trans.) Boston: MIT Press.

Gadamer, H.-G. (1995). Foreword to Jean Grondin, *Introduction to philosophical hermeneutics* (pp. ix–xii). New Haven: Yale University Press.

Gadamer, H.-G. (2001). *Gadamer in conversation: Reflections and commentary* (R. Palmer, Trans.). New Haven, CT: Yale University Press.

Gardner, H., & Boix-Mansilla, V. (1994). Teaching for understanding in the disciplines. *Teachers' College Record, 96*(2), 198–218.

Gilligan, C. (1993). *In a different voice: Psychological theory and women's development.* Cambridge MA: Harvard University Press.

Godbout, J., with Caille, A. (1998). *The world of the gift.* Montreal and Kingston: McGill and Queen's University Press.

Goodman, K., Bird, L., & Goodman, Y. (1991). *The whole language catalogue.* New York: Glencoe, McGraw Hill.

Greene, M. (1978). *Landscapes of learning.* New York: Teachers College Press.

Greene, M. (1988). *The dialectic of freedom.* New York: Teachers College Press.

Greene, M. (1993). Diversity and inclusion: Toward a curriculum for human beings. *Teachers College Record, 95*(2), 211–221.

Gregory, B. (1990). *Inventing reality: Physics as language.* New York: Wiley.

Gregory, V. (1992). *Through the Mickle Woods.* Boston: Little, Brown.

Grondin, J. (1995). *Introduction to philosophical hermeneutics.* New Haven CT: Yale University Press.

Grossman, D. (1988). *The yellow wind* (H. Watzman, Trans.). New York: Bantam Doubleday.

Grumet, M. (1993). The curriculum: What are the basics and are we teaching them? In J. Kinchloe & S. Steinberg (Eds.), *Thirteen questions: Reframing education's conversation* (pp. 5–22). New York: Peter Lang.

Habermas, J. (1972). *Knowledge and human interests.* Boston: Beacon Books.

Heidegger, M. (1968). *What is called thinking?* New York: Harper & Row.

Heidegger, M. (1971). *Origin of the work of art.* New York: Harper & Row.

Hillman, J. (1979a). Notes on opportunism. In J. Hillman (Ed.), *Puer papers* (pp. 152–158). Dallas: Spring Publications.

Hillman, J. (1979b). Senex and puer: An aspect of the historical and psychological present. In J. Hillman (Ed.), *Puer papers* (pp. 3–53). Dallas, TX: Spring Publications.

Hillman, J. (1982). Anima Mundi: The return of soul to the world. *Spring: An annual of archetypical psychology and Jungian studies* (pp. 174–188). Dallas, TX: Spring Publications.

Hillman, J. (1983). *Healing fiction.* Barrytown, IL: Station Hill Press.

Hillman, J. (1991). *Inter/Views.* Dallas: Spring Publications.

Holt, M. (1996). A cautionary tale: School reform in England. *Journal of Curriculum and Supervision, 12*(1), 4–6.

Hood, M. (1996). *Getting lost in a book.* Unpublished manuscript.

Hyde, L. (1983). *The gift: Imagination and the erotic life of property.* New York: Vintage Books.

Ingram, C. (1990). *In the foot steps of Gandhi: Conversations with spiritual social activists.* Berkeley, CA: Parallax Press.

Inhelder, B. (1969). Some aspects of Piaget's genetic approach to cognition. In H. Furth (Ed.), *Piaget and knowledge: Theoretical foundations* (pp. 9–23). Englewood Cliffs, NJ: Prentice-Hall.

Jackson, G. (1991). The pleasure of forgetting things. *Globe and Mail,* Toronto, p. A20.

Jardine, D. (1990). Awakening from Descartes' nightmare: On the love of ambiguity in phenomenological approaches to education. *Studies in Philosophy and Education, 10*(1), 211–232.

Jardine, D. W. (1992a). A belling ringing in the empty sky. *Journal of Curriculum Theorizing, 10*(1), 17–37.

Jardine, D. W. (1992b). "The fecundity of the individual case": Considerations of the pedagogic heart of interpretive work. *Journal of Philosophy of Education, 26*(1), 51–61.

Jardine, D. W. (1992c). *Speaking with a boneless tongue.* BragCreek, Alberta, Canada: Makyo Press.

Jardine, D. W. (1992d). Immanuel Kant, Jean Piaget and the rage for order: Hints of the colonial spirit in pedagogy. *Educational Philosophy and Theory, 23*(1), 28–43.

Jardine, D. W. (1992e). The pedagogic wound and the pathologies of doubt. In B. Levering, M. VanManen, & S. Miedema (Eds.), *Reflections on pedagogy and method, Vol. II* (pp. 97–112). Montfoort, Netherlands: Uriah Heep.

Jardine, D. W. (1994a). Student-teaching, interpretation and the monstrous child. *Journal of Philosophy of Education, 28*(1), 17–24.

Jardine, D. W. (1994b). "Littered with literacy": An ecopedagogical reflection on whole language, pedocentrism and the necessity of refusal. *Journal of Curriculum Studies, 26*(5), 509–524.

Jardine, D. W. (1994c, December). *"Signs of the former tenant": On reading, composure and character.* Paper presented at the National Reading Conference, San Diego CA.

Jardine, D. W. (1994d). The ecologies of mathematics and the rhythms of the Earth. In P. Ernest (Ed.), *Mathematics, philosophy and education: An international perspective, Studies in mathematics education* (Vol. 3, pp. 109–123). London: Falmer Press.

Jardine, D. W. (1995a). On the integrity of things: Ecopedagogical reflections on the integrated curriculum. In G. Vars (Ed.), *Current conceptions of core curriculum: Alternative designs for integrative programs* (pp. 33–38). Kent OH: National Association for Core Curriculum.

Jardine, D. W. (1995b). "The stubborn particulars of grace": Meditations on curriculum integration, ecological wholeness and the interpretability of the world. In B. Horwood (Ed.), *Experience and the curriculum: Principles and programs* (pp. 261–275). Dubuque IO: Kendall/ Hunt.

Jardine, D. W. (1995c, November). *Pedagogy and the power of address.* Presented to the Faculty of Education, Louisiana State University, Baton Rouge, LA.

Jardine, D. W. (1996). "Under the tough old stars": Pedagogical hyperactivity and the mood of environmental education. *Canadian Journal of Environmental Education, 1* (Spring), 48–55.

Jardine, D. W. (1997a). American Dippers and Alberta winter strawberries. *Raising the stakes: The planet drum review.* Special issue on "Mainstreaming Watersheds," #27, 8.

Jardine, D. W. (1997b). The surroundings. *The Journal of Curriculum Theorizing, 13*(3), 18–31.

Jardine, D. W. (1998). *"To dwell with a boundless heart": On curriculum theory, hermeneutics and the ecological imagination.* New York: Peter Lang.

Jardine, D. W. (2000). *"Under the tough old stars": Ecopedagogical essays.* Brandon, VT: Psychology Press / Holistic Education Press. (Vol. 4 of the Foundation for Educational Renewal Series, Catalogue Number 4177).

Jardine, D. W. (in press). Welcoming the old man home: Meditations on Jean Piaget, Interpretation and the nostalgia for origins. *Taboo: A Journal of Education and Culture.*

Jardine, D. W., Clifford, P., & Friesen, S. (1999). "Standing helpless before the child." A response to Naomi Norquay's "Social difference and the problem of the 'unique individual': An uneasy legacy of child-centered pedagogy." *Canadian Journal of Education, 24*(3), 321–326.

Jardine, D. W., & Field, J. C. (1992). "Disproportion, monstrousness and mystery": Ecological and ethical reflections on the initiation of student–teachers into the community of education. *Teaching and Teacher Education, 12,* 127–137.

Jardine, D., Graham, T., LaGrange, A., & Kisling-Saunders, H. (2000). Staying within the lines: Re-imagining what is "elementary" in the arts of elementary schooling. *Language and Literacy: A Canadian On-Line E-Journal.* Available at: http://edu10.educ.queensu.~landl/papers/stayingwithin.htm

Kay, A. C. (1995). Computers, networks and education. *Scientific American Special Issue: The computer in the 21st century*, 148–155.

King, T. (1992). A *Coyote Columbus Story*. Toronto, Canada: Groundwood Books.

Koestler, A. (1959). *The sleepwalker*. New York: Penguin Books.

Lazere, D. (1992). Back to basics: A force for oppression or liberation? *College English, 54*(1), 7–21.

LeGuin, U. (1987). *Buffalo gals and other animal presences*. Santa Barbara, CA: Capra Press.

LeGuin, U. (1989). Woman/wilderness. In J. Plant (Ed.), *Healing the wounds*. Toronto, Canada: Between the lines press.

Lugone, K. (1996). Internet message. *Kidsphere*. March.

Ly, Y. (1996). *Family tree*. Unpublished story.

Mahdi, L., Foster, S., & Little, M. (1987). *Betwixt and between: Patterns of masculine and feminine initiation*. LaSalle IL: Open Court.

McMaster Website (1998). Found at www.humanities.mcmaster.ca/~global / themeschool / globaliz.html. McMaster University, Hamilton, Ontario, Canada.

Meier, D. (1992). Reinventing teaching. *Teachers college record, 93*(4), 594–609.

Miller, A. (1989). *For your own good: Hidden cruelty in child-rearing and the roots of violence*. Toronto, Canada: Collins.

Minh-Ha, T. (1994). Other than myself/my other self. In G. Robertson, M. Mash, L. Tickner, J. Bird, B. Curtis, & T. Putnam (Eds.), *Travellers' tales: Narratives of home and displacement* (pp. 9–26). London, England: Routledge.

Moore, D. S. (1990). Uncertainty. In L. Steen (Ed.), *On the shoulders of giants: New approaches to numeracy* (pp. 95–137). Washington, DC: National Academy Press.

Nandy, A. (1987). *Traditions, tyranny and utopia*. Delhi: Oxford University Press.

Negroponte, N. (1995). *Being digital*. New York: Knopf.

Norris-Clarke, W. (1976). Analogy and the meaningfulness of language about God. *The Thomist, 40*, 176–198.

Okri, B. (1991). *The famished road*. Toronto, Canada: McLelland and Stewart.

Palmer, P. (1993). *To know as we are known: Education as a spiritual journey* (2nd ed.). San Francisco: Harper.

Papert, S. (1993). *The children's machine: Rethinking school in the age of the computer*. New York: Basic Books.

Piaget, J. (1952). *Origins of intelligence in children*. New York: International Universities Press.

Piaget, J. (1965). *Insights and illusions of philosophy*. New York: Meridian Books.

Piaget, J. (1968). *Six psychological studies*. New York: Vintage Books.

Piaget, J. (1970a). Piaget's theory. In P. Mussen (Ed.), *Carmichael's manual of child psychology* (Vol. 1, pp. 703–732). Toronto: Wiley.

Piaget, J. (1970b). *Structuralism*. New York: Harper & Row.

Piaget, J. (1971a). *Genetic epistemology*. New York: Norton.

Piaget, J. (1971b). *Biology and knowledge*. Chicago: University of Chicago Press.

Piaget, J. (1971c). *The construction of reality in the child*. New York: Ballantine Books.

Piaget, J. (1972). *Judgement and reasoning in the child*. Totawa, NJ: Littlefield & Adams.

Piaget, J. (1974). *The child's conception of the world*. London, England: Paladin Books.

Piaget, J. (1977). The mission of the idea. *The essential Piaget*. New York: Basic Books.

Piaget, J., & Inhelder, B. (1969). *The psychology of the child*. New York: Harper & Row.

Piaget, J., & Inhelder, B. (1976). Gaps in empiricism. In B. Inhelder & H. Chipman (Eds.), *Piaget and his school: A reader in developmental psychology* (pp. 25–35). New York: Springer-Verlag.

Plato (trans. 1956): *Phaedrus* (W. G. Helmbold & W. G. Rabinowitz, Trans.). New York: The Liberal Arts Press.

Postman, N. (1995). *The end of education: Redefining the value of school*. New York: Knopf.

Professional standards for teaching mathematics. (1991). Reston VA: National Council of Teachers of Mathematics.

Sarason, S. (1982). *The culture of the school and the problem of change.* Boston: Allyn & Bacon.

Sarason, S. (1990). *The inevitable failure of school reform: Can we change course before it's too late?* San Francisco: Jossey-Bass.

Schmidt, W., McKnight, C., & Raizen, S. (1997). *A splintered vision: An investigation of U.S. science and mathematics education.* Norwell, MA: Kluwer.

Schrift, A. (Ed.). (1997). *The logic of the gift: Toward an ethic of generosity.* New York: Routledge.

Smith, D. (1999). *Pedagon: Interdisciplinary essays in the human sciences, pedagogy and culture.* New York: Peter Lang.

Smith, D. G. (1988). Children and the gods of war. *Journal of Educational Thought, 22A(2),* 173–177.

Snyder, G. (1977). *The old ways.* San Francisco: City Lights Books.

Snyder, G. (1980). *The real work.* New York: New Directions Books.

Snyder, G. (1990). *The practice of the wild.* New York: North Point Press.

Sumara, D. (1995a). Counterfeiting. *Taboo: A Journal of Education and Culture, 1(1),* 94–122.

Sumara, D. (1995b, December). Understanding response to reading as a focal practice. Paper presented at the *National Reading Conference,* New Orleans.

Sumara, D. (1996). Using commonplace books in curriculum studies. *JCT: An Interdisciplinary Journal of Curriculum Studies, 12(1),* 44–50.

Tannahill, R. (1975). *Flesh and blood: A history of the cannibal complex.* London, England: Hamish Hamilton.

Tennyson, A. (1986). *The lady of Shalott.* Oxford, England: Oxford University Press.

Trungpa, C. (1988). *Cutting through spiritual materialism.* San Francisco: Shambala Press.

Turner, V. (1969). *The ritual process.* Chicago: Aldine.

Turner, V. (1987). Betwixt and between: The liminal period in rites of passage. In L. Mahdi, S. Foster, & M. Little (Eds.), *Betwixt and between: Patterns of masculine and feminine initiation.* LaSalle, IL: Open Court.

Usher, R., & Edwards, R. (1994). *Postmodernism and education.* London: Routledge.

Van Gennup (1960). *Rites of passage.* Chicago: University of Chicago Press.

Voneche, J., & Bovet, M. (1982). Training research and cognitive development: What do Piagetians want to accomplish? In S. Modgil & C. Modgil (Eds.), *Jean Piaget: Consensus and controversy* (pp. 83–94). London, England: Holt, Rinehart & Winston.

Wallace, B. (1987). *The stubborn particulars of grace.* Toronto, Canada: McLelland and Stewart.

Weinsheimer, J. (1987). *Gadamer's hermeneutics.* New Haven, CT: Yale University Press.

Werner, M. (1994). *Managing monsters: Six myths of our time.* (Transcriptions of The Reith Lectures, BBC Radio.) London, England: Vintage Books.

White, J. (1989). Student teaching as a rite of passage. *Anthropology and Education Quarterly, 22(1),* 177–195.

Wittgenstein, L. (1968). *Philosophical investigations.* Cambridge, England: Blackwell.

Author Index

Subject Index